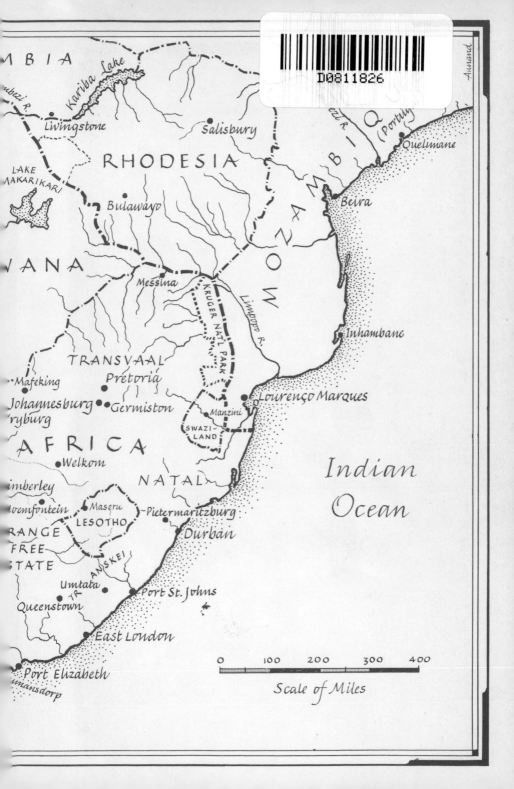

THE
SEPARATED
PEOPLE

Other books by *E. J. Kahn, Jr.*

THE

SEPARATED

PEOPLE

A Look at Contemporary

South Africa

E. J. KAHN, JR.

W. W. Norton & Company, Inc.

New York

FOR *Terry*

Author's Note

I spent three months in South Africa at the end of 1966. I wish I could properly thank all the South Africans—White, African, Colored, and Indian—whose information and insights were so helpful to me. But some of them might conceivably get into trouble if it became known they'd been fraternizing with a prying foreign journalist, and others might be embarrassed. My friends there—and I made some good friends there—know who they are, and if they read these lines they will, I hope, realize that the gratitude I herewith extend applies to them. South Africa today can inspire convulsive arguments, but there is surely one unarguable aspect of that many-faceted country: it stands second to none when it comes to gracious hospitality. Thank you all very much.

E.J.K.

THE
SEPARATED
PEOPLE

I

The late Jan Smuts once described South Africa as a laboratory for the social sciences. Of the thirty-seven independent nations of Africa, South Africa—in Prime Minister Smuts's day a union and since 1961 a republic—has lately attracted a lion's share of attention, even though it is sovereign over less of the acreage of that continent than, among others, the Sudan and Chad, and though it has only eighteen and a half million inhabitants. Nigeria has three times as many. What prompted Smuts's observation is the peculiar composition of South Africa's population, which has given the country its character and its controversiality. There are four principal kinds of South Africans. Largest in number and least in influence are its twelve and a half million black-skinned people. There are almost two million others, of mixed blood, who are

11

known as "Colored." Their skins range in hue from white to black, but whatever a Colored man's color, his rights are meager. There are slightly more than half a million Asiatics, most of them of Indian ancestry and all of them second-class citizens. First class is reserved for three and a half million Whites, who, as they never forget, constitute the largest concentration of white people in Africa. Johannesburg, the Republic's main metropolis, with a total population of 1,250,000, has the biggest white population of any city on the continent. Johannesburg also has the biggest black population. It is in large part because of such unique distinctions that contemporary South Africa is so uniquely vexed.

The mere identification of the various categories of South Africans can confuse outsiders. The Whites—who rarely have anyone else in mind when they use the term "South African"—are often known as "Europeans," although in fact most of them have firm African roots; some of their family trees were planted in African soil a dozen generations ago. (The few Japanese in South Africa also rate as Europeans, because most of them are businessmen and it suits the South African government to treat them—although Chinese do not get the same break—as honorary Whites.) In the Transvaal province—wherein are located both Johannesburg and Pretoria, the country's administrative capital—"non-European" means "non-White." In the province of the Cape of Good Hope, however, wherein lies Cape Town, the country's legislative capital (the highest judicial body sits in still another province, at Bloemfontein in the Orange Free State), the only non-Whites considered non-European are the Coloreds, most of whom live in the Cape. Throughout South Africa the darkest and most downtrodden of its residents are called either Africans, as they themselves prefer to be designated, or Bantu, as the government prefers to designate them (in many African languages, "Bantu" means "people"), or natives, or kaffirs, a word of Arabic origin that means infidels and is akin to the American "niggers." Only bigots and Africans use "kaffir."

South Africa is extremely conscious of the variety and disparity of its inhabitants. Where else on earth would the head of a government refer, as Prime Minister Balthazar John Vorster did in the winter of 1967, to "my country and my *peoples*"? In Pretoria

12

a lesser government official said to me, "How can the rest of the world expect us to have in one orderly framework the Afrikaner, the English, the Colored, the Indian, and eight Bantu tribes, if in western Europe they can't even agree on an economic union?" The man, like most government officials, was an Afrikaner—a member of the politically dominant white group whose primary language is Afrikaans. "Afrikaner" is simply the Afrikaans word for "African." Black men can't be called "Africans" in the Afrikaans press, because if they were they would come out sounding white. When the Afrikaans press mentions the now outlawed political group called the African National Congress, it avoids any possible confusion by putting the organization's name in English. Most of the Coloreds in South Africa speak Afrikaans, and they are sometimes known as "brown Afrikaners," to the indignation of many non-brown Afrikaners. The more enlightened among the latter don't care much who gets called what, but they are wont to complain that nobody outside their realm ever seems to understand who they are or what they are. "We Afrikaners are merely another tribe of Africans," one white tribal elder told me, "just like Xhosas or Zulus or Basutos or any of the others. We happen to be white, which is unfortunate. We could have been much better understood if we'd been black."

Among the 1,800,000 Afrikaners who comprise 60 per cent of the white South African population, there are of course differences, but some traits most of them share. Practically all of them have rural origins. They are descendants of the eighteenth-century Voortrekkers—themselves descendants of seventeenth-century Hollanders—who drove their oxcarts inland from the southern tip of the continent and began tilling the soil. When the pioneers made camp, they would form a circle, or *laager,* of their ox wagons to protect themselves against attacks from hostile natives. Contemporary Afrikaners who have never seen an oxcart except in anniversary processions still have a *laager* philosophy. They are forever defending themselves against real or imaginary incursions, and doing so with what their assassinated prime minister, Dr. Hendrik F. Verwoerd, described admiringly as "their spirit of tenacity." At a party, they are apt to sit in a broad circle. It inhibits conversation, but it gets their backs closer to the walls. In the last

13

thirty years or so, more and more of them have become urbanized—"detribalized" is a word some of them fancy—but the stereotype of the Afrikaner remains the rugged, individualistic farmer who wants to live out of sight of his neighbor's chimney smoke, who is bitterly opposed to paying taxes, and who sees no earthly use in ever reading anything except the Bible, which he interprets literally. There is no doubt in his mind that he is one of the chosen people, and indeed Afrikaners sometimes refer to themselves, though their theological leanings are toward Calvinism, as the Israelis of Africa.

The Afrikaner is also quite fond of black people, in their place. It would never occur to him—nor to the majority of other white South Africans—to solicit the black Africans' views on what their place should be. The Afrikaner is sometimes compared to the Irishman. He has the same feeling about land, with which he or his ancestors have ceaselessly struggled and which comforts him as it torments him; he has something of the same sardonic sense of humor; and he is apt to be a pretty good storyteller, since, with his sparse library, whatever nonbiblical yarns he chooses to spin have to come out of his own head. Like the Irish, moreover, he is apt to be quite outspoken, a characteristic that he concedes may have contributed to his generally low repute in the rest of the world. "We Afrikaners are honest to a degree where we often say too much and deny too little," one Afrikaner told me.

The Afrikaners' Dutch ancestors arrived in what is now South Africa in 1652. Most of the other principal white group, the English-speaking South Africans, trace their African origins back to 1820, when the first British settlers materialized. (French Huguenots had been on the scene even earlier—in 1689—but left little legacy beyond a thriving wine industry and surnames like de Villiers and du Plessis, which now belong to some pre-eminent Afrikaners.) Today's English-speaking South African is very much a South African whose primary language happens to be English; he should not be thought of as an Englishman who happens to live in South Africa. The English group now contains a number of Europeans from continental Europe, including one major subgroup: the Jews. *Their* progenitors, mostly from eastern Europe, arrived a century ago and became itinerant traders, peddling merchandise

14

to scattered farmers. There are over a hundred thousand Jews in South Africa today. They play important roles in commerce, finance, and real estate, and they are very conscious of their Jewishness. Since more than a few of the incumbent rulers of South Africa had manifest pro-Nazi sentiments not so long ago, the Jews in South Africa are uneasy, but this does not make them especially singular. Practically everybody in South Africa is uneasy.

South Africa withdrew from the British Commonwealth in 1961. But the influence of English-oriented people, who for much of the country's history dominated its political, economic, cultural, and social life, is still evident. South African cities have double-decker buses, and vehicular traffic keeps to the left. All over the country, its citizens are enjoined by signs to *"hou links"* —"keep left." (Poor South Africans—constantly being reminded to *hou links* while the government steers them ever more sternly in the opposite direction!) In the reception rooms of the big mining-house offices in Johannesburg, the visitor has his choice of *Punch* or *Country Life*. In Natal, the most British of the four provinces of the Republic, there are coastal resorts called Ramsgate and Margate; and in Durban, Natal's major city, there are districts called Hyde Park and Marble Hill. Durban, where schoolboys wear boaters, is so doggedly British that whereas at the Rand Club, Johannesburg's stuffiest retreat, one sees a portrait of Queen Elizabeth II, at the Durban Club one sees George VI and his Elizabeth. (The Netherlands Club in Cape Town, where the Dutch influence is still a factor, displays Queen Juliana.) A meal at the very British Mount Nelson Hotel in Cape Town is apt to conclude with some such savory as pilchards on toast, and to include somewhere along the line the sort of tasteless Brussels sprouts that many places in Britain itself stopped serving when the Empire fell apart. At South African country clubs, lawn bowls is a sport much in favor, and in the clubhouses, when a second drink is urged upon a guest (South Africans drink a great deal, and are especially fond of brandy), he is invited, as if he were in London, to "have the other half." The English monetary system has vanished from South Africa, but it has influenced its successor; the rand, the basic unit of South African currency,

15

was—until the British devalued their currency in the fall of 1967—worth ten shillings. That made it easy for Englishmen to figure out the cost of things, but it can be tough on others, including Americans, who are likely to equate a rand with a dollar when actually the rand is worth a dollar-forty.

English-speaking South Africans often refer to their Afrikaner compatriots as "they" or "them." It is not uncommon elsewhere on earth for people to use a third-person plural pronoun without antecedent to refer to strangers, or to enemies, but in South Africa the practice seems unusually prevalent, and there are a staggering number of "theys." Afrikaners thus refer to non-Afrikaner white South Africans. All white South Africans use "they" for all Blacks, and the Blacks return the compliment—or, depending on the context, the insult. To South African white liberals, "they"—in this instance, a pejorative "they"—often means the government. "They" is also used by South Africans, in appropriate circumstances, to refer to the remainder of Africa or indeed to the remainder of the whole wide uncomprehending world.

A newly arrived visitor to South Africa generally hasn't been there for more than a few hours before he is asked—and the question is repeated interminably—for his impressions of the country and its people. South Africans make the inquiry much in the fashion of a child who, coveting attention or affection, will pester his peers with "Do you like me?" The impression that many South Africans seem to have of themselves would indicate that they are on a different intellectual wavelength from most of mankind. In an allusion to the national policy of apartheid, Prime Minister Vorster said in the fall of 1966, soon after succeeding Dr. Verwoerd, "We do not ask the world to subscribe to it or even to understand it, because it is intended to deal with a situation peculiar to South Africa and is something others cannot understand." The black people of South Africa understand apartheid all too well. It was Dr. Verwoerd's special, bitter prescription for them after he had diagnosed their predicament, and he gave it to them with a curt "Take it; it's good for you." The alleged ignorance of the outside world is one of the few subjects on which Mr. Vorster would seem to agree with one of his most peppery and articulate opponents, Laurence Gandar, the editor-in-chief of

16

the principal English-language daily, the *Rand Daily Mail*. "The outside world doesn't understand what we're talking about," Gandar says, "and we don't understand what it's talking about." Some people who think they understand at least something about South Africa believe that the place might be more comprehensible if it had a name that wasn't a mere geographical description, and that South Africa would stand a much better chance of being accepted by the community of nations if it itself had long ago adopted some such identification as, say, "Arcadia," or perhaps "Good Hope."

It has been suggested by some observers of the South African scene that the main difficulty with the country is that it has somehow fallen a century or so behind the rest of the world, and that if the rest of the world would just mark time for a hundred years South Africa would very likely catch up and be able to communicate with it. It might not take that long; a mere forty years after miniature golf burst upon other sectors of the Western world, South Africa embraced the sport. In the big South African cities these days, three kinds of car-window stickers are popular. There are those saying "Charge or Release!," a protest against the government's nasty policy of locking up people it doesn't like without accusing them of anything or giving them a chance to defend themselves. There are stickers—for rear windows—that say, "You are behind me. I am behind Ian Smith. Let's go forward together." And there are stickers that proudly proclaim, "I play putt-putt!" Some cars display both the first and the third, some the second and the third. The first two together would be an unlikely combination.

South Africans have some grounds for being resentful about the outside world's attitude toward them. Most white South Africans are aware that they are often—and wrongly—depicted as presiding sadistically over one huge concentration camp, like as not brandishing whips or their stout clubs called *sjamboks*. As they view the indisputably serene environment most of them live in, they find it unfathomable that, in a world racked with hostility and violence, anyone could be annoyed with *them*. Thus, when Prime Minister Vorster now receives visiting delegations from abroad, his opening words are apt to be, "Welcome to the happi-

17

est police state in the world." But if outsiders know little about South Africa, when it comes to ignorance South Africans are a match for any group. Ostriches are indigenous to their country, and the analogy is obvious. Of late, South Africans have been talking more and more about getting acquainted with the rest of the globe and about making the rest of the globe more aware of what they are like. Specifically, Mr. Vorster not long ago urged South Africans to write letters to overseas friends describing the kind of lives they lead. The *Rand Daily Mail* promptly invited its readers to send their letters to the paper for publication, and it ran a sheaf of them, a good many of which described South African life in terms that would hardly be calculated to improve any country's image anywhere.

Some South Africans are astonishingly obtuse about anything beyond their borders. An American diplomat recently visited a fair-sized South African country town and was asked to lunch at the mayor's house. The guest commiserated with his hostess about a drought that had parched the area. "I guess you never have to worry about droughts in the United States," the mayor's wife responded, "with your big rivers like the Mississippi and the Amazon." The same American found himself not long afterward at a lunch in Cape Town, given by a member of Parliament. On learning that the man at her right was from the United States, a woman evinced mild interest in his country, and asked him what the name of its capital was; she had apparently never heard of Washington, D. C. I myself was somewhat taken aback, in the course of a luncheon at Pretoria, when the wife of a professor at the university there remarked pleasantly that she didn't care a fig for outside information. "I never read the newspapers except to find out what's playing at the drive-in," she said.

Prime Minister Vorster has made only one trip outside South Africa. He took a cruise across the Atlantic, and briefly went ashore at Brazil. Many South Africans, of course, have traveled far more extensively. I had a chat at a wayside inn one day with an East London couple just back from a trip "overseas," by which they, like most of their compatriots, meant Europe. They were glad to be home, where one could get one's luggage carried free. In France some cheeky French porter had charged them a

18

franc a bag, and what was more, wherever they had gone, they had run into a wall of ignorance about South Africa. "They don't want to understand us," the husband said over his brandy. "It's aggravating," said the wife. Some Afrikaners, raised to be suspicious of the outside world, are perplexed when they examine it at firsthand and find it not quite so alien as they'd expected. An English-speaking South African university professor was in London not long ago and visited South Africa House, at Trafalgar Square. Coming out, he ran into a former student, a young Afrikaner man. The Afrikaner was looking glum, and his teacher asked him why. "I feel so awful because I'm in London and I feel so at home here," the Afrikaner said.

The majority of Afrikaners are quite content not to broaden their horizons. While I was visiting their country, there was a big flap when the administrator of the Transvaal province, a man of solid standing in the ruling National Party, viewed with alarm the granting of traveling scholarships to young South Africans by Rotary International. (The National Party is often called the Nationalist Party, but the latter terminology is fancied mainly by its detractors; some Republicans in the United States do the same sort of thing when they refer to their opposition as the "Democrat Party.") The Transvaal man didn't like the idea of "spiritually defenseless young people" being exposed to foreign mental processes. To some South Africans, even Rotary International can be an outfit that warrants careful scrutiny.

White South Africans are intensely and unashamedly chauvinistic. At Christmas time they decorate their shops with, among other holiday sentiments, "This year give a South African present." They are enormously proud of the high level of their self-sufficiency. They are determined to show the rest of the world that whether or not it can get along without South African gold, diamonds, and other minerals, South Africa can make do with its own resources. Recently South Africans were advised that one of their pharmaceutical companies had started concocting its own salicylic acid. It was a breakthrough; South Africa would no longer have to import aspirin. It is hard to believe that in a world as complex and interdependent as ours a highly industrialized and economically surging country like South Africa could completely

19

hole up behind its boundaries, but there are some rigid-thinking and influential South Africans who believe that would be a splendid notion. The prospect makes other South Africans shudder. Not long ago one of the more forward-thinking of the country's journalists, the political commentator Stanley Uys, deplored the possibility of South Africa's ever becoming a white nation "withdrawn down here at the southern tip of a black continent, isolated and sullen, the lost people of the twentieth century."

In *Anatomy of South Africa,* a book published in Johannesburg in 1966 and written by three white South African social scientists (Drs. William Hudson, Gideon Francois Jacobs, and Simon Biesheuvel), the authors observed, "In the welter and stress of political change within the past twenty years, we South Africans have grown disenchanted to the point of indifference. World events have taken us unawares. . . . What is it that impels us to pursue a path so unpopular with the world around us—fear, self-interest, prejudice, delusion, or a penetrating judgment which is being denied to the rest of the world, bemused by a misguided humanism?" Most South Africans of all colors, answering the question, would probably skip its caudal ironies and vote in favor of fear. Hardly anyone, black or white, *looks* fearful in South Africa. It is a warm, sunny, prosperous nation, and peoples' outward appearances tend to reflect their environment. But fear is everywhere.

"Make no mistake about it," one law professor told me. "This is a frightened country." After a dinner one night, three of the other guests—all of them white—were kind enough to drive me back to my hotel. I asked them in for a nightcap. It was a hot evening, and one man wasn't wearing a tie. The head porter said he couldn't enter the lounge without one. I said I'd run up to my room and get one of mine. The porter said no, my friend couldn't go in the lounge anyway, because he was wearing a sports coat and slacks; he would need a suit. I thought this was all foolish, and began to say so, but my companions deterred me. "No," they said, "this is South Africa," and they went meekly off into the night. Another time, I spent a weekend at the home, outside Johannesburg, of an English-speaking couple who have a nineteen-year-old son. He drove off on a date Saturday night, and when he

20

hadn't returned by four in the morning, his mother telephoned the police. It was not his being in a car, she told me later, that made her anxious; he was a good driver. It was not alcohol or women; he was old enough and responsible enough to handle those situations himself. What upset her was the possibility that he might have gone to an interracial party and been picked up in a raid and thrown into jail. I refer to the parents as English-speaking because it would never occur to most Afrikaner families that a son of theirs would do any such thing.

White South Africans with the cleanest consciences imaginable —not that too many of them can be said really to have them— suffer from fear. One middle-aged woman of impeccable deportment told me that her heart had skipped a beat one morning when she received a phone call from the secretary of a high-ranking police officer whom she'd met socially a few times and who wanted to talk to her. What could she possibly have done?, she wondered. Was she about to be told to report for ninety days' detention, or worse? She was much relieved when the policeman came on the phone and jovially invited her to dinner. When white South Africans write letters to visitors containing names, addresses, or telephone numbers of people who might conceivably be in bad with the government, the recipients are urged to destroy the communications after reading them. A good many people in South Africa think their phones are tapped; maybe they are and maybe they aren't, but the people *think* they are, and that is enough to make them circumspect, if not downright furtive. One Johannesburg businessman who served on a social-welfare committee heard from a friend that a member of the security police had said the committee was infested with Communists. "I'd like him to tell me that to my face," the businessman said. A few days later, he learned that a lunch date had been set up to do just that. The policeman told him, moreover, that his department had spies within the committee and, in fact, had spies everywhere. "I'm afraid to talk candidly to *any* South African now," the businessman told me. He is not alone. As the head of the now impotent Liberal Party of the country has put it, "Evasion has become our national sin."

Most white South Africans are mainly afraid of Blacks. It is

21

strange in a way that they should be; never was there a group of people who had more reason to be angry and who were so placid. Of course, it usually takes leadership to provoke people with even real grievances into violent action, and most of the country's African leaders are either in prison, or in exile, or banned, or under careful surveillance. En masse, contemporary black South Africans are fairly resigned and apathetic. One night Mrs. Helen Suzman, the celebrated single member in Parliament of the relatively progressive Progressive Party, visited a friend's home. Because not one of the country's twelve and a half million Blacks is represented in the legislature and because Mrs. Suzman persistently speaks up for them, she is sometimes said to have the largest constituency of any legislator on earth. When an African maid brought in tea, her mistress identified the guest and told the servant, "This is the lady who has been trying to do so much for you in Parliament.

"She's wasting her time," said the maid.

Individual Africans are quite capable of brutality—the majority of these assaults, like most Negroes' crimes in America, committed against victims of their own color—and this is one reason why most white South African men have firearms and why most white South African stores are screened and shuttered at night and white South African homes fitted out with burglar alarms. But the fear is mainly not of individual Blacks but of Blacks in bulk. There are so many of them that the ruling white minority can never feel wholly comfortable. The Afrikaners feel the worst. The English-speaking South African may come from a family that for generations has not left Africa, but he has a vague affinity with the Commonwealth and reasons that in a pinch he could always go to England, or Canada, or Australia. The Afrikaner has no affinity with any other part of the globe, and he is afraid of any threat, real or fancied, to dislodge him from what he quite properly thinks of as his homeland.

His attitude is not quite the same as that which prevails in parts of the United States South, although there are similarities. "Every white South African woman has an anxiety complex about—ah—certain aspects of our situation here," a white South African woman told me. (Actually, far more black women are assaulted by white men than are white women by black men.) Most South African Whites are not at all truculent toward non-Whites, and the Whites make a big point of how they do not go in for lynchings. "You have racial hatred; we only have racial fear," one white South African told me. "I visited your country once and went to Little Rock and hadn't been there twenty minutes when a man came into a bar and announced, 'They just dynamited a Goddam nigger's house,' and everyone there was pleased. It really shook me. South Africans wouldn't have reacted like that even in the narrowest-minded portions of the Orange Free State. Our cruelties are impersonal."

Outsiders sometimes find it hard to comprehend why any people living as cozily as white South Africans do could be so inwardly trembly. When G. Mennen Williams was America's Assistant Secretary of State for African Affairs, he was not allowed in South Africa—he had publicly endorsed "Africa for the Africans"—but he visited the adjacent British High Commission territories and met with some South African reporters there. The first question asked him was, "Do you think the white man's expendable in South Africa?" Williams said he thought that was a silly question. Afterward one Afrikaner reporter came up to him and said, "Why did you say that was a silly question? Every black man is a Communist, and every Communist wants to kill every white man." Williams said he thought *that* was even sillier. Later he told an English-speaking South African about the exchange. "Well, the Afrikaner bloke may have put it a little exaggeratedly," the man said, "but that's what many people in our country believe."

I talked one morning with a white lawyer in Johannesburg. He has not been banned—not yet, anyway, as far as I know—but he is certainly not one of the government's favorites, having devoted much of his time to defending Africans accused of subversive activities. He comes as close to being a friend of the black man as any white South African. "Most Whites are simply scared to death of all Africans nowadays," he said. "Ten years ago it was considered a sport by some of our more bigoted citizens to push Blacks off bicycles or to ride past black pedestrians in a car and clout them on the head. No longer. For one thing, we've grown more civilized—most of us, anyway. For another, there's too

23

much risk of getting clouted back. It is currently an accepted legal defense in South Africa for a White to say, 'I didn't stop after I knocked down the deceased, because the area was full of natives.' Just now, on my way to meet you, I saw something that was revealing about how white people feel. A black man and a white man were having a fist fight in the street. There were a bunch of Blacks standing around enjoying it hugely, and urging the black man on. But every white man who passed by quickened his pace to get out of there as fast as possible."

"How did the fight come out?" I asked.

"I don't know," he said. "I was one of those white people who got the hell out of there."

If Africans aren't quite as servile as they used to be, most of them still jump when a white man snaps his fingers. I called on the editor of a newspaper published for Africans. He was white, but most of his staff was black. He wanted me to meet one of his principal African subordinates, and asked a secretary to have the subeditor stop by his office. A moment later the African came in. The three of us chatted for fifteen minutes or so, at which point the African said he wondered if we would excuse him; he had been in the middle of an important phone call when he was summoned, and he didn't want to keep the other party waiting any longer. There was no reason at all why he couldn't have finished his call before coming by, except that it would never have crossed his mind to keep his white boss waiting. Africans still say "boss" and "master" to Whites all the time. But the overtones have changed slightly. Soon after I arrived in South Africa a white friend of mine was driving me around Johannesburg, and went through a red light. An African bystander yelled out, "Whoa, baasie!" I remarked to my companion that that was the first time I'd actually heard the word used. "I think it was said with a certain amount of derision," my friend said.

Swart gevaar is the phrase in Afrikaans—black danger. To avoid having to think about the danger any more than necessary, the white South Africans rely on apartheid. Some say there are two kinds of apartheid—big and petty. The first kind relates to the grandiose government scheme of trying to separate people of different colors and let them develop, in theory, along parallel

24

lines in their own areas. The petty kind is what one hears most about—the mean, niggling debasement of the non-White through an endless series of laws and administrative regulations. But grand or small, apartheid is based on the notion that the black man—at least when his services are not required—is to be kept out of sight. Out of sight, he is out of mind, and the white man can breathe easier.

The practice of apartheid did not begin when the National Party, which seems to get stronger and stronger with each successive election, was first voted into power in 1948. As good a date as any for the origin of apartheid is 1660, when a wild-almond hedge was planted on a hill above Cape Town, where the Dutch had settled eight years earlier. Beyond that hedge, and a pole fence extending from it, no Hottentot was supposed to venture. The color bar was at first not too vigorously enforced; as late as 1857 South African communicants of the Dutch Reformed Church sipped, whatever their color, from the same communion cup. Now, the church is militantly segregationist. The word "apartheid" itself is fairly recent, having been coined in 1944 by Prime Minister Daniel F. Malan. Afrikaners don't like the word "apartheid" any more; they prefer "separate development" or "separate freedoms" or "multiracial coexistence." The use of the word "freedom" to describe the conditions under which black South Africans live doesn't strike most white South Africans as strange. They are inclined to torture the language in many respects. To describe, for instance, the six hundred thousand or so Africans from other countries who work inside South Africa as migrant laborers, white South Africans have come up with the peculiar phrase "foreign natives."

South Africans often complain that they don't see why there should be so much to-do about their policies of racial discrimination—they prefer "differentiation"—when the same sort of thing exists in so many other places, and in some of them has led to so much more drastic consequences. Watts, California, is one of their favorite cases in point. When South African Whites chide Americans for their treatment of non-Whites, the Americans usually point out that in the United States the indignities heaped upon Negroes are often in direct contravention of federal laws, whereas the South African Parliament has enacted law upon law

25

piling indignity upon indignity. To this rejoinder, South Africans, who think they have a case and have no qualms about articulating it, quickly retort that it is all well and good, in a nation like America, for a white power structure to legislate to protect the rights of people they outnumber by some nine to one, but that in a nation like theirs, where there are nearly five times as many non-Whites as Whites, the minority's self-interest demands that it protect itself against being overwhelmed by the majority. The idea of universal franchise does not lend itself to extensive discussion in South Africa, because most Whites dismiss it out of hand as utterly preposterous. "If Africans got the vote, they'd vote black," one reasonable white South African told me. "I'm afraid that what's happened in other parts of Africa lately—not to mention your own Negroes' epidermal reaction to that Adam Clayton Powell business—doesn't make the prospect encouraging. However liberal one's feelings may be about race, one can't ignore the consequences of a switch in power. Whatever their color, people ultimately are swayed by self-interest. I really don't know why the rest of the world expects South Africans to be different."

Back in 1908 Olive Schreiner, a white South African novelist and essayist of considerable discernment, said, "All persons born in the country or permanently resident here should be one in the eye of the State. . . . South Africa must be a free man's country. The idea that a man born in this country, possibly endowed with many gifts and highly cultured, should in this, his native land, be refused any form of civic or political right on the ground that he is descended from a race with a civilization, it may be, much older than our own, is one which must be abhorrent to every liberalized mind. I believe that an attempt to base our national life on distinctions of race and color as such will, after the lapse of many years, prove fatal to us."

For someone who is white, South Africa can be an extremely pleasant place to visit, and after a few weeks there, whatever one's views about apartheid, one gets used to it. It simply becomes part of the environment, like the gorgeous scenery of which South Africans are so justly proud and which they often talk about when they can be diverted from their two favorite subjects.

These, in order of precedence, are race relations and rugby. (Sex, cricket, scenery, and political matters not involving black-white relationships are distant also-rans.) Apartheid is everywhere. An American minister assigned to South Africa began soon after his arrival to clip the newspapers for petty-apartheid material, but after a few weeks he stopped. It was getting to be a full-time job. "There are very few countries where you can count on being appalled by something in just about every issue of every paper," he told me. In one South African newspaper a recent visitor to the country could read that a lecture for doctors on venereal diseases had been canceled because its sponsors had been too late in asking the Department of Community Development in Cape Town for permission to have two colored physicians attend. From another paper one learned that a Johannesburg sporting event called an Ecumenical Golf Tournament had been canceled because it was too ecumenical; the Minister of Bantu Affairs and Development had told its sponsors that an African Roman Catholic priest who'd been playing in the tournament for years would no longer be allowed to do so.

One of the saddest aspects of apartheid is its wastefulness. "Is there not a better way of using our human and material resources?" an editorial in the weekly *Post,* an African paper, has plaintively inquired. Separation of peoples leads almost inevitably to duplication of facilities; South Africa has a Bantu Animal Welfare Society. Even the blind, who presumably couldn't care less about skin color, are taken into consideration. South Africa has a Colored and Indian Blind Welfare Association. Eleemosynary apartheid. (The standard annual government pension for a blind White is $372.58. For a blind Colored or Indian, it's $130.59, and for a blind African $37.06.)

One day I visited a subterranean tourist attraction called the Cango Caves—the South African equivalent of the Carlsbad Caverns. A bush-jacketed guide who took me around said that nobody knew just how extensive the underground chambers were. It *was* known, he said, that there were a good many unexplored caverns close to the one through which we were traipsing. These, however, could be made accessible only if tunnels were blasted through to them, and inasmuch as the area had been proclaimed a national historic monument, all further blasting in the vicinity had been forbidden. The guide went on to describe the dimensional glories of the main cave, where a German chorus had not long before put on a concert for I forget how many thousands of auditors, who my escort said had fitted into the place very comfortably. "Now we're blasting a new entrance into this chamber," he went on, with sunny South African inconsistency.

"Blasting?" I asked. "But you were just saying——"

He interrupted me. "It's to be a new entrance for non-Whites," he said, "so they can come in at their own hours with their own guides. When we get it finished, there'll have to be no communication at all between them and us."

Speleological apartheid.

Apartheid is not always rigorously enforced. Since most of the black-skinned messengers who scurry around the big cities are on errands for Whites, nobody particularly minds if they ride in elevators marked "Whites Only"; that way, they get their work done faster. But buses, which Africans mostly use before the beginning and after the end of their work days, are something else again. In Cape Town, Whites and non-Whites are allowed on the same buses, but in different sections. (This can make some Whites feel uncomfortable, especially if there are empty seats in their section and elderly nonwhite women have to stand because the seats in *their* section are all occupied.) In Johannesburg, though, white buses and nonwhite buses ply identical routes, and sometimes one sees one of—rather, for—each color traveling in tandem, with only a handful of passengers in each. In many instances, Whites' and non-Whites' buses are painted different colors. Sometimes, when white buses begin to get decrepit, they are repainted and pressed into nonwhite service. (In South Africa, "separate" does not mean "separate but equal"; indeed, there are laws prescribing just the opposite.) "I don't remember ever sitting in a new bus," a South African Indian told me in Durban one day. "Some of the buses they assign to us here are so old they can't make the hills. People who've queued up at a bus stop won't board some of the vehicles that come by, because if a bus breaks down halfway up a hill you have to get out and queue up again and you don't get your fare back."

Most white South Africans wink at apartheid when it becomes economically awkward. Drive-in theaters are supposed to be segregated, but on weekdays, when attendance is light, some theater proprietors are grateful for any kind of patronage and don't carefully scrutinize the faces within approaching vehicles. On weekends, however, when there's a good chance of a capacity audience of Whites, non-Whites are turned away. At some monuments and memorials, there are separate sight-seeing hours for non-Whites, and a few zealous advocates of apartheid have proposed that stores set up separate sections for white and nonwhite customers. "Fine," was one African's reaction. "Let's have separate working days, too." The loudest opponents of separate shopping are the people who own the stores. To have segregated stores or segregated sections of stores might entail carrying cumbersome inventories and hiring extra staffs. Thus, most stores serve all comers. (I once saw the Chinese proprietor of a small corner grocery ignore a white woman customer to wait on a black man, and none of the three of them seemed concerned.)

Quite a few salesclerks in the larger department stores are Afrikaner housewives who've moved from country to city, and it is sometimes painful for them to have to adjust to tending to the wants of Africans, whom they have never known before except as people who were supposed to tend to *their* wants. The biggest chain of stores in the country, the O. K. Bazaars, has a training program for junior executives, each of whom is supposed to put in some time behind a counter. One trainee was doing his stint when an elderly African woman approached him and asked, "Where are gloves?"

"Three counters down, Madam," he replied. Dumfounded at his using that kind of word to that kind of person, a white saleswoman standing nearby slapped her own face so hard she left finger marks on it. However, in South Africa, as elsewhere, economic pressures can affect social attitudes. In the Cape Town open-air market, for instance, I heard a white auctioneer who was selling dinner plates for seventy-five cents a dozen refer aloud to an African customer as "the lady in blue."

Most of the amenities that one associates with big cities are denied to urban Africans. A nonwhite Cape Town woman returning

29

from a European vacation said that what she had liked best about the trip was to be able to go to any theater of her choice. It should be added, however, as an illustration of the affection even circumscribed South Africans have for their country, that she also said that she'd love to go abroad again some time but there was really no place like home. "In South Africa we have everything overseas people could wish for," she said, "except freedom to do certain things."

In Johannesburg, shortly after noon one day, a white acquaintance drove me from a native township outside the city to a downtown lunch appointment. In the car ahead of us sat a black man and black woman, faultlessly dressed. I wondered offhandedly if they were planning also to have lunch in town. "Only if they're carrying it in a paper bag and plan to sit in the gutter," my companion said. He was exaggerating slightly. There are a few restaurants in Johannesburg that cater to non-Whites, but most of these are tacky fish-and-chips establishments on the fringes of the city. (When one sees a sign in the middle of any South African city advertising a New Anglo-African Tea Room, one knows that only Anglos are welcome.) Some Africans are luckier than others. One of them who has an executive job in a large and enlightened corporation might have some personal difficulties did not his boss happen to have a private washroom, which he shares with his African deputy. The two of them, though, cannot have a business lunch together in any restaurant; when they want to eat together, they eat at the boss's desk. There are no park benches in Johannesburg on which a non-White, even if he happens to have his lunch in a paper bag, may lawfully sit.

The three-quarters of a million non-Whites in and around Johannesburg are served by just one hotel. It has thirty-eight rooms, six with private baths. South Africa has an enormous coastline and is a vacation land par excellence. Notwithstanding, it is only just recently that the government has even begun talking about setting up any seaside facilities for its African population. In 1967 it was still possible in a nation 80 per cent nonwhite for a small hotel outside Durban to bill itself the "only fully licensed non-European beach front hotel in South Africa." Beach fronts, like everything else, are rigorously segregated. Durban has an Indian beach, a

30

Colored beach, and an African beach. The only amenity the African beach has is a single water tap at the edge of the road that leads to it. The other non-white beaches are a little better, but not much. I asked an Indian there, a businessman of considerable means who lives in an elegant home, how he felt about having to swim at the only stretch of strand allocated to him. "I don't go swimming," he said.

There are several splendid beaches for Whites close by the big white hotels and a big amusement park for Whites. (The non-Whites in Durban derive whatever amusement they can from a "Europeans Only" sign outside an establishment called Caves of Terror and Horror.) At the white beaches another sign says "Dogs Prohibited." Any further posted restrictions would be supererogatory, but at other locations South Africans like to waste money reminding themselves of what they all already know. Thus, telephone booths in Whites-only areas have Whites-only warnings stenciled on them; the same goes for coin-operated weighing machines at the Whites-only amusement park in Durban. No non-White would be foolish enough to respond to a help-wanted notice posted at one of the nearby beaches: "Young lady required to operate portable suntan sprayer at South Beach." Classified ads in the newspapers are more specifically worded: "Colored Female Clerk," "European Matriculants," "Non-European Chemical Technician," etc.

Right in the middle of Durban, located much as Central Park is in New York, is a huge race track, where the nation's most celebrated horsey event, the July Handicap, is run every South African winter. (One visitor to South Africa, who had heard about its requiring most of its citizens to carry identification papers with them at all times, saw a notice in a shop window, "Buy Race Cards Here," and was momentarily taken aback until he realized it had to do with horse racing.) The track is huge, two and a half miles in circumference, with an eighteen-hole golf course in the infield. The spectators' stands are separated—the Whites' at the finish line, the Africans' so far from it that they have to wait for an announcement to tell them which horse has won, the rest not too much better situated. I asked one Indian lawyer how he felt about enjoying such a poor view. "I don't go to the horse races,"

31

he said.

Apartheid can be inconvenient, and even dangerous. Ambulances are segregated. A so-called European injured in an automobile accident may not be picked up by a non-European ambulance (nor may a non-European by a European one), and if a white man has the misfortune to bleed to death before an appropriate mercy vehicle materializes, he can comfort himself in extremis by reflecting that he will most assuredly be buried in an all-white cemetery. (Nonwhite South African doctors may not perform autopsies on white South African corpses.) The South African obsession with total racial separation to and even beyond the bitter end was neatly encapsuled some years back by the writer Herman Charles Bosman, who turned out many short stories about Afrikaner life. In one of them, "Unto Dust," Bosman had a narrator tell of a black-white war in the course of which a white man and a black man died while in hand-to-hand combat. Some time later the white victim's widow wanted to give him a decent burial, but when her friends went to the scene of battle they found only a jumbled mess of skin and bones. All the bones were very white and all the skin had been turned black by the sun. The widow interred some of the bones and some of the skin, but she must have guessed wrong, because a dog belonging to the dead black man began hanging around mournfully at the grave. "I remember one of our party saying that that was the worst of these kaffir wars," Bosman had his narrator remark. "If it had been a war against the English, and part of a dead Englishman had got lifted into that coffin by mistake, it wouldn't have mattered so much."

Apartheid wastes a lot of time. The trains that run in and out of Cape Town leave from a single central station, with separate cars for Whites and non-Whites. There are also separate station entrances for the two groups. After the non-Whites have gone a long way around they end up on the same platform with the Whites. At one white entrance there is a sign that says "Forwarded baggage for Whites tendered by non-Whites." After getting accustomed to such absurdities, one comes to take almost anything in stride. Along a mall in Cape Town that leads past a botanical garden to the Houses of Parliament, one does not know

32

quite what to make of a cage full of pigeons, just outside of which there are apparently identical pigeons flying around free.

South African apologists like to think of themselves as comprising one big happy separated family, and indeed the country's motto is "Unitas." What unites South Africans more than anything else, perhaps, is unanimity on the nature of the problems that it faces. In a recent poll conducted among South African Whites, nearly three-quarters of them agreed that the color question was their paramount contemporary issue, and one would hardly expect non-Whites to consider it any less consequential. Important as race relations may be to all South Africans, few of them, though, *have* many race relations. The vast majority of white South Africans rarely talk *to* any Blacks, except their own servants; they mostly just talk *about* them. A white man who not long ago publicly urged his fellow Whites to make a point of establishing some meaningful contact with at least one non-White was considered eccentric, if not radical.

Most Whites would regard it as simply unthinkable to sit down to a meal with a non-White, though attitudes may be changing. After all, their Prime Minister not long ago had lunch at the Mount Nelson Hotel with the black Prime Minister of the newly independent neighboring state of Lesotho. But that was high-level diplomacy, not day-to-day social intercourse. Outside of South Africa, curiously, many white South Africans go out of their way to hobnob with non-Whites—forbidden fruit and all that. Lourenço Marques, in neighboring Mozambique, is a popular weekend spot. Mozambique is integrated, and white South Africans can date dark girls there. The same holds true in the High Commission territory of not-quite-yet-fully-independent Swaziland, which is surrounded on three sides by South Africa.

The entire white South African attitude toward interracial sex is bewildering. It is perhaps not surprising that a country with foreign natives should also have, by inference at least, moral brothels. Among the laws peculiar to South Africa is an immorality act that makes it a criminal offense for people whose colors do not match to have sexual relations. Nevertheless, there are establishments where white males can enjoy nonwhite female companionship. The places are called immoral brothels, a phrase that anywhere but in South Africa would have a tautological ring. While I was in the country, no one seemed to think it particularly odd that one of the popular stage attractions should be an old-fashioned minstrel show (*that* dates South Africa) in which blond girls cavorted with blackface partners. I guess it was considered all right because it was make-believe. At one Afrikaner university a girl student who'd spent a year in the United States told me with equanimity that while over there she had dated an American Negro and had thought not too much about it. She hadn't even felt all too bad about dating a South African Zulu who was also studying in the States. In South Africa, of course, she wouldn't —she *couldn't*—have had any meaningful contact with either of them.

Few Whites, however, know much at firsthand about the non-Whites' humiliations and frustrations. There used to be a far greater number of integrated groups than there are now, and the last few holdouts are either disappearing or diminishing in importance. Yet the visitor never stops being told how well the white South Africans get along with their black brethren. "You journalists just don't understand," a woman told me at a cocktail party. "We have a marvelous relationship with our servants. Not all Africans are perfect—there are those political types—but some of them are as loyal as you could wish." Loyalty was the theme she stressed. Her remarks were addressed to me at one of the few kinds of interracial parties the ordinary visitor gets to attend. This particular one, held at a private club, was a fund-raising occasion. Some Whites were trying to raise money to support an African cultural movement. The entertainers included five African singers who, among other numbers, sang one song, with great feeling, that included the words "So take my hand and walk this land with me." I saw no physical laying-on of hands as a result. A lot of interracial meetings arranged with great difficulty prove when they take place to be plain awkward. There is a determinedly nonpolitical club in Cape Town whose members are composed of white and nonwhite men who get together once a month to talk about rugby and cricket. Once a year it is their practice to invite their wives and have a buffet supper. They have been assured by lawyers that this is perfectly all right provided that no Whites and

34

non-Whites sit down while they are eating in the same room. So they eat standing up. There are elderly white South African liberals who used to see a great deal of Africans. I talked with one woman who had once spent a weekend with the late Chief Albert Luthuli. "I couldn't do that sort of thing now," she said. "I don't even *know* the leaders."

Just about the only interracial gatherings of any consequence in South Africa today are the parties given by the United States diplomatic representatives there. Our ambassador holds open houses, as a rule, at Pretoria on George Washington's birthday and at Cape Town on the Fourth of July. All colors are welcome. To avoid subjecting high South African government officials to the embarrassment of declining an invitation, since they wouldn't dream of attending such affairs, they are simply not invited. A good many American businessmen stationed in South Africa stay away, too; they seem to think attendance might offend some of the South Africans they have to do business with. There is considerably less agitation in South Africa now, however, than there was when the parties began in 1963. For two years after that, the stubborn American practice of indulging in interracial hospitality was much discussed in the news columns and editorial pages of the South African papers. Now the parties are covered routinely on the society pages.

An individual—a visiting journalist, say—can entertain non-Whites in his hotel room, but the glare of the desk clerks as he ushers his guests onto the premises can be something chilling. There are a few—a very few—private homes of white South Africans where it is still possible to meet Blacks. (Even under their own roofs Whites are not supposed to offer non-Whites alcoholic beverages, so if the police pop in while drinks are being served, the Africans pretend that they brought their own liquor.) Attending such a gathering, one feels almost conspiratorial, and—inasmuch as these occasions are subversive of the separation policy that the government holds so dear—one probably is being conspiratorial. It is very difficult these days for a visiting white person in South Africa to sit alongside a black man at a dinner table without thinking to himself, "Hey, look at me!"

35

II

Physically, South Africa is one of the loveliest spots on earth. It has in abundance all the different kinds of scenery that anyone could possibly ask for, plus, of course, an eye-opening assortment of wild animals. It is far enough below the Equator so that in most portions of the country the temperature is rarely oppressively hot; it is not so far south that the weather is ever excessively cold. With its seasons the reverse of those in the northern hemisphere, it holds an all-iris show in October. Since South Africa has both a mild climate and more automobiles than any other nation on its continent, one would think convertibles would be much in evidence. The only ones around are apt to belong to sporty foreigners. Some think the absence of convertibles is attributable to South Africans' *laager* philosophy. An equally plausible

36

explanation may be merely that South African women don't like to get their hair mussed.

Nature has been kind to South Africa except in one respect: the country periodically suffers from severe droughts. When Prime Minister Vorster assumed office his country had long been without substantial rainfall, and he said that his biggest concern at that moment was the drought. Some Afrikaners were annoyed because the English press reported him as having said that his biggest concern was internal affairs. During protracted droughts, the Dutch Reformed Church sometimes calls for national prayers, with the country's president, who is largely a ceremonial figurehead, leading his nation in supplication. When their prayers for rain are rewarded, South Africans are jubilant. At the torrential end of one particularly long dry spell, a staid Afrikaner farm family stripped naked, as did their black servant girl, and they all went out and danced together in celebration. When the rains come, they often come savagely, and strip off the farmers' precious topsoil. Part of the northern Transvaal province, where the extremes of weather are notably grievous, is called the Belt of Sorrow.

Of all the big South African cities, Johannesburg is most affected by the droughts, because it has no natural water supply. Its lawns turn brown and its flowers wilt. I was there during a drought, and heard much admiration expressed for the resourcefulness of one suburban housewife. Hearing that her butcher was cleaning out his freezer, she rushed over and helped herself to some of his ice scrapings. She dumped them on a flower bed, and when they melted, not only did her garden perk up but there was an unexpected bonus: her dogs found some tasty scraps of meat. To escape the censure of neighbors who might think they are violating water-rationing regulations, some Johannesburg householders with private wells post signs at the entrances to their homes saying "This property has its own borehole."

Nearly every suburban place also has a sign at its entrance attesting to its being protected by this or that burglar-alarm system. Johannesburg must be one of the world's prime markets for burglar alarms. Not long ago a new security fence was advertised there. It was composed of sections of wire on frames that revolved at more than thirty miles per hour, and it was augmented by an infrared device that would sound an alarm if a man or large animal approached within a hundred yards of the installation. The white residents of Johannesburg are so distrustful of Blacks, including often their own servants, that they normally keep their liquor cabinets securely locked; some of the wealthier residents have night watchmen equipped with walkie-talkies who patrol their grounds at night accompanied by savage dogs. Even private automobiles are fitted out with alarms. During a cricket match one day at the Wanderers Club, the license number of a car was announced over a public-address system, followed by the request, "Would the owner of the car kindly go and shut off the hooter? Somebody tried to break into your car and it's blowing like mad."

Johannesburg, which South Africans of all colors familiarly call Joburg, is a fast-growing and modern-looking city. Its central district, like that of almost any contemporary metropolis, is laid out in orderly rectangles, with one exception—a street that runs diagonally and that has been named, with typical South African practicality, Diagonal Street. Excavations are now under way for a new, grandiose civic project that, like Rockefeller Center, will swallow up a couple of existing streets. Covering five acres, the venture in progress is called Carlton Center. It will have a fifty-store office building, a thirty-story hotel, and seven levels below ground. South Africans like to speak of their own achievements in superlatives. "The basement is a job the like of which the world hasn't seen before," one Carlton Center engineer told me. Compared to basements in the rest of the world, the forthcoming one has a further distinction: it will contain separate canteens for Europeans, Africans, Coloreds, and Indians. The Center was designed by Skidmore, Owings & Merrill, in association with a firm of South African architects. American engineers have also been involved, to the distress of some chauvinistic South Africans. One National Party city councilman in Johannesburg said, "Why must we follow American building techniques? They voted against us at the U.N."

Digging deep holes into the earth is what caused Johannesburg to be where it is in the first place. It is where gold was first mined in 1886, and another name for it is the City of Gold. All around the city are massive, ziggurat-shaped, man-made hills of mine tailings. The present-day Johannesburg stock exchange is a hundred yards from the site of the first productive local gold mine. There has been so much digging around Johannesburg that the ground trembles all the time, and every now and then a sinkhole will open up perilously near someone's house. The city is also notorious for the violence of its spring and early-summer thunderstorms.

By day, the streets of Johannesburg swarm with Africans, most of them thoroughly Westernized. Even those Africans who while in town cling to some of their tribal customs compromise to a degree with city ways. One may see walking down a street a straight-backed, arm-swinging, head-high, multiple-ankleted African woman in native dress, but she is likely to have balanced on her head a cardboard box containing a lady's handbag. Or, in a curio shop normally patronized by foreign tourists, one may come across an authentic female witch doctor accompanied by a young disciple who during her novitiate is required to assume a kneeling position whenever her superior talks to anyone. I saw such a couple one day trying to shop for a leopard skin and an *assegai,* a native spear. The white saleswoman waiting on them was quite agreeable about selling the fur, but told the witch doctor regretfully that before the store could sell her the weapon she would have to obtain a permit from the Department of Bantu Affairs and Development.

By night the streets of Johannesburg are all but deserted. In theory, all non-Whites have to be out of the city by eleven o'clock, except for those who have live-in jobs or are employed as night watchmen and ride around on bicycles. These latter are called the Black Watch. The curfew ends early—at 5:00 A.M. —because that is when the Africans start coming back to work from their homes outside the city. The Whites, after dark, retreat to their own suburbs, to rest up. Most white South African men of the upper middle class or higher work quite hard. They have to; because non-Whites are generally permitted to advance only so far, there aren't enough competent Whites around to handle the nation's managerial affairs. So white South Africans knock themselves out at the office every day, rush home to play tennis

39

energetically at an altitude of six thousand feet, stay up a good part of the night drinking brandy, and take perverse pride that they have the highest per capita male coronary-thrombosis rate on earth.

There are poor Whites in South Africa. I had a car-hire driver one day who was sixty-five years old and worked, he said, from six every morning to ten thirty every night, holding down a full daytime job as a clerk in a brewery and then putting on a chauffeur's cap. He said it was the only way he could make ends meet, and he was quite bitter about the government for spending as much money as it does on non-Whites and paying so relatively little heed to the likes of him. There are even white beggars in South Africa. Most of the beggars one sees on the streets—and one doesn't see too many of them—are crippled Africans, but there are white panhandlers, too, and they have a slight advantage. I was having a drink on the veranda of a Durban hotel one day when a grubby white beggar approached and made a terrible nuisance of himself. None of the African waiters who were standing around could do anything about him—in South Africa, a non-White doesn't shoo a White away—so he was able to wheedle with impunity until a white doorman came along and sent him packing. I had already given him twenty cents, on the theory that any white man in South Africa who has to beg must really be in trouble.

For surely nowhere else on earth can there be, for most white people, such easy living. In South Africa, for a man to have a two-car garage and a yard boy is not necessarily a sign that he is prosperous. It just means that he is white. Some white liberals are recurrently disturbed at being so comfortable as the result of a system they find morally indefensible. But most of them don't fret too much; life is too good. Sixty-two per cent of all white South African families have domestic servants, and this despite the refusal of quite a few Afrikaner households to employ servants on the ground that it would be incompatible with their devotion to separation of the races. (One per cent of black South Africans have domestic servants.) One can hire an African servant in South Africa for about two hundred dollars a year.

White South Africans are quick to point out, however, when

40

foreigners raise their eyebrows at this rate of pay, that it often takes two or three African employees to do what might elsewhere be considered a single person's work. And some of the domestics' habits are unpredictable. Quite a few of them, for instance, even those who have long been living in a Western environment, cling to many of their tribal beliefs, including witchcraft. I spent one evening at the home of a Johannesburg couple who apologized because their manservant was unavailable. He had gone home, my hosts told me, because one of his four wives was ailing. The last time he'd had a sick wife, though he himself when ill would go to a conventional doctor, he had taken her to a witch doctor, who had produced a live frog and convinced the husband that it was the creature leaping around inside his wife that had made her sick. Another time, I visited a farm family who, in the course of telling me how well they treated their help, complained that they had once put in a bathroom for their Africans but that the Africans wouldn't use it. What apparently had not occurred to the farmers was that there might be some people on earth who would rather be granted a wish than a wash.

In theory, South African cityfolk may keep only one live-in servant, who must sleep in quarters detached from their employer's premises. In practice, there are apt to be a good many more friends or relatives of the servant's visiting or staying on the premises than the employer knows about or the government condones. Most white housewives wink at these petty transgressions, but one of them, disturbed by what seemed to her excessive commotion in her servant's quarters, complained to her maid that perhaps she might be a little bit more circumspect about receiving men at night. "Well, Madam," the maid replied, "if you and your husband can entertain your friends whenever you feel like it, I don't see why I can't."

There are all kinds of backstairs dramas. One housewife took me to her servant's quarters one day to show me a newborn baby belonging, she thought, to a neighbor's maid. The day before, my hostess' maid had asked her if she could call an ambulance for a friend, who was in labor. The housewife had no clear idea what was going on, but called anyway. She was asked at first whether the ambulance was for a European or a non-European. When she

41

said it was for a non-European, the next question was, "Will they pay cash?" The housewife said *she* would pay. Twenty-four hours later, the mother and her newborn child were back in the servant's quarters, and when I left the housewife had no idea exactly what she was going to do with them.

The government, which is dedicated to controlling the influx of Africans, of all ages, into urban communities, is ever alert. Where post offices in other countries might stamp envelopes with some such legend as "Support your Community Chest," South African post offices use "Have you registered your Bantu servant?" Periodically, the police raid suburban areas, looking for Africans who are not supposed to be there, and carting them off by the vanload. Frequently, a cook or houseboy will disappear from his place of employment during the night, and his employer will spend the rest of the night trying to find out where he has been taken and to bail him out. After one Western diplomat whose country enjoys friendly relations with South Africa had gone sleepless trying to retrieve one of his servants, a South African government official apologized to him for the inconvenience. "Not at all," said the diplomat. "It's an experience all foreigners should have in your country at least once."

Only 26 per cent of all white South African women do any kind of work at all—one of the lowest percentages in the Western world. Surrounded—except during droughts—by flowers, and by servants, they lead a delightful, leisurely existence. At a dinner party I attended in Johannesburg the talk got around to reincarnation. One white businessman, asked in what guise he'd like to return to earth if he had the opportunity, said, unhesitatingly, "I'd like to come back as my wife." (Another male guest said, *"I'd* like to come back as a black man living somewhere on the coast with its beautiful scenery and good fishing, with plenty of women and children around to do all the work, and if I got tired of my wife I'd get me another. But of course if I were a black man, I wouldn't have enough energy to fish.") Many inland white South Africans have second homes along the seashore where they spend a good part of the summer months of December and January. A Pretoria man whose vacation place is on the edge of Cape Town, where the waters teem with shellfish, told me that it never bothered his wife and him if a dozen or so Sunday-afternoon guests there decided to stay on for supper. "I just step outside and walk into the water and grab enough crayfish to handle the crowd," he said.

The white suburbs of the big South African cities are like a synthesis of Grosse Pointe, Beverly Hills, and Scarsdale. Not only do a great many of the houses have their own swimming pools, but there is an extraordinary density of private tennis courts. South Africans of all colors are extremely sports-minded. Early in 1967 a South African cricket team defeated a traveling Australian team in an international test match. It was the first such South African triumph in sixty-four years. Afterward one rooter for the victorious home side rose to his feet in a bar and exclaimed, "Anybody who is not merry by now is not a South African!" He must have meant any White, because non-Whites have taken to cheering for all non-South African teams that come to the country. It is one of the few ways they have had of expressing their resentment at sports apartheid. Not too long ago there were quite a few mixed South African teams, and spectators of all colors were welcome at South African arenas. Now, with a few exceptions, white events are supposed to be watched by Whites only, and nonwhite events by non-Whites only.

Race tracks are open to all comers, but because they are kept separated, there can be complications. At the Durbanville course outside Cape Town there is a maze of fences, set up to let both Whites and non-Whites get to the paddock by different routes, and also to permit Whites to get to an all-white restaurant that happens to be located in a nonwhite area. (Some nonwhite punters grumble that the bookmakers in their area—the bookies who work at the tracks are all white—discriminate against them by laying worse odds than they do for white bettors.) The rules governing sports vary from province to province. In Natal, Indians are still allowed to watch white soccer games, because they have traditionally been soccer's most loyal supporters and the sport probably couldn't survive without their backing. Elsewhere, where there are fewer Indians, soccer audiences are segregated.

South Africa was barred from the 1964 Olympic Games because of apartheid. The only two South African sports organizations that currently have international recognition are in the fields of weight lifting and table tennis. (The South African Table Tennis Board, which enjoys favor abroad, is composed mostly of non-Whites; the comparable white group, the South African Table Tennis Union, is frowned upon.) Looking toward the 1968 Olympics in Mexico City, many South Africans hoped that their new prime minister, a sports-minded man, would adopt a less unbending attitude toward mixed sports than his predecessor, and, to the surprise of many others, Mr. Vorster has done just that. He has decided that South Africa may send a mixed team to Mexico City, though it is to be selected in a curious way—its white contingent by white committees, and its nonwhite contingent by white ones. He has declared furthermore that although domestic teams must continue to be segregated, visiting foreigners may use their own judgment about who represents them. This would seem to indicate that, also in 1968, South Africa might get to see one of its athletic heroes back in action in his native land. He is Basil D'Oliveira, a colored cricket player who now lives in England, and who will probably be picked for a challenge team the British are planning to send down for a test-match series. (Dolly, as he is popularly known, visited South Africa in 1966 to supervise some cricket clinics, but these were only for colored players.) For adopting his comparatively relaxed attitude, Mr. Vorster, at a meeting of some members of his own political party in Pretoria, was called a Judas.

Vorster is primarily a golfer, though he is not unacquainted with other sports. In the course of one recent diplomatic exchange he remarked, "The ball is now in the United States court." He has a thirteen handicap at golf. He likes to have pictures of himself taken while he is on the links, wearing a pair of shorts and a battered felt hat pulled down over his ears. His predecessor, Dr. Verwoerd, was aloof and humorless. Mr. Vorster is fond of relating comical anecdotes about himself. One has to do with a colored caddie who goes around with him in the Cape province, and who allegedly told the Prime Minister after one good shot, "You know, Master, with my brains and your brawn we could go far." On another occasion, as the Prime Minister tells it, after another

44

good shot, the caddie said, "Ah, my dear sir, if it wasn't for this bloody apartheid I'd shake your hand." A sharp-penned cartoonist for the *Cape Times,* Dave Marais, used to show Dr. Verwoerd, an otherworldly man, speaking on a telephone whose wire extended up to heaven; he now often shows Mr. Vorster with a bag of golf clubs. In one drawing the woods had cloth covers bearing the numerals 1, 2, 90, and 180—these last two referring, as South Africans didn't have to be told, to the infamous detention laws that Vorster invoked and enforced while holding a cabinet portfolio that South Africans straightfacedly call the Ministry of Justice. South Africa's only weekly newsmagazine, a fairly irreverent journal called *News/Check,* handed out some tongue-in-cheek tributes not long ago and gave Vorster the Eisenhower Award for 1966. Mr. Vorster is said to have kept four golf dates during the height of the Rhodesian crisis in November 1966, and he once cut short a meeting with a prominent newspaper editor because he had a golf date with Gary Player.

Player is probably the most celebrated South African athlete who still lives in South Africa. A physical-fitness and health-food faddist, he runs the Gary Player Health Center in Johannesburg. He has also lately written an autobiographical book. It has received some adverse criticism because, along with crediting God and the proper diet for his success, he goes out of his way to praise his government. He won the 1961 Masters, he says, because God wanted him to; he won an important match-play contest in 1965 because he got to thinking about his country, "maligned, misunderstood, pilloried by people who can tell us how to order our affairs from a range of six thousand miles without ever coming down to South Africa and seeing for themselves, and trying to understand."

One of the oddest things about the book is that one scans it in vain for any mention of a man who, but for South Africa's rules about sports, would quite possibly be a golfer as formidable as the author. This is an Indian pro, Sewsunker Sewgolum, whose nickname is Papwa. Now, Gary may have skipped over Papwa because, like many other South Africans, Player sometimes seems to have a special frame of reference. He has spoken in public appearances of the three million inhabitants of South Africa, as if

45

there were no others than Whites. Papwa belongs to the other fifteen million. He began his career in Durban as a caddie, moved ahead, and in time won the professional championship of the Netherlands. He used to play in quite a few tournaments, except for those held in the Orange Free State, where no Asian is allowed to stay more than twenty-four hours in any circumstances. In 1963 Papwa won the Natal Open, beating a hundred and thirteen white players. But now the government is making it increasingly difficult for him to play outside of nonwhite circles. He can't as a rule sharpen his game by practicing on decent courses, and he can't make enough money in nonwhite tournaments, which he usually wins handily, to enable him to tackle the international circuit. He did get to the United States, in May 1967, for the Houston Open—an Indian businessman in Durban underwrote his expenses—but he found the competition a bit stiff and finished out of the money. Sometimes the nonwhite tournaments he is largely confined to at home are held on white courses. In such cases, non-Whites are barred from the club house and Whites may not follow the nonwhite players around. When Papwa was playing in one recent such competition, the white members of the club at which it was held were restricted to their club house, from which they tried with binoculars to follow his progress as well as they could. The *Johannesburg Star* has cited Sewgolum as a shining example of the difficulty of a man's trying to develop separately under the South African system of separate development.

The inconveniences that beset Sewgolum are the result of a series of Group Areas Acts that the South African legislature has been passing since 1950 and that decree who shall live where and do what where. Indians are supposed to stay, and play, with Indians. (Instead of "Group Areas," the government has lately been talking in terms of "Community Development," which sounds nicer.) A nonwhite senior technologist at a hospital lived in a part of Cape Town that for years had been occupied largely by Coloreds. The government proclaimed that it would henceforth be a white area, and the Department of Community Development offered him another residence. He couldn't move to it because it had no telephone and he was on round-the-clock call. He was hauled into court, where a magistrate agreed that he was essential

46

to the hospital and then sentenced him to a fine of a hundred and fifty dollars or fifty days in prison. The sentence was suspended for eighteen months on condition that the man move. Still, he was found guilty.

It is sometimes bitterly said by non-Whites in South Africa that the only piece of soil on which they can be sure of having permanent occupancy is the grave. Some have been luckier than others. The Malayans of Cape Town, for instance, continue to live in the same cobblestone-street sector of the city that has been theirs for the last hundred and fifty years. In shuffling around its various population groups, the government has, to be sure, moved many people from dismal slums into reasonably decent housing. South Africa, in fact, has probably done more to provide new housing for non-Whites in the last decade than any government anywhere. But the people it moves at will and seemingly at whim do not always appreciate the change; nobody likes to have no choice about his residence. The government's arbitrariness has particularly riled South Africa's Indian population. Quite a few Indians acquired substantial land holdings in areas that were subsequently designated white. When they were obliged to sell, the prices the government set were, the Indians insist, demonstrably unfair. Nearly all the Indians live in Natal, the most tropical of the country's provinces. "In Natal, we just sort of aim to survive from October to March," one Durban man told me. The Indians tend not to complain too much, but few of them are happy. They don't mind living apart. They almost always have. "We don't want to live with white people," one of their community leaders told me. "Just give us a place we can be proud to live in." Moreover, Indians customarily live in large family units, with grandparents, cousins, and other relatives sharing the same roof; the houses to which the government wants them to shift have been designed to suit the less gregarious, Anglo-Saxon way of life.

The forebears of South Africa's contemporary Indian community came to Natal in 1860 as indentured workers for the province's sugar-cane plantations. With close to half a million Indians in and around Durban, the city has a spicy Asiatic character. Mosques are everywhere. The principal Indian market offers a dazzling variety of curry powders—Hell-Fire, Atomic, Mother-in-

Law, Delayed Action, and, of relatively recent origin, Rock 'n' Roll. The Indian market is located right alongside the principal African market, but the juxtaposition does not mean that the two groups are necessarily chummy. They have been likened to two caged animals, both of which detest their zookeeper, but, realizing they are impotent to hurt him, turn on one another. In 1949 some of the Africans in Durban went on an anti-Indian rampage that caused much bloodshed.

There has lately been little overt animosity, although one cultured Indian man did surprise me a bit by saying, "It's in the heart of the African to kill and pillage. He will only obey tribal laws. Until he changes, he can't be part of the civilized Western world." He sounded more like an Afrikaner. Indians and Africans work side by side in Natal factories that manufacture shoes, carpets, and handbags. Quite a few Indians used to make a living by running trading stores in largely African-inhabited areas. Now, under the Group-Areas regulations, these Indians are being removed from their business locations, and they don't like it. From time to time there has been talk about some of them emigrating to India, and the South African government has offered to provide those who wished to return with their fare. Very few South African Indians availed themselves of the opportunity. "We're not Indians," one of them told me. "We're South Africans."

It has only been since 1961 that the South African government has formally conceded that they are. But merely as inferiors. "How can you give your best to a land in which you're not allowed to function as a full-fledged member?" an Indian doctor said to me one day. "My little boy, aged five, said to me recently, 'Dad, why can't *we* find a place where we can restrict the *Whites* from having things?' I don't know; I've sent my sister and her children abroad, but I have my mother here with me, and she's too old to move and make new friends I've been to America and to England and to Canada, but, damn it, this is my home. I'm a South African. And the time may come when I'll be needed here, so I guess I'll probably stay. But it isn't easy. It's never easy when you can't tell your boy why he can't go in the kids' paddling pool at the amusement park. My sons think I'm being stingy and don't want to pay the money."

The doctor thought that the consulting rooms he had to use were putrid, although he conceded that a couple of African doctors who had stopped by rather admired them. At that, though, the Durban doctor considered himself better off than a colleague in Pretoria, which has a small Indian population. The doctor there had an office only a mile from the nearest hospital, but since it was an all-white hospital, he had to associate himself with one fifty miles away. (Many of Pretoria's Indians have for years lived in a slum called Asiatic Bazaar, a twelve-by-six-block area that is a slum largely because the government has done nothing to improve it since 1880. South Africa, like any up-to-date Western nation, is crisscrossed with handsome highways of which the country's leaders are very proud; the streets of Asiatic Bazaar aren't even paved. And since nonwhite members of the South African Medical Association can't attend that group's meetings, which are normally held at the exclusive University of Pretoria, the only way those doctors can keep abreast of the Association's activities is to invite one of its sympathetic white members to their homes and ask for a recapitulation.) "The morbid side of all this apartheid legislation is not its material aspects, though they're bad enough," the Durban doctor told me, "but the emotional and intellectual ones. Until I went abroad I was almost beginning to feel that I was a second-rate human being." The doctor had a little anecdote to tell me, too—about a disturbed Afrikaner who'd come to his office one day and then, without waiting to be examined, had rushed off shouting that he was going to commit suicide. The Indian had called in a policeman and urged him to try to find the fellow before he killed himself, but the policeman had said he didn't see what he could do about it, since no crime had been committed. Upon which, the doctor said, his African servant had exclaimed, "Master, if they treat their own people like that, what hope is there for you and me?"

"Oh, we love apartheid!" an Indian businessman told me at his Durban home. "It gives us spanking new schools and hygienic houses and other amenities that we never had before, and at the same time it crushes our spirits, thus giving us an excuse to revolt. There aren't many of us who are really militant, but it's hard for any of us not to feel some sympathy for groups like the African National Congress. The government has forced us into this alliance. We're between the devil and the deep blue sea, in more senses than one." It was a splendid home, in a suburb of Durban that has been set aside for Indians, and a not uncommon home, because although the majority of South Africa's Indians live marginally, quite a few of them have done extremely well in business and in professions. No matter how much of a financial success any of them may have become, however, they can never attain higher standing in the Durban Chamber of Commerce than that of associate membership. If they were full-fledged members, they might want to attend the Chamber's annual banquets, and that could be awkward.

Some of the more prosperous Indians seem quite content with their lot. "Even with apartheid, the standard of living of nonwhite South Africans is better than that of all the rest of Africa, and better than that of all of Asia, except Japan, and better than that of much of the United States," one Indian businessman told me. "We don't condone anything, but we must recognize facts. South Africa is a young country, and the opportunities here are enormous for us, as well as for everyone else. We businessmen never had it so good." He had not gone so far in approving the National Party, however, as to associate himself with a group called the Indian National Council, which the government established in 1963 and which supposedly speaks for the Indian community, though in fact it has no influence, serving at best in an advisory capacity. But he spoke rather charitably, on the whole, about the government. "There isn't really so much that's so bad about South Africa," he said. "We Indians can still talk reasonably freely. The government *wants* us to express our opinions. Some people think that our acceptance of things as they are smacks of expediency. Our answer to that is, what choice do we have? We have to live here. It's not a question of political theory. When I was in London a few months ago and I saw how the Indians there were living, I began to wonder, do they with their freedoms enjoy a better life than we do here? The answer is no. In England Indians can't get jobs unless there are no Whites available for them. And when it comes to that, when I was last in Washington, D. C., a friend of mine and I were chased from a theater because our skin

50

was dark. We should have had the sense to wear turbans instead of hats. I ran into an acquaintance in London who had gone into exile because of his feelings about the government here. He urged me not to make the same mistake he'd made. 'Keep your nose clean and carry on,' he told me."

It is central to the theory of separate development that such political rights as non-Whites enjoy are to be conferred on them only in their homelands. It can be argued that Africans, most of whom have specific tribal affiliations, do have homelands, although the argument is not very persuasive to a third- or fourth-generation urban African who has never laid eyes on his so-called homeland and in whose eyes environment looms larger than heredity. Indian South Africans have no discernible homeland— New Delhi or Bombay being just about as remote to them as New York or Boston—and neither do the much larger group of South African colored people. All they have is mixed blood, and they got that because somewhere along the line they had white ancestors. It is an old joke among South African Coloreds that the answer to the question "When did the colored race begin?" is "Exactly nine months after van Riebeeck landed"—Jan van Riebeeck being the leader of the 1652 Dutch expedition. Cape Town is the hub of the colored nonhomeland. "Ninety-nine per cent of the bloody white people in Cape Town are not bloody white, which is what makes us so bloody mad," one Cape Colored told me.

In South Africa everybody has to be *something,* but inasmuch as many Whites have rather dark complexions, and as many Coloreds are quite fair, the dividing line between them is occasionally fuzzy. Between 1911 and 1921, when it was easier to switch classifications than it is today, some fifty thousand individuals disappeared from the colored population rolls. Presumably, they elected to become white. Such a switch is still possible. I met one elderly colored man who had lived and worked in the same small town for thirty-five years. Now the town was being proclaimed a white area, and the government had said he would have to move. When he complained that his grandfather and father had lived there before him and that he had no idea where to go or

51

what to do, a government official suggested that he avoid all the fuss by getting himself reclassified white. He declined, on the ground that if he did the Whites who had thought of him all along as colored would reject him and so would all his colored friends. There are few such cases nowadays. There are many more, most of them heartbreaking, of people who had thought of themselves all along as white suddenly being reclassified as colored. An eleven-year-old girl from an Afrikaner family in the Transvaal was sent home from the white boarding school she attended because the authorities decided she looked colored. Technically, she could continue living with her family only if they gave her the status of a servant. The courts eventually declared her white, under a new law that says the child of two white parents is automatically white, but at last reports the girl was having trouble getting back into a white school, and whatever happens to her education she is apt to go through life perplexed.

In South Africa, a prizefighter may try to beat the brains out of only an opponent of his own race; the career of one professional boxer was jolted when he was reclassified from white to colored. Some light-skinned colored people like to fool the authorities whenever they can. It is the practice on South African airlines, for instance, for all seats to be assigned, even in the economy section. This is to make certain that all non-Whites are put at the rear of the plane. One white man who was traveling with a colored friend from Cape Town to Johannesburg asked to be placed next to him, and assumed they would both be at the back. The seat-assignment clerk, though, after looking at the colored man and assuming that he, too, was white, gave both men seats up forward. They had splendid service from the white stewardess, who was all the more attentive when she discovered that the colored man spoke fluent Afrikaans. As the men were leaving, the Colored told the stewardess, truthfully, that he'd never had such good treatment on a flight before, and she beamed. When she was out of earshot, he told his companion, "I'll bet she thinks I'm a deputy Nat minister on my way to Pretoria."

Some South African Coloreds are resentful of Africans; for all the latters' subservience, at least they have an identity. Some Coloreds once formed an organization called the South African Colored National Convention, which had as one of its purposes the establishment of their nonexistence as an authentic group. "Let nobody say that because we are organizing a convention as a colored group," they announced, "we are recognizing and accepting the fact that we are a separate group, nor that we wish to be so regarded in the laws of the land. We repeat that we are a separate group by exclusion, by discrimination, by virtue of laws which we regard as wrong. And it is to destroy this false, separate identity that we are dedicating ourselves in this convention." Most South African Coloreds would like to be part of the white group. They wear the same clothes, enjoy the same sports, eat the same food, observe the same religion, and speak the same language. Afrikaans has traditionally been the principal colored language. As a form of political protest, however, many of them are now turning increasingly to English. Not long ago there was a conference of Coloreds at Johannesburg, held under government auspices, and as a result the proceedings were conducted in Afrikaans, which the colored participants all spoke perfectly. During intervals for tea and meals, though, they all pointedly switched to English. The government doesn't really know what to do about them or with them, and there are many of them—nearly two million. "There is not a single responsible leader in South Africa in or out of government who doesn't think that the Coloreds and the Whites will come together, and soon," a government spokesman in Pretoria told me one day. "But no one will admit it publicly now, and no politician will be able to enunciate it for fifteen years, and if you say I said so I'll deny it till I'm blue in the face. But that is the way things are, and I'd be extremely grateful if in my official capacity I could say to you what I'm saying to you today."

Few colored South Africans take that kind of talk seriously, on or off the record. Most of them are resigned to an indeterminate future of nothingness. "The Lord shook the dice and they fell badly for us," one of their own poets, Adam Small, has written. "That's all." It is a measure of the Coloreds' disillusionment that among them they have attained a truly heroic rate of alcoholism. In South Africa the rate for Africans is four per thousand and for Europeans five per thousand. For Coloreds, it is thirty-five per thousand. They are loyal employees. After trying to drink themselves into oblivion over a weekend (Cape-made wine is their staple beverage), they will report to work reeling on a Monday morning and try to fulfill their obligations on their hands and knees. Some thoughtful employers have them gently escorted home. Living as most of them do near the coast, they have become expert fishermen, but so many of them have been undone by drink that outside Cape Town, African fishermen not indigenous to that area have had to be brought in to work the fishing boats—some of these being inland men who look upon fish as inedible snakes. The government is trying hard to keep Africans out of the Cape province, because that is not their homeland; nonetheless, at the moment there are about a hundred and thirty thousand African contract workers on that scene. They are not allowed to bring their wives or children with them, and the social consequences of that particular kind of separateness are obvious. When one of the government's colored allies expressed misgivings about fraternization between these migratory African workers and Cape colored women, an African wrote a letter to the *Cape Argus,* saying, "How in the world can 131,414 men be put in a camp and be told not to mix with women? . . . We never wanted segregation in the first place. . . . I think that as long as it is not illegal for an African to be in love with a colored person the authorities should stop losing sleep about it. Or will the time come when we will be told where to love and whom to love?"

As with the Indians, the government has spent a good deal of money for the South African Coloreds on homes, hospitals, schools, and other facilities. But many of these are jerry-built, and to few of them do the Coloreds feel any sense of affinity. They used to have more or less the same educational program as the Whites. Now the Coloreds have many spruce new school buildings, but their educational program is prescribed by the federal government in Pretoria, and their teachers are disheartened. "We're underpaid and oversupervised, and if we speak up, we risk our livelihood," one of them told me. "Then we begin to worry that we may be cowards, and this is bad for us psychologically. There's still some prestige attached to being a teacher, but our intellectual standards have deteriorated badly. That's why so many of us have left the country."

54

In the province of the Cape of Good Hope, Coloreds used to have some voting rights. The Union of South Africa would never have come into being in 1910, in fact, had not the other provinces agreed to the demands of the Cape negotiators that their colored residents continue to enjoy the franchise. The government took away the Coloreds' vote in 1955. Now the Cape Coloreds are represented in Parliament by four white men. It is hard for the Coloreds to forget their disenfranchisement; the Parliament buildings are right in the middle of Cape Town, at the head of Adderley Street. (It is named after a man who led an 1835 protest against the importation of British convicts to South Africa; eventually they went to Australia instead.) There are colored policemen in Cape Town, and some of them would now and then be assigned to traffic duty at Parliament. They have since been deployed elsewhere. It was too unsettling for some National Party M.P.'s, going to and from their work, to be given directions by men who had lost the right to direct their actions in any more significant fashion.

Cape Town's attractiveness is legendary. It sits at the foot of a flat-topped crag called Table Mountain, which frequently has tufts of clouds—they are known locally as tablecloths—clinging to its peak. The air is bracing. Everybody in Cape Town professes to be in blooming health and attributes this condition to the prevailing southeast wind, which is known as the Cape's doctor. While I do not believe in witchcraft, or even superstition, I must admit that I went out into a southeast wind with a terrible head cold and thought I was going to die that night and awoke the next morning, without having seen a human doctor, feeling fine.

Cape Town, with more than three hundred years of history, is proud of its relative antiquity. Capetonians like to call to visitors' attention an old Dutch windmill that has been operating for two hundred years—one hundred and twenty years, they add pointedly, before Johannesburg even existed. Cape Town thinks Johannesburg is a foreign and probably a heathen city. Cape Town is sometimes called the country's Mother City; when feeling especially maternal, Capetonians are apt to refer to Joburg as a precocious, noisy brat. Johannesburg people, on the other hand, say that when they go to Cape Town they take pains to walk on tip-

55

toe so they won't wake anybody up.

One of the once most picturesque and liveliest sections of Cape Town is known as District Six. It is a sort of Soho, where Coloreds used to live and Whites would come to shop and play. District Six is still a colored area in fact, but under the Group-Areas laws it has been handed over to the Whites. Few of the landlords, accordingly, have done anything lately to maintain the quarter's buildings, which are sadly disintegrating. Perhaps fifty thousand colored South Africans still live there (at least one of them, it was interesting to observe, has a black sheep for a pet), and will continue to for quite some time to come, since the government doesn't have enough housing elsewhere to move them into. "You are now in fairyland," says an ironic sign painted on one wall.

Among the landmarks of District Six that will presumably soon disappear is the rehearsal hall of the Eoan Group, possibly South Africa's best known theatrical organization. An all-colored company, the group was founded in 1933. Its members rehearse and perform, as a rule, in their spare time, most of them being employed as teachers or factory workers. In the old, comparatively easygoing days, when Cape Town was as close to a multiracial city as anything South Africa had, Eoan would put on operas and ballets at the city hall, to mixed audiences. The government stopped that in 1955. In the winter of 1967 the group did *Oklahoma!* It set a precedent by putting on the musical at a downtown theater that normally caters to white audiences exclusively. Coloreds were not permitted to watch their colored friends and relatives perform there, but the company got permission for a special invited audience to attend a dress rehearsal. Most of the colored guests arrived early, to be sure of getting seats. When the later arrivals, the majority of them Whites, turned up, the theater manager was so flustered he ushered them up into the balcony, which all agreed afterward was a most un-South African thing to do.

In South Africa cultural apartheid is the norm. There is a good deal of intellectual ferment in the country, but most of it must perforce be segregated, although every so often a bunch of painters will resolutely have an interracial exhibit on a Johannesburg sidewalk, and Whites now and then turn up at Dorkay House in the same city, where African musicians affiliated with a group called Union Artists meet and rehearse. Most Afrikaners take a dim view of this sort of thing. The legitimate theater has fallen on fairly bleak times, in part because many English and American playwrights have refused to let their works be produced in the country. (This is too bad, in a way, because it is the relatively liberal South Africans who have traditionally supported the theater.) Movies are very popular, and for good reason: South Africa has no television. The reason for *that* is that unless South Africa wanted to go to the prohibitively expensive trouble of creating all its own programs, it would have to use stock material, and that would be in English rather than Afrikaans. And *that* would presumably not sit well with the government. At least one government supporter I spoke to, however, had a different explanation. "We saw televison in England," he told me, "and we don't want it here until it's technically perfected. Besides, I'd rather have my children play out-of-doors." One joke to which nongovernment supporters are partial has it that South African children are disadvantaged, compared to children elsewhere, because they don't know two letters of the alphabet—"TV."

Having no competition from television, South African movie exhibitors have an advantage over *their* counterparts elsewhere. They show B pictures as single features. South Africans make some movies of their own, and these are loyally supported. One I went to was accompanied by a newsreel containing a sequence praising the very picture it supplemented. The feature had been shot in Cape Town; the denouement took place in a Table Mountain cable car. In reviewing it, a critic for one paper said, "One of the points that surprised me was that nobody appears to inhabit Cape Town who is African or colored." (He was wrong; I had detected a little colored boy extra who was shown leading a blind old white man into a courtroom.) In keeping with the nation's bilinguality, there were two newsreels, actually—one in Afrikaans and one in English. There was also a short subject, *This Is Rhodesia,* produced by the Rhodesian Information Services. Showing that in South Africa seemed to me tantamount to showing a Nantucket travelogue on Cape Cod, but the film was enthusiastically applauded, possibly because its commentator said that in all of Africa Rhodesia ranked second only to South Africa when it came to caring about the welfare of black people. There were no Blacks in the audience.

Not only does South Africa have no television; it doesn't have much in the way of radio. There are plenty of programs, but they are all controlled by a government monopoly, the South African Broadcasting Corporation, as unbending an entity as the communications field has ever known. It banned the Beatles. It fired one part-time employee, a university student, for having had the temerity to invite Senator Robert F. Kennedy to speak at his dormitory. It gives the government's formal political opponents, the United Party, short shrift. During the Republic's last country-wide elections, in the spring of 1966, the National Party got all the air time it wanted; the United Party could get no more satisfaction than to have the gist of its leader's speeches carried as news items. One difficulty was that there were twenty or so Nationalist ministers and deputy ministers making news every day, whereas the other side was represented as a rule only by the lonely voice of its principal spokesman, Sir de Villiers Graaff.

The S.A.B.C. puts on programs in various languages, and has one network, called Radio Bantu, which addresses itself exclusively to Africans. No South African organization adheres more firmly to apartheid than does the S.A.B.C. The chairman of its board has said that there must be no cultural integration among the races "in no matter how limited a field." Its strict views are enthusiastically echoed by an Afrikaner cultural outfit called the Federasie van Afrikaanse Kultuur Vereenigings, one of whose officials said that the "kaffir can be our cultural servant as he is our farm servant."

A daily S.A.B.C. highlight is a news commentary, *Current Affairs,* which in the narrowness of its viewpoint is impressive even for South Africa. In 1966, a publishing house of which Prime Minister Vorster was chairman of the board brought out a book advocating world supremacy for white Christians. "We must reduce every other race and sub-race to servitude and dependence," its author wrote in part. He thought it a pity that slavery had ever been abolished in the United States, since he believed Blacks to be "permanently inferior" and "not human beings in the sense we normally convey by that term." Such statements, and

58

others like them, were too much even for South Africa to stomach. The book was banned. But before that happened, the program *Current Affairs* had acclaimed the volume as "the battle hymn of the Republic of South Africa—a clarion call to stand fast against the onslaught of red communism, pink Western defeatism, and colorless shapeless internationalism as embodied in the United States."

Book censorship comes under something called the Publications Control Board. This consists of eleven men, most of them professors and all of them Afrikaners. The chairman hails from the University of Potchefstroom, a straitlaced institution; before its athletic teams go out on a trip they have to sign a pledge that they won't dance off campus. The Board scrutinizes around twelve hundred publications a year. Four votes out of the eleven are usually enough to clear a book, or condemn it. (The one that S.A.B.C. liked was read by all eleven members; it is not the kind of book that is ordinarily banned in South Africa, and, besides, the Prime Minister was involved.) The Board is divided into a literary committee and a political-affairs committee. The literary men look chiefly for obscenity. The political men usually reject anything that deals with African nationalism. (Some years ago South Africa's censors tossed out *Black Beauty* and *The Return of the Native,* apparently not having delved beyond their titles; the incumbent censors are more sophisticated.) The Board concerns itself mostly with imports. Local publishers generally just don't print anything that might be objectionable. Local writers can usually get away with more than aliens. Afrikaner writers, that is; Nadine Gordimer's novel *The Late Bourgeois World* has been banned in her own country. The censors are especially wary of paperbacks, on the theory that Africans, who have less money than other readers, are more likely to buy these. Some observers of the South African literary scene think that the censors are wasting much of their time, inasmuch as the majority of Africans who read any books stick pretty much to James Bond and how-to works.

The Board bans about seven or eight hundred books a year, and a man in Pretoria has done quite nicely for himself by issuing a periodic list, at fifteen dollars a year, for librarians and other

59

subscribers who want to keep abreast of what's in and what's out. Books by Africans in exile from South Africa, like Bloke Modisane's *Blame Me on History*, are out; so is the excellent recent *Against the World*, Douglas Brown's study of white South African attitudes. The list of contraband includes *The Blue Negro and Other Stories*, all issues of *Boxing Life*, a Jayne Mansfield calendar, *Classical Hindu Erotology*, the *Gag Writer's Private Joke Book*, *Gene Autry and Champion*, *Peyton Place*, *Return to Peyton Place*, *Sex and the Single Girl*, *Too Black for Heaven*, *Too Hot to Handle*, *Too Many Girls*, *Too Many Sinners*, *Too Many Women*, *Too Much Woman*, *Too Scared to Live*, *Too Soon to Die*, *The Woman of Rome*, *A Woman of Paris*, *A Woman of Bangkok*, *Women of Vietnam*, *Women of China*, *Women of Korea*, *Women of the Shadows*, *Woman of the Underworld*, *Women of Evil*, *The Woman of Danger*, and *Women of the Whole World*; books by Pearl S. Buck, Truman Capote, Simone de Beauvoir, J. P. Donleavy, Jack Kerouac, William Manchester, Karl Marx, Mary McCarthy, Carson McCullers, Henry Miller, George Orwell, Ellery Queen, Harold Robbins, and Billy Rose; and all books, newspapers, magazines, phonograph records, and postage stamps from the Soviet Union.

It is not customarily considered an offense to own a banned book, but to sell or lend one is forbidden. However, the police are known to look with suspicion on any premises they may raid that contain banned books, and if they happen to see a student reading a book about the Russian revolution on a train they may ask him a few searching questions. The Publications Control Board doesn't handle books written by people who have been banned themselves. Their books are automatically banned when they are. One South African literary magazine had to snip out a page of one of its recent issues; the writer of the page had been banned after the magazine went to press. The Johannesburg office of the United States Information Service puts out a catalogue of films it keeps in its library. In one catalogue it had to black out a mention of a twenty-minute newsreel because the contents included a shot of the Nobel Prize being awarded to Chief Albert Luthuli, who died banned.

Newspapers have to be watchful about what names they men-

60

tion. One editor keeps a card file of a thousand names—95 per cent of them non-Whites' names—in three colors. People whom the government has identified as Communists are pink (naturally); people who've been singled out under a law called the Suppression-of-Communism Act are green; people who have been forbidden to attend public gatherings are white. None of the lot may be quoted in any publication, except under circumstances favorable to the government. If, for instance, a South African exile in London whom the government has pinpointed as a Communist says that violent revolution is the answer to apartheid, the South African Minister of the Interior is apt to authorize publication of his statement, on the ground that such incendiary talk shows what devils the country's enemies are.

and third-class citizens? Does skin color determine the scope and quality of a man's life or does it not? Remember, if the truth is not found in what we say, it will be revealed in what we do."

Fifteen years ago, the white people's newspapers in South Africa rarely carried news about black sports or politics, and a black man's picture was hardly ever published. The English-language papers have since then tried to curry favor with African readers. Most of the big English-language papers have special editions for those readers and have at least one or two African reporters on their staffs. The *Rand Daily Mail* used to run a weekly column by the African Nat Nakasa, who committed suicide in New York in 1965. Now it has a similar feature by Stanley Motjuwadi. One day the papers carried a story about an unidentified African body that was lying at the morgue. It was the body of a messenger who had been stabbed on the street and had staggered back to his employer's office, where he died. He was unidentified because nobody at the premises where he worked had ever bothered to learn his name. This incident prompted Motjuwadi to reflect that when he had visited the office where his own father had worked for more than forty-five years, nobody knew *his* surname; to the people in his office, he was just Old Joe. A columnist like Motjuwadi has a better chance than most of his white counterparts of being able to write about what it's like to be arrested.

Africans are especially partial to evening and Sunday newspapers, because they contain more advertising and are bulkier. Thus, after being perused, their pages can be used as tablecloths, for lining shelves, and, on cool nights, for supplementing blankets. Along with the *Sunday Times,* which has a circulation of four hundred and fifty thousand, there are several substantial Afrikaans-language Sunday papers, which do quite well in spite of occasional pronouncements by ministers of the Dutch Reformed Church who believe that the Sabbath should be reserved exclusively for God's words. One church elder suggested not long ago that the reading of Sunday papers should be deferred until Monday and that God-fearing parents should refuse to let their children distribute the Sunday press.

Although Afrikaners constitute 60 per cent of the white South

African population, there are thirteen English-language dailies and only five Afrikaans-language ones. Some English-speaking South Africans read the Afrikaans press; many Afrikaners read the English-language press. It often turns them purple with rage. One of the few times I lost my temper in South Africa was when a government booster told me flatly one evening, "All journalists are leftists." Usually, such charges are leveled only at English-language journalists. The country's Minister of Posts and Telegraphs thinks there is an international plot to slant outside news coming into South Africa; the villainous operatives are Communists employed in London by Reuter's. After delivering one such unbridled attack on the English-language press on the floor of Parliament, that minister tried to tone down his remarks by having them amended in the official transcript of the proceedings. The English-language press promptly picked him up on it.

The papers ordinarily deal more with policies than personalities, but nonetheless National Party M.P.s frequently arise in the legislature to characterize English-language journalists, by name, as liars, besmirchers, or traitors. The English-language papers carry on unabashed, though with some circumspection. When an editor has a piece he wants to run that he thinks might upset the Secret Police, he is apt to show it to them first and to solicit their comments. The more removed correspondents are from big cities, the more cautious they are apt to be. A rural stringer for one big-city paper sent in a dispatch about a train wreck that began, "A Bantu on a bicycle collided with a train here today." Then, apparently feeling that his lead might be thought to express excessive sympathy for a non-White, he went on, "It is believed he was on his way to commit a robbery."

But the boldness of some of the country's editors is refreshing. One of the most outspoken of the lot is a young man named Donald Woods, of the *East London Daily Dispatch*. He grew up in the native homeland called the Transkei; his nurse was a witch doctor who would amuse the children in her charge by going into trances and rolling bones. When he went off to college he was so hidebound a racist that on being asked his solution to the race problem, he said, quite seriously, "Shoot every kaffir in the country and you won't have a problem." There was an American

65

Negro on the campus at the time, and Woods was so flabber-gasted on being exposed to an educated, civilized black man that his attitude underwent a formidable change. His paper is ideal for him. Its founder decreed, "The editorial policy is independent, free from any political ties, and advocates the preservation of South Africa's traditional links with the Western world. It favors a liberal policy toward the nonwhite races, a policy represented by the idea of Cecil Rhodes: 'Equal rights for all civilized men.' " Quintuplets were born in East London in 1966 and the *Dispatch* quickly sewed up the exclusive rights to their story. It built the babies and their parents a house in a native township—the quints being African—and provided a trained nurse for them. The com-pany that owns the paper has been diversifying lately, because opponents of the government can never be sure what will happen next; the quintuplets are among the diversifications.

East London is not a liberal city, even by South African stan-dards. The country's only known branch of the John Birch So-ciety was spawned in East London. Woods frequently gets irate phone calls embodying threats to himself and his family, but a couple of times a week there are compensating calls from African readers who say something like, "Keep up the good work," and it heartens him further that sometimes trucks delivering his product to nonwhite areas are greeted with cheers. Indisputably South African though he is, Woods displays Winston Churchill's picture in his office, and is in demand at parties for his knack of simul-taneously playing Afrikaner nationalist songs on the piano with his right hand and African nationalist ones with his left.

In 1950, two years after the National Party assumed power, a commission was appointed to make a study of the South African press. Twelve years passed before it issued a report, and no won-der; the commission undertook to count, read, and appraise every word filed abroad about South Africa for more than five years. The ascertainable total came to 9,088,489 words, but that was only a part of the output, for the commission discovered, to its annoyance, that not every single reporter who had filed an airmail dispatch during the period in question had bothered to keep a carbon. Before its scrutiny was done, one member of the com-mission had gone blind.

The English-language press, not surprisingly, came in for the heaviest criticism. On the basis of their dispatches, reporters were graded "good," "faulty," "bad," or "very bad"—the mere categories suggesting a predisposition toward dissatisfaction. Of four full-time Associated Press correspondents who received a word-by-word going-over, three were judged very bad. In rummaging through the back files of cable offices, the members of the commission even studied, and quoted from, service messages that reporters sent to their editors. Noticing that a stringer for the *London Daily Mail* had once cabled his editor, "The *Daily Herald* stringer was arrested today and my position is getting dicy," the commission's report put a "(sic)" after "dicy" and followed this with "(dicky?)." Bad to very bad.

In more than a dozen ponderous and preposterous volumes of its report, the exact number of words in which nobody ever quite got around to adding up, the commission complained, *inter alia,* that in covering one South African riot foreign reporters had neglected to pass along to their readers that some Africans had burned a nun and eaten part of her. More generally, the commission was peeved that reports sent overseas "looked upon all differentiation as an unjust discrimination," and it went on, "the desire and need of people of the same race, civilization, and language to consort in a manner that excludes strangers, i.e. persons of other races, civilizations, and languages, were generally described as racialism or racial intolerance. The need to protect race, civilization and language groups against the invasion of the privacy they enjoy when consorting with their own kind was represented as an interference with the basic liberties of the citizens of the State and, at times, described as a desire for racial isolationism. The fact that people can and do use certain public amenities in common was generally regarded as proof that all differentiation was unnecessary and that such differentiation as existed was illogical and unfair. These circumstances led foreign correspondents to mis-report the South African political and racial scene and to ascribe false motives to the Whites in general and more in particular to the Afrikaner, the present Government, and the members of the National Party."

South Africa has several newspapers for non-Whites. One of

them, a biweekly published in Durban, was founded by an African doctor who'd been to the United States and wanted to influence Zulus—who are the principal Africans of Natal—toward emulating the American Negroes' way of life. It was called *Ilanga Lase Natal,* Zulu for "Sun of Natal." After a while, the paper got to be known for short, among English-speakers, as *Ilanga Lase.* To Zulus, "Sun of" sounded silly, not to mention incomplete; so the name became plain *Ilanga.* The biggest African papers are two tabloids, the *Post* and the *World.* The *Post,* a weekly, claims a circulation of a hundred and seventy thousand—the largest of any nonwhite paper in South Africa. Its proprietors put out a companion weekly, called *Drum,* that also has editions distributed in other parts of Africa. (These are printed in London; most independent Africans wouldn't touch anything from South Africa.) *Drum* was the first paper edited by Whites for nonwhite readers, and its chief editors are still white. Most of its reporters are Africans, and they have to be resourceful and durable. The beats they cover are not notably tranquil (six *World* reporters, for instance, were assaulted in the line of duty last year), and Africans do not always have ready access to transportation or telephones. The African newspapers are breezy; if a reporter wants to describe a girl as "scrumptious" in a news story, that is not considered editorializing but merely sprightly writing. Sensationalism is their stock in trade. The *Post*'s lead story is apt to bear some such headline as "SCHOOL PRINCIPAL WIFE IN BED WITH ANOTHER PRINCIPAL!" Some reticence is observed, however; the editors prefer to keep mentions of both race and rape out of their headlines.

Drum used to be a crusading paper; it ran fiery exposés of the conditions under which African farm laborers worked and of the conditions they experienced in prison. Now both these papers are tamer. They don't profess to be pleased with the government, but they take the editorial line that everybody in South Africa is going to have to manage somehow to get along with everybody else. " 'Let's march together' would summarize our attitude, I guess," one of the *Post*'s editors said to me. When I asked whether he meant marching shoulder to shoulder or in tandem, he changed the subject.

South Africa's Africans are much better informed than were their parents, or even their older brothers. In 1964 the *World* was a weekly with a circulation of thirteen thousand. Now it is a daily with a circulation of eighty thousand, and it claims five readers for each copy. (The *Post,* when it comes to that, claims 7.2 readers a copy.) Both papers, despite their growing readership, have to struggle to make ends meet. They get very little advertising revenue. Whereas South African companies spend about forty million dollars a year on advertising in the white press, they allocate only a million and a half to the nonwhite. One shoe chain declined to advertise at all in nonwhite papers because it was afraid its ads might bring in business and it didn't want its white fitters to have to kneel before nonwhite customers.

The *World* and the *Post* run everything in English. *Ilanga* is printed partly in English and partly in Zulu; its editors hope that by using two languages they can help to create a bridge of understanding between Whites and Blacks. The newspapers that serve the white community have tried from time to time to build similar bridges between *its* components, but as a rule do not communicate much back and forth. When the English-language papers quote their Afrikaans-language counterparts, it is much in the fashion that the *New York Times* quotes *Pravda.* One Afrikaans-language Sunday paper has an English-speaking feature writer. His mere existence there is considered freaky, much as if he were a white gorilla. Some Afrikaans-language editors take a condescending view of their English-language brethren. The Afrikaners like to point out that the English press, while more widely read than theirs, and while blessed with more advertising revenue, has on the whole very little influence. "They irritate the government, but they don't persuade the governed," one Afrikaner editor told me. The *Cape Times* and *Die Burger,* though, often translate and reprint one another's editorials. A few of the English-language papers even run short daily lessons in Afrikaans.

Everyone in South Africa is acutely conscious of the importance that bilinguality, or the lack of it, plays in the nation's affairs. Some Africans, to get ahead, have to be *trilingual*—to become fluent in English and Afrikaans along with their own ver-

69

nacular. Some menus are trilingual, too. The Langham Hotel restaurant in Johannesburg lists its offerings, like any cosmopolitan eating establishment, in French; to the left of the French the dishes are described in English, and to the right of the French in Afrikaans. Not long ago there was a furor at a resort hotel when an Afrikaner politician checked in and then stalked out because it had a menu that was printed in English only and not in Afrikaans as well. He could read English all right, but it was a question of patriotism. He was not mollified by the proprietor's explanation that 99 per cent of his patrons were predominantly English-speaking. The controversy went on for days, and one result was a proposal for a law that all public eating places *had* to offer bilingual menus. The stoutly progovernment daily, *Die Transvaler,* headlined one of its accounts of the incident, "There is still a struggle."

The two white men's languages have long struggled for preeminence in South Africa. Afrikaans, the only language of European origin that is not spoken in Europe, has Dutch roots, but it is linguistically somewhat closer to Flemish. Early in South Africa's history, Afrikaans was regarded as a kitchen tongue. Its partisans began the battle to win it front-parlor acceptance in 1875, but for quite some time after that it was still considered socially unacceptable, and all white South Africans, whether Afrikaans- or English-speaking, looked on the public use of English as a sign of good breeding. Afrikaner schoolteachers were fired for addressing their Afrikaner pupils in Afrikaans, and the children were punished for using it outside their homes. A lot of resentment was engendered, and it lingers on. A few years ago, when an English-speaking woman was imprisoned under the ninety-day detention law, one of the Afrikaner policemen who interrogated her kept saying bitterly that when his mother had been a schoolgirl, every time she spoke Afrikaans in class her teacher would hang a sign saying "Donkey" around her neck, and she would have to wear it until some other Afrikaner child made the same lapse and the stigmatic placard could be transferred.

The Afrikaans language might never have got anywhere had not the English-speaking South Africans insisted, while they were in power, that their language be used exclusively in schools and churches. Their disdain for the indigenous language made its users all the more eager to have it accepted. This was all part of the *volk* feeling that was and is so endemic to Afrikanerdom. After their defeat in the Boer War, the Afrikaners had little left that they could call their own *except* their language, and they cherished it and fought for it more than ever. By 1914 they had managed to get it approved as a second medium of instruction in South African public schools. In 1916 it replaced Dutch as the language of the local Dutch Reformed Church. In 1925 it became, along with English, an official national language. In 1926 Afrikaner scholars began to compile the first Afrikaans-language dictionary. (By 1966 the editors of *Die Afrikaanse Woordeboek* had got only as far as the letter "I," but they had already produced four volumes containing 2,681 triple-column pages.) In 1933 the Bible was translated into Afrikaans for the first time. Since then, nearly three million Afrikaans Bibles have been printed.

There is still, in many Afrikaner eyes, a lamentable imbalance between the two now official languages. Of late, the South African Academy of Arts and Sciences, an Afrikaner group that goes back to 1909 and is considered the final authority on Afrikaans spelling and usage, has been complaining that because of insufficient translations less than 20 per cent of the textbooks prescribed for Afrikaner universities are in Afrikaans. "If people study in English, they start to think in English," an Academy spokesman has said. Outside of South Africa itself, Afrikaans is hardly spoken at all. In the fall of 1966, South Africans were delighted when a course in Afrikaans began in Portugal, one of the few nations with which their country has amicable relations. On the occasion, the South African ambassador in Lisbon described his homeland's language as "forever our own, a medium of human intercourse in which we can most effectively communicate our innermost feelings to our God and to our fellow men." Presumably an all-out Afrikaner, even a thoroughly bilingual one, gets less out of reading the Bible than *die Bybel*.

Although Afrikaans has been a written language for only fifty years, and although there are only three million human beings who can read a word of it, a quite respectable body of Afrikaans

71

literature exists. Afrikaners take nearly everything that is written in their language seriously; if Irving Wallace wrote in Afrikaans, he'd be taken seriously. English literature began with *Beowulf*; poets also blazed the trail of Afrikaans literature. Novelists are in the forefront now; one of the principal ones, Etienne Leroux, said recently that "there is a very clear and typical Afrikaans tradition, more powerful perhaps than anything similar in the Western world because of our isolation—and I don't allude to this in any derogative sense. Even when the Afrikaans writer tries to transcend his world, he is still bound to the invisible substratum from which he derives his incantations. In our portrayal of the tragic we are inspired by what seems anachronistic to others; our satire is based on situations that are often incomprehensible to the outsider. . . ."

Leroux, an Orange Free State farmer whose father was a cabinet minister under Dr. Verwoerd, can expect to sell eight to ten thousand copies of a novel at home; in South Africa, that is a best-selling performance. Many contemporary works of Afrikaner fiction are indeed thought to be anachronistic; they sound as if they'd been written elsewhere in the 1920s and '30s. But the current crop of Afrikaner novelists are, by their own national standards, so emancipated that their cultural elders have lately been annoyed with them for the forthrightness of their work. It is possible for a student at an Afrikaner university to be told one day by a liberal Afrikaner lecturer that so-and-so's new novel is fresh and challenging, and to hear the next day from a conservative Afrikaner lecturer that the book is obscene and unpatriotic trash. The Afrikaner writer, one cultural conservative declared not long ago, should make the struggle of the nation *his* struggle; the issuer of that pronunciamento would probably have been horrified if somebody had said he seemed to be following an old Communist Party line. For the most part, Afrikaner writers have not yet got themselves too involved, on either side, in the national struggle; when it comes to political action, and even to writing about politics, they are far behind some of the better-known English-speaking South Africans, notable among these being Alan Paton. "I don't think we're interested in contemporary South African politics," a highly respected young novelist there told me. He was

72

writing a book about the Spanish Civil War.

South African writers are customarily lumped together by decades. In the 1930s there were the Dertigers; in the '60s there are the Sestigers. They are a diverse group, in age as well as creativity. One of the more articulate of the Sestigers, the poet and short-story writer Uys Krige, was also a Dertiger. Krige is an uncommonly worldly Afrikaner. He has traveled extensively and has tried to build his own cultural bridges by translating French, Italian, and Spanish poetry into Afrikaans. He deplores the tendency of many young Afrikaner writers to refuse, no matter how strongly they may say they feel about moral issues, to break with the reigning National Party. "Surely what happens to the colored man is the acid test," says Krige, who lives in Cape Town. "Surely you've got to break with the Nats over that."

Krige broke with them long ago, and many of them broke with him during the Second World War, when he joined the army at a time when the majority of Afrikaner men were either sitting out the war or trying to subvert the Allied effort. For his betrayal of his *volk,* he was chastized in the Afrikaans-language press, and the *Transvaler,* of which Dr. Verwoerd was then editor, ran letter after letter disapproving of his behavior. One was from a man who said his little daughter had been a devoted Krige fan, but now she had asked her daddy to remove the poet's picture from her bedroom wall. "Uyssie, why do you do this to my little girl?" the letter writer concluded.

There is one colored man among the Sestigers. He is Adam Small, a twenty-nine-year-old poet and essayist who is head of the department of philosophy at Western Cape College, which the government established sixteen miles outside of Cape Town in 1960, after decreeing that the races should be educated separately. The difference between Western Cape—which many Coloreds refer to caustically as Bush College—and the preapartheid universities can be ascertained by looking at a telephone directory. Its nearest academic neighbors, the universities of Cape Town and of Stellenbosch, are to be found under their own names. Western Cape is listed in the government section under the subheading "Colored." Small is a conspicuously political writer. "I always say that politics is everything and everything is

73

politics," he says. "But politics shouldn't have to legislate about everything just because it *is* about everything. The government has even legislated about making love. The Immorality Act is the most vicious legislation we have. Even the Group-Areas Act and the Suppression-of-Communism Act aren't as mischievous. Here a completely individual right is brushed aside by law. It's a negation of the whole meaning of law. So I don't keep the peace; I talk."

Small, who studied for a while in London a few years ago, seriously considered leaving South Africa permanently, but he finally decided to stay on. "It's important for someone with true critical intent—in the Socratic sense—to be around," he says. "And I have a duty toward my students—not the government's version of duty but duty to let my students know what exactly are the main currents of thought in the world; to make them realize that there *is* an outside world, and that through me they are not cut off from it. I see my function as that of inculcating at least some universal values, and of developing a critical sense. I don't care whether I give them philosophy or not; I want to give them the equipment for true criticism. Some day I'd like to see some of them take part in a national convention for a dialogue on race. I think that many people who talk about liberal values don't really know what they mean by liberty or freedom. I wish everybody interested in liberal values could get together and find out what we're talking about when we talk about freedom. The government knows what *it* wants."

Small is the only non-White on the Western Cape teaching staff; all the other instructors are Afrikaners. His academic colleagues are pleasant enough to him, but his relations with them have to be circumscribed. The chief scholarly body of any South African university is its senate, composed of the heads of each department. By federal law, no non-White may belong to a senate, so the philosophy department isn't represented at Western Cape senate meetings. True, the law also provides for an advisory senate, which was designed to accommodate non-Whites, but an advisory senate at Western Cape would consist solely of the university's rector, its secretary, and the head of its philosophy department, and wouldn't make much sense even to a nonphilosopher. In 1966, Small was invited to read a paper to a philosophical congress at the University of Natal. His own senate gave him its blessing, but on a higher administrative level the proposal got disapproved, on the ground that if he attended the congress it would become a mixed affair, and that that would be in conflict with government policy. Small is a gifted linguist. He writes his philosophical treatises and occasional newspaper articles in English; he does some of his literary work in Afrikaans and some in a Cape-colored dialect that is a cross between those two languages and is called Gammattaal. He has been writing since he was thirteen and has received high praise for his creativity. During the first nine months of 1966 the total income he received from all his nonjournalistic writings came to ten dollars and ten cents.

For all the creative writing of which South Africa can boast, no really great fictional Afrikaner character has yet emerged, unless one counts Oom Schalk Lourens, the narrator of many of Herman Bosman's short stories. In a way, the chief fictional Afrikaner character is a fellow whose surname—he has no first name—is Van der Merwe, the South African equivalent of Smith. There is a solid page of Van der Merwes in the Johannesburg phone book, and in Pretoria, which has fewer people but more Afrikaners, the roster is even longer. After Dr. Verwoerd's death a special election was held to fill his seat in Parliament; both candidates were named Van der Merwe. Including the winner, there are now five Van der Merwes in Parliament. The South African Broadcasting Corporation has a situation-comedy show called *Leave It to Van der Merwe.*

The biggest van der Merwe of them all, not counting the captain of the South African cricket team that recently defeated Australia, is the surname-only chap who is the hero, or the butt, of innumerable comical stories. He is a country bumpkin, an ignoramus, an engaging Afrikaner lout; contemporary South African humor often seems utterly dependent on him. Van der Merwe, for instance, is an astronaut aboard a two-man spaceship. His partner goes outside for a space walk while Van der Merwe, inside the capsule, reads the *Sunday Times*. After a while, the partner hammers on the hatch. "Who's there?" asks Van der Merwe. Van der Merwe goes to Rhodesia, where the censorship

75

imposed by the Ian Smith regime has had the effect of news-papers' publishing some editions with blank spaces in them. "Hell," says Van der Merwe, "the papers here are good. There are papers for people who can read and for people who can't."

The Mayor of Bloemfontein, the principal city of the Orange Free State and a fortress of Afrikanerdom, was rebuked not long ago by the English-language press for telling a Van der Merwe joke, while presiding over the opening of a new wing on an abat-toir, that his critics thought was in shabby taste. In this one, Van der Merwe was in London, where a crippled beggar with only one arm and one leg approached him. Van der Merwe gave the man twenty cents, walked on, turned around, and gave the man a much more substantial sum. When the beggar asked him why he'd been so generous, Van der Merwe said, "This is the first time I have seen an Englishman *opgedondered* to my complete satis-faction." There are anti-Semitic jokes in South Africa about a character called Van der Cohen. The captain of the Australian cricket team was Bobby Simpson. During the test series, the *Rand Daily Mail*'s political cartoonist, Bob Connolly, had one cricket fan saying to another, "Heard any good Van der Simpson stories lately?"

Some South Africans have been truly bilingual since childhood. In the family of one man I know, the father always spoke to his children in Afrikaans, and the mother in English. When I asked my friend in which language his parents communicated between themselves, he said, "It depended on whoever started the conver-sation." Lately, English-speaking South Africans have had to learn Afrikaans if they want to get anywhere in politics. Twenty years ago, though, before the Nats took power, a reporter could cover Parliament without knowing a word of Afrikaans, and there were English-speaking cabinet ministers who could follow speeches in Afrikaans only through interpreters. Now, one can at-tend a National Party Congress and, although most of the partic-ipants are conversant in English, be unlikely to hear a single word of it spoken.

Afrikaners, for their part, had to learn English not too long ago if they wanted to get anywhere outside of politics. An Afrikaner professor of engineering at the University of Pretoria still does his

76

calculating in English, because it was in that tongue that he learned his mathematics. His wife grew up on a farm and as a girl spoke only Afrikaans. When her best friend went to an English-language school, she insisted on going along, and at the same time that she learned English she learned Latin in English. Then she went to an Afrikaans-language university and forgot nearly all her English.

English is still the basic language of business. Companies that are largely owned and managed and staffed by Afrikaners nonetheless hold their board meetings in English. "You can't organize an overseas contract in Afrikaans," one corporation executive told me. There is a constant switching back and forth between the languages. "When I'm tired, I find it very difficult to speak English," one Afrikaner editor told me, in perfect English, while feeling rested. There are more white South Africans who speak only Afrikaans than there are who speak only English, and most bilingual English-speaking South Africans don't speak Afrikaans as well as the bilingual Afrikaners speak English. Children are supposed to go to schools where their primary home language is taught. Some Afrikaner public-school teachers are so rigidly pro-government that enlightened Afrikaner parents have taken to speaking English at home so their children can get a somewhat more flexible education than they might otherwise receive.

It is getting harder and harder to find schools, however, where predominantly English-speaking teachers preside. In today's teachers' colleges, more than 80 per cent of the lecturers don't have English as their home language. Nearly three-quarters of all white elementary public-school teachers are Afrikaners. The result of this imbalance is beginning to make itself statistically felt. While a few years ago 73 per cent of the white South African population was bilingual, now the figure is only 66 per cent. In the Cape province, there are only thirteen teachers with English-speaking backgrounds scattered among eighty-four primary schools, and in the Orange Free State, once the most bilingual of all of South Africa's provinces, 95 per cent of the teachers come from Afrikaans-speaking homes.

"There is this one country which belongs to all of us," Dr. Verwoerd said in 1961, though he apparently was thinking only of

77

white folks. "In particular it must be emphasized that we have two languages: not one language belonging to some and another belonging to others, but two languages belonging to all of us, and of value to all of us." Three years later he said, "I hope the time will come when all of us will not only understand both languages, but will look upon both languages as the languages we own and love, as the languages of our country as one unitary whole."

Bilingualism has been burdensome. There are all those apartheid signs, and they are all up in two languages. A bakery must also proclaim itself a *"bakkery,"* and a school a *"skool."* Bilingualism can also be diverting; the sign "Gents Here" outside a men's restroom does not mean exactly what an American might think it means; *"here"* is the Afrikaans word for "gents." Some South Africans, like Japanese, carry calling cards with their names and other information in English on one side and in Afrikaans on the other. Many official and other printed documents begin at one end in English and at the other, when turned upside down, in Afrikaans. Their conclusions meet in the middle. As Afrikaans is the basic language of the National Party, so is English that of the opposition United Party. Political partisanship has affected speech habits. I met several English-speaking women who refused to speak Afrikaans at all because of their antipathy for the government. An English-speaking man of similar viewpoint told me that whenever he gets angry at anyone he curses him in Afrikaans. "I figure it will help our side," he said.

Soon after Prime Minister Vorster assumed office he said, "I can sincerely say that the relations between the English-speaking and the Afrikaans population of this country have never been better." But his opinion is not universally shared. An editorial in the *Johannesburg Star* said afterward, "Afrikaner nationalists really must make up their minds about English-speaking South Africans. Are they allies or enemies, compatriots or foreigners? They cannot continue to be both." It is probably true that relations between the two segments of white South African society are smoother than they were a generation ago, but there is still a good deal of discernible thorniness. The city of Pretoria not long ago announced that it was going to change the names of its streets to Afrikaans names; 90 per cent of them had been English. Some observers of the contemporary South African scene think that the South African Institute of Race Relations, an admirable organization whose researches into black-white relations have been thorough and dispassionate, devotes too little attention to the equally crucial matter of white-white relations.

Since the Afrikaners currently enjoy political power, most of the complaints about unfairness come from their English-speaking compatriots. An English-speaking farmer in the Orange Free State, for instance, groused not long ago that when the provincial authorities there decided to build a new highway, they ran it through his land because he was the only non-Afrikaner in the area. Sometimes the two groups jest about their differences. After a lunch at which the country's difficulties were inevitably discussed, one of the guests said to me, "There are worse places on earth." "And he's an Englishman," an Afrikaner in the group said gleefully. The skirmishing between the two factions takes strange twists and turns. A town council in the Transvaal province recently debated at length as to whether it should shift its municipal bank account from an English-owned bank to an Afrikaner-owned one, even though 80 per cent of the employees of the first bank were Afrikaners. The English bank won out, in spite of the impassioned declaration of one councilman that "we must start to realize that we have been weaned from the White Cliffs of Dover." The two principal white groups in South Africa would probably be even more divided than they are had they not their mutual apprehension of Blacks to keep them edgily together.

One thing that disturbs reflective Afrikaners is their own rate of breeding. Dominant they may be, but in comparison to the other groups in their country their numbers are decreasing. In 1966 some of their tribal elders urged all of them who could to have babies, as a patriotic gesture. The chairman of something called the Federal Council of Afrikaans Coordinating Committees, aware that some Afrikaner families were resisting the exhortation because if they had too many children their high standard of living might diminish, urged the government to grant subsidies to parents who cooperated.

Fighting on two fronts at once, the government has been trying

79

to lower the rate of nonwhite births. The government is preparing a film on contraception to show to African audiences, and has been extolling the glories of the Pill. The propaganda has produced something of a backlash, as similar propaganda has in American black-power circles. "Our fecundity may be a social problem," one African father told me, "but the white man's solutions are not socially but politically motivated, and therefore must be opposed. Why should the Republic be advocating free nursing homes for Whites, and birth control for Blacks? I heard one Afrikaner say that we Africans shouldn't have as many children as we do because we're interested only in mating and not in love. I took that to mean that he thought we were beasts, and to me that was an insult to every African."

As a further step toward keeping white South Africans from being numerically overwhelmed by non-Whites, the government has been encouraging white immigration and offering generous subsidies to families willing to swell its ranks. The government would like to attract about fifty thousand white immigrants a year, but it has been getting somewhat less than that. Moreover, a good many of the settlers who do turn up are from Mediterranean countries. It is all very well to have Greeks and Portuguese and Italians come to South Africa—they have brought artichokes and asparagus and good coffee with them—but some of them are darkish-skinned, and may be Catholics to boot. The Coordinating Committees think that at least 59 per cent of all immigrants should be "potential Afrikaners," by which they mean people from northern European countries like Holland and Germany.

What's worse, to become a naturalized South African citizen, an immigrant is required by law to learn to speak one of the country's two official languages, and most of the newcomers, if they don't already know English, generally turn to that one. Less than 3 per cent of recent immigrants have chosen to affiliate themselves with the Afrikaner community. Addressing itself to this worrisome point, *Die Vaderland* said editorially, "Our Afrikaans-speaking people would be more realistic if we accepted that the great mass of immigrants will not integrate themselves in the Afrikaans groups unless we ourselves behave in such a positive, virile, and superior manner that the Afrikaans group exercises a spontaneous attraction for the immigrants." The Society for the Maintenance for Afrikaans (*Die Genootskap vir die Handhawing van Afrikaans*) wants Parliament to make it obligatory for immigrants to learn *both* official languages, and has said that anyone who doesn't learn Afrikaans is a "half-baked and a dangerous citizen." One M.P. has proposed that the government take over all existing private nursery schools, the net effect of which would be to impose Afrikaans on some 60 per cent of young immigrant children at their most impressionable age.

Not all the immigrants who come to South Africa stay there. For the most part, they find the materialistic aspects of their new lives every bit as agreeable as South African recruiting literature makes them out to be. But they also sometimes find it hard to become socially assimilated and adjusted. The thinning of their new-formed ranks, even so, poses a less serious threat to the future of the country than the emigration of quite a few of its indigenous white people. Most of the immigrants are artisans. Most of the native-born South Africans who leave are professionals. The brain drain is much on South African minds these days.

There are two ways of getting out, by passport or by exit permit. The government is capricious about passports, which it gives and takes away with little seeeming rhyme or reason, and an exit permit is a one-way ticket. Anyone who leaves South Africa in that fashion can never lawfully return. It is hard for the South Africans in power to comprehend why any South African of any color should ever wish to leave the land of his birth. When an architect who'd been detained in jail for ninety days was finally released, a warden asked him what his plans were. "To get the hell out of this country as soon as possible," the detainee said. "You can't do that," said his jailer. "We need talented people like you."

But South Africa, for all its inequities and iniquities, has a potent, compelling attraction for those who were born there. One meets the man who is sick at heart and thinking of emigrating because his five-year-old daughter not long before looked out of a car window and said to him, "That's not a man, Daddy; that's a Colored." One meets a woman who says, "I'm South African, and I'm in South Africa, but I don't feel that I'm a part of it, and if I

81

knew how to get out I would. There's nothing about the life here to make me want to stay except its comforts, and they're corrupt." But just as often one meets, say, an Indian South African whose daughter is studying medicine abroad. He himself has been imprisoned for an alleged political offense, but he is determined that his daughter shall come home to practice, because South Africa is her land as well as his.

And one also meets the liberal white businessman who says, "I've brought up my children to think of apartheid as distasteful, but when I hear them starting to say that *everything* about South Africa is distasteful, I find myself arguing with them about their lack of patriotism and insisting that many things here are good. No one is more aware than I am that South Africa is a place where as nowhere else on earth is prejudice a daily part of life. But I love this country, and whenever I go away from it I can't wait to get back to it. I know it's awful, but every time I read in the papers that Gary Player has won another tournament I feel good—and I'm not even a golfer."

IV

"Treat him as a human being. He is one." Thus begins a guide list drawn up, for white South African employers of Africans, by a Johannesburg labor-relations consultant. The document is called "50 Things to Do with Bantu Workers," and the bosses are told, among other things, "Stand up for them. They have no Unions and no one to speak up for them unless you do"; "Call him by his name. A man's name is his personality—it marks him out from all other people"; "Respect his beliefs. They may be superstitious, but it's the best he has"; "Remember he has a tough life—travel, township conditions, laws which might be broken by forgetfulness; these things worry him"; "Speak clearly to him. Europeans often mumble more than they realize"; and "Keep off larking with him. His father would never do that and you are in the place of his father. He is terribly embarrassed when a white man larks around."

"Treat him as a human being. He is one." Perhaps only in South Africa would it occur to anyone that anyone else should have to be reminded of the essential humanity of mankind. After all, the Africans are hardly unnoticeable; twelve and a half million strong, they outnumber the Whites by more than four to one. The Africans have been around a long time. A thousand years ago, some four hundred years after they moved down from Central Africa toward the bottom tip of the continent, these Africans had a flourishing iron-age culture. In the eyes of many white South Africans, the black man's origins are unexceptionally pastoral. It is true that the iron-age culture disappeared, but nonetheless it was there ten centuries ago, when forerunners of today's black South Africans lived in stone-walled municipalities and smelted metal.

South Africa's contemporary Africans are a mixed lot. Some of them live more primitively, and less enterprisingly, than did their sophisticated counterparts of A.D. 1000. Some are far more sophisticated, and far abler, than a good many of their white compatriots. Taken as a group, all of them are far better off—materialistically—than any other national group of black men on the continent. Low as their wages are, compared to Whites', these are still so high by the continent's standards that around six hundred thousand black men from neighboring countries seek employment in South Africa each year.

Slightly over 40 per cent of the Republic's Africans live in their tribal homelands, where the government professes to hope that nearly all of them will eventually live, in conformity with its policy of separate development. A third of the Africans dwell and toil on white men's farms. The remaining quarter of them reside in, or on the fringes of, urban white settlements. What makes the Africans of South Africa so uniquely anguished a group is that, for all the statistical advantages they can rightly be said to enjoy over so many other inhabitants of their continent, they have very little say about where they live or where they work or practically anything. "Apart from everything else," said an editorial in one of their newspapers, "to consult people on matters which affect them makes them feel that they count as human beings."

The Africans of South Africa are by no means a homogeneous group. There are Xhosas and Zulus, Ndebeles and Swazis, three kinds of Sothos, and a multitude of tribal subdivisions. Many white South Africans sincerely believe that if the Blacks were left to their own devices they'd soon be at one another's throats. "If it hadn't been for the white man, they'd all have murdered each other long ago," one government official told me. There certainly used to be fierce tribal wars, not unlike those that have lately beset Nigeria, and nowadays in South Africa there are black men who loathe each other for no ascertainable reason other than that their ancestors were enemies. Many black South Africans, however, scoff at the notion that, given the opportunity to move around freely, most of them could not get along with the sons and daughters of alien tribes.

Some think that, given a really big opportunity, they could even establish a modus vivendi with Whites, whose comfort and serenity they admire and envy. Like a good many United States Negroes, many Africans in South Africa would seemingly like nothing better than to be white. With a few exceptions, they resent products aimed at them as Blacks. It would be the commercial kiss of death for a South African manufacturer to proclaim that this cigarette or that soft drink had been created specifically for African tastes; Africans would automatically think that there must be something wrong with it. A medical-supply house not long ago brought out a Band-Aid-like product tinted brown, for dark skins. It was test-marketed in a nonwhite area and was an utter flop. The only kind of flesh-colored skin dressings most Africans would use were those designed to match white skin.

The exceptions have to do mostly with products purportedly endowed with blanching qualities. Accordingly, billboards in non-white residential areas eulogize one cosmetic lotion with "Lighter, Lovelier Skin *Fast* . . . the American Way!" The weekly *Post,* whose readership is almost exclusively African, ran a letter not long ago from a heartsick young man who said that he was in love and wanted to get married, but his mother and his sister— African society, for a variety of reasons, is apt to be matriarchal —wouldn't give their blessing because his sweetheart was too dark. "I keep telling my mother that I love my girl and that the color of her skin does not matter to me," the dejected swain wrote, "but in vain."

It is surprising how cheerful South Africa's Africans can be, and frequently are. From afar, one visualizes them walking along the streets, tremulously and dourly, stepping carefully out of the path of their passing white masters. That is not the case at all. Africans assert themselves boldly on the sidewalk—not to mention in automobiles—and they not only often smile in public but laugh uproariously. So, of course, did Pagliacci. "When you're around Africans, things look good on the surface," one white South African told me. "But you can't really tell what's going on underneath. Maybe the Africans are smiling because they feel it's expected of them."

Some Africans smile simply because they feel merry. They like jokes, especially ones of which Whites are the butts. The government ministry that has the most direct impact on Africans' lives, for instance, is the Department of Bantu Affairs and Development. In newspapers written for Africans, the Department is often identified by the impish acronym "BAD." (There is a department for Colored Affairs and Development that lends itself to the same treatment.) African humor can be plaintive, or ironic. One day I went to a township outside Johannesburg in the company of a white woman who was a volunteer worker at a day center for very young children with no parents to look after them during working hours. The children at this particular center spoke no English, but had been taught a few songs and phrases in English by an African woman who looked after them. (One that I heard sounded like a cross between *My Fair Lady* and Dr. Seuss: "The cat on mat looks funny in the hat.") When my companion and I drove up, a dozen or more tots came to welcome us, and, at a signal from their teacher, they rendered a brief new musical greeting she had just taught them. "Good morning, how are you, Mrs. Fletcher?" the children chanted. "We are still alive."

The nursery school—or crêche, as this kind of institution is called—was one of thirty-odd such places in the principal African residential area outside of Johannesburg. The crêches are sponsored not by the government but by an organization called the Af-

86

rican Self Help Association. White women furnish most of its money and much of its help. Originally, the schools met in private homes, but the government has lately insisted that separate buildings used for no other purpose be constructed. A few of the African women who supervise the children have had some training as teachers. At present some twenty-five hundred children seven years old or younger spend their days at crêches, often getting there at seven thirty in the morning and staying till five in the evening. Their parents are supposed to pay for this protracted babysitting, but the fees are modest, rarely coming to more than a couple of dollars a month per child.

The children are fed at the crêches—often that is where they get most of their nourishment—and in the course of a day may receive some milk, soup, and mealie meal, the staple African dish, which is corn mush. Each crêche has at least one white patron, who stops by every week or so and usually brings some treats, perhaps candy or fresh vegetables. My escort had brought along some apples and oranges and a new spoon, which she'd heard the children needed. The woman in charge of the crêche was delighted with the spoon. (The children's benefactress also had with her some horse meat. She had been distressed, she told me, at the obvious malnutrition of the township's dogs. One of her own dogs had died not long before, but she hadn't told her butcher to reduce her regular horse-meat order so that she would be sure of always having a surplus she could take to the township with her.) She had also brought some ringworm medicine. The children didn't seem to care one way or another about that, but the African woman in charge of them was overjoyed to have it.

Many white South Africans are concerned, for a variety of reasons, with the health of blacks. Some, like the ladies of the Self Help Association, have genuine humanitarian motives. White farmers who treat their African hands somewhat brusquely when they're robust will, when they're ailing, drop everything to drive them to a hospital that may be hundreds of miles away. When an African woman walked into a rural clinic with Siamese twins, to which she had just given birth without any assistance and which puzzled her because they wouldn't come apart, the babies were flown to a Cape Town hospital, where a team of topflight white surgeons did successful surgery on them. (Almost at once South Africans began to circulate the joke that Pretoria was delighted with the episode because it was so striking a demonstration of the virtues of separate development.)

Others look at the situation from an economic slant. The black man, after all, provides the labor that primes the pump of the continent's most throbbing economy. (The ordinary South African white man, in any event, does not hate the black man. He may be frightened of him, and he may regard him as inferior, but he knows he will always be living close to him, and he does not plant bombs under the hood of the black man's car.) In employers' eyes, the healthier African worker is the stronger and more productive worker. The standard African diet of mealie meal is nutritionally unsatisfactory, consisting mainly of carbohydrates. Many rural Africans are afflicted with a disease called kwashiorkor, which hits children when they go off mother's milk—sometimes as late as their third year—and go onto mealie meal. Its symptoms are lethargy, distended stomachs, skin splotches, and loss of hair. (The infant mortality rate among Africans in South Africa is two hundred and seventy per thousand.) Such protein-rich foods as fish and eggs readily circumvent kwashiorkor, but there are African families who believe that eating fish makes children grow beards, and that eating eggs makes them bald.

The South African government has done probably more than any government in Africa to curb kwashiorkor. It is the only country on earth where doctors are supposed to report cases of it they encounter. The government, moreover, has tried to improve its black peoples' diet, in spite of their predilections, by promoting the sale of mealie meal into which skimmed milk has been induced, and also by trying to persuade Africans to buy bread that has been enriched by deodorized fish meal. But even many Africans who know what they or their children should eat cannot afford to do anything about it; their incomes are so low that they are forced to live beneath what all statisticians proclaim to be the local poverty level.

The principal attack upon kwashiorkor and malnutrition has been mounted by a nongovernment, nonprofit organization called

Kupugani. This remarkable group, whose name is a simplification of the Zulu word *"kuphukani,"* which means, roughly, "uplift yourself," began in 1962, when a South African farmer who was concerned about agricultural surpluses met a South African doctor who was concerned about the inadequacy of many South Africans' diets. Kupugani began buying unmarketable food at extremely low prices; it would then sell it through various outlets at a cost far below what similar food would have commanded at ordinary stores. The organization permits only the needy to be its customers. White people have to prove their indigence; non-Whites are assumed to be needy.

Kupugani's main objective is to provide one meal a day for every school child in South Africa. It is already doing that for more than a quarter of a million nonwhite children, at a cost of only a cent and a half per meal. True, the repast consists of no more than a cup of soup and a biscuit, but both are fortified with protein. In its sixty or so urban retail outlets, most of them extremely modest establishments in dowdy neighborhoods, Kupugani offers bargain-hunting housewives a couple of dozen kinds of items: the fortified biscuits and soup powders (these come in five flavors, and a pound, priced at only sixteen cents, can be stretched into thirty-two nourishing cups), peanuts, peanut butter, fish paste, fortified candy, and a precooked ready-to-eat powdery substance called ProNutro, which is made of mealie meal, fish, milk, bone meal, peanuts, soya, and yeast and which has been acclaimed by its sponsors as the perfect food. Two ounces of it a day, consumed in any one of a number of fashions, is supposed to give an African or anyone else all the nutrition he needs.

South Africans who are concerned with dietary matters have also been paying a good deal of attention lately to a comestible called Bantu beer, as well they might. In the urban centers of the country alone, a hundred and ten million gallons of the stuff are consumed each year. A government agency called the Council for Scientific and Industrial Research, which has done considerable research in diet deficiencies and how to cure them, has also tried to devise a standardized, healthful formula for the drink, and to that end has conducted numerous taste tests among African miners. The Council still has a small research unit, at one of its laboratories outside Pretoria, that devotes itself to brewing Bantu beer. Made largely from sprouted corn, the beer is acrid, flat, and sour and has a 3 per cent alcohol content. It costs twenty cents a gallon. It has such tonic qualities that doctors sometimes prescribe it for white patients with ulcers and other internal complaints. Some Whites put sugar into it to make it more palatable.

In former times, much Bantu beer was made by the proprietors of back-room drinking establishments, women known as shebeen queens, in their back yards, in forty-four-gallon-drum lots. Its composition was variable, and it was sometimes lethal. Now all Bantu beer is made, in theory at least, under government-controlled conditions, and is distributed through municipal administrations. Companies that make ordinary beer are not allowed to make Bantu beer, and the profits reaped from its sales are supposed to be used for Africans' welfare. The drink is so popular among non-Whites in South Africa that one white food-products distributor has been toying with the notion of exporting it, specifically aiming it at the American Negro market. He has already decided that if he goes through with his plans, to avoid any possible political fuss he will call his export not Bantu beer and not even South African beer but just plain African beer.

Thanks to both public and private agencies concerned with his welfare, the African's body is probably more robust today than it ever has been, but his soul is still emaciated. When Prime Minister Vorster calls South Africa "the happiest police state in the world," it is a white man's joke. For in truth South Africa is not, for most white-skinned people, a police state. The African tends to look at the matter quite differently. He is not a free man by any conceivable definition of freedom that would be acceptable outside South Africa. He has no vote. To earn a living he may have to live alone, since his family is apt to be barred from being with him. He is always pretty much at the mercy of his employer. Even if he happens to be a lecturer at a university, he must have the passbook that he, like all Africans, is required to carry at all times signed once every week by his boss. If he is caught without his pass, he can be put in jail or fined or "endorsed out"—sent, that is, to a so-called homeland he may never have seen and to which he has no ties. Seven hundred thousand arrests are made annually for pass-law violations, and eighty thousand Africans are endorsed out.

As long ago as the start of the nineteenth century, Africans in southernmost Africa had to carry identification documents. The idea then was to curb vagrancy, but the practice was abolished under missionary pressure. Now the South African government has all but abolished missionary pressure. It is not just Africans who must carry identification papers. Since August 1, 1966, every person over eighteen in South Africa has been required to carry a card. Every African over sixteen must have on his person what is called a reference book, a bulky document measuring five by three and a half inches and containing ninety-five pages. As a rule, it is only Africans who are stopped by the police and asked to produce their passes. "The African must be a collector of documents from the day of his birth to the day of his death," says a publication issued by a liberty-loving South African organization called the Black Sash. His passbook must contain particulars about every job he has had, every tax he has paid, and every X-ray he has taken. He would be well advised, the Black Sash has suggested, not to let himself get too far away from his birth certificate, baptismal certificate, school certificates, employment references, housing permits, hospital and clinic cards, prison discharge papers, rent receipts, and, the organization has added sarcastically, death and burial certificates.

Some Africans' pants pockets have permanent bulges from their passbooks. An African is frequently required to produce his documents for some bureaucrat's scrutiny, and when he asks for them back, the Black Sash says, "(a) He is told that he did not leave them there; or (b) The official denies all knowledge of them; or (c) He is told that they are now the property of the Department of Bantu Affairs and Development." The government insists that its reference-book system is fair and necessary, and the Bantu Affairs and Development Department has said that the pass laws were "created for safeguarding the Bantu against unemployment, unscrupulous exploitation, squatting, and the creation of slums." But, argues the Black Sash, "no system

91

which causes so much suffering can be justified. A nation cannot be great when it builds on the misery of its people."

One can get a sense of the misery and confusion that besets so many non-Whites in South Africa by visiting a Black Sash office. The organization, originally called the Women's Defense of the Constitution League, began in 1955, in protest against the government's then having taken away the Coloreds' right to vote. The name "Black Sash" derived from the habitual costume of the group's members, who would drape themselves in big mourning bands and stand in silent reproach outside government buildings. They would "haunt" cabinet ministers by going to airports and railroad stations and forming double black-sashed lines through which the officials had to pass. The women, most of them white and many of them elderly, stood their ground despite occasional assaults from young pro-government toughs. The Black Sash was the personification of the conscience of white South Africa. Now, like most liberal organizations in South Africa, it is a feeble group. In 1955, when it wanted to present a petition to the government, its members collected a hundred thousand women's signatures in ten days. "Today we couldn't get a hundred," one Black Sash woman told me.

But the Black Sash has been allowed to go on functioning, in part because many of its leaders are ladies of impeccable social standing. Other organiations have fared less well. The Defense and Aid Fund, for instance, which began in 1960 during South Africa's celebrated mass treason trials and which devoted itself to obtaining legal counsel for people accused of political crimes, was declared unlawful in the spring of 1966. More recently, the government has reminded itself that it has on its statute books a 1962 proclamation to the effect that people who ever belonged to any banned group like Defense and Aid were breaking the law *now* if they belonged to any other organization that even discussed—let alone criticized—the government. This 1962 law has not yet been much invoked, but it is there. Presumably, the government could use it to cripple the Black Sash if it wanted to.

The Sash, as many of its members fondly call it, has its headquarters in Johannesburg, but it functions principally out of its

Athlone Advice Office, a cramped and grubby installation on the outskirts of Cape Town not too far from that city's two African townships. The office is open every weekday morning and is staffed by three paid African workers and a changing guard of white volunteers. The office handles four thousand cases a year. Most of them involve people who are already in trouble with the authorities and are looking for last-minute intercession to avoid being endorsed out of the area. In some way or other, they have violated a law that says that no African may stay in an urban area for over seventy-two hours without permission, unless he was born there, has lived there uninterruptedly for fifteen years, or has been working for the same employer there for ten uninterrupted years. The Black Sash has found out that women who buy sewing machines on the installment plan stand a better chance of not being endorsed out than women who don't; the receipts that the machine owners have for their periodic payments are generally regarded as evidence of suitably long residence. Many African women—and men, too—never quite seem to have all the documents that the government demands of them. In South Africa, the people who are least likely to keep meticulous records are usually those most dependent on them.

Some of the Africans who come in to the Athlone office are luckier than others. A woman well advanced in pregnancy turned up while I was there. She had lost her pass and was about to be shipped off, having no acceptable substitute documents. Happily for her, the Black Sash knew that the government-owned South African Railways won't accept an endorsed-out passenger who is more than seven months pregnant, and the one document the woman did have was a doctor's certificate attesting that she was thirty-two weeks with child. Next came an eighteen-year-old boy who said he had been born near Cape Town but couldn't prove it. He was told to go to the church his parents had attended at the time of his birth and try to find a baptismal certificate, and to ask various friends and neighbors to make affidavits to the effect that he'd been born where and when he said he had.

Then there was a widow who had lost her passbook, she said, in a fire. She didn't want to be endorsed out because, having lived in the Cape province all her life, she didn't know any African language, although she was fluent in both English and Afrikaans. The Black Sash didn't think it could do much to help her; she would probably end up in a native homeland where she could hardly understand a word that anyone was saying. There was a sixteen-year-old girl who brought her illegitimate baby with her. She'd been born in the Transkei but had come to Cape Town when she was fourteen, after her parents had been evicted from their home for lack of funds. Now she was working, illegally, as a domestic servant, and when she turned sixteen she had never got around to applying for a reference book. Hopeless case. She had nowhere to go, really, but she would have to go anyway.

Organizations like the Black Sash are constantly under the surveillance of the South African Security Police, but the Sash has been comparatively fortunate; it hadn't been raided since July 1965. The police are fond of raids, which they call swoops. There are three principal kinds. There are swoops calculated to thwart vice and gambling and that sort of thing. There are swoops aimed at uncovering alleged threats to the security of the state. And there are swoops to round up non-Whites who are where the government says they shouldn't be. (The government seems to be convinced that this represents a threat to the security of the state.) When raiding a white man's home, the police are apt to be deferential. They usually won't search such a house unless a white person is in it. They went to one home at midday, knowing that the head of the family customarily came home for lunch. The man in question happened to have a business lunch that day, so the cops just went away and never came back.

Every now and then the police will organize a catchall swoop in a white suburban residential area. They come with a large van, being confident from past experience that they will be able to fill it up with servants or friends of servants whose papers are not in order. One white South African woman I know has an African manservant whose documentation is faulty. Whenever there's a raid in her neighborhood, if she has sufficient warning, she hides the African in her bedroom. She knows that no white South African policeman would ever dream of searching a white woman's bedroom for a black man.

94

The South African police has a strength of more than thirty thousand. Half its members are Africans. "Why do they join the police, Mummy?" I once heard a small white boy ask his mother. She replied that some Blacks join up because it's a job, because they like to wear uniforms and have authority, and because there are natural bullies of every color. She added, presumably to try to cheer the lad, that there was a good side to it all; African policemen sometimes tip off other Africans when a raid is scheduled. (There is another side: the police are reliably thought to have hundreds, if not thousands, of nonuniformed African informers who tip *them* off.) On the police force, as in every phase of South African life, no black man may ever rise above a white man. Thus a senior African policeman with twenty years' experience on the force may never outrank the downiest-faced eighteen-year-old fledgling Afrikaner cop. The senior police officials are all white, naturally, and they sometimes say odd things. One of the highest-ranking of them all not long ago created a stir by declaring that communism was the highest form of capitalism. "I ask you," another top policeman said, "what has an innocent man to fear by answering questions, and how are our liberties protected by making criminals and suspects a privileged class? The activities of criminals and saboteurs are a far more serious invasion of our privileges and liberties than those of the police." It was perhaps illustrative of police thinking that his "suspects" in one sentence had so smoothly become "saboteurs" in the next.

The police have a good deal of hard-core crime to cope with. South Africa averages nine known murders a day. The country still has capital punishment, and in 1966 a hundred and twenty-four people were hanged—eighty-nine African men, thirty-two colored men, two white men, and one African woman. South Africa also still has whipping. In the last twenty years the courts have ordered one million strokes inflicted, mostly on black backs. It is no news that disenchantment, unhappiness, and hopelessness can lead to crime, and it is no surprise that most of the crimes in South African are committed by Africans. "Another 13 Murders" is a routine headline for a Monday-morning African newspaper. The principal service station in Soweto, the main African township area outside Johannesburg, has underground chutes along side its gas pumps so that money taken in can be tucked away before it is taken off. A lot of Africans carry home their pay in their shoes. In the Johannesburg area, a thousand people are knifed to death each year.

Whites run scared. One outspokenly liberal white South African woman told me, "If you meet an African at the other end of an axe at three in the morning it's a terrifying experience, no matter how you were brought up." Non-Whites are often equally afraid. The African daily, the *World*, which once described a six-murder weekend as "a quiet weekend for Soweto," has also recounted how residents of that area don't dare help people who appear to be bleeding to death right outside their homes at night. The people inside have no telephone and are too frightened to open their doors. One *World* reporter thought he heard a man being stabbed to death outside his house one night, but waited until morning to investigate, when on opening his curtains he was relieved to find no body outside. "He might have crawled into a nearby yard to die," the *World* man wrote. "Thank heaven, not ours!"

The Security Police, which deals with more refined matters, is unobtrusive but omnipresent. "You can't even have a meeting of three people without the Special Branch knowing about it," one antigovernment man told me. "You get to recognize their faces. You learn to live with these boys." The boys turn up in university classrooms. "I haven't got any spies in my class this year—as far as I know," I heard one professor tell another over tea. The year before, the speaker had had a spy who was easy to detect. The undercover student had a notebook, but he only used it when the professor mentioned nonwhite political figures. There are spies in churches. To keep tabs on one Anglican minister whose nontheological activities it frowned upon, the Special Branch not long ago placed an agent in his confirmation class. The ruse came to light when the agent got religion and asked the minister for a bona fide confirmation.

When the Robert Kennedys were in South Africa in the spring of 1966, at one point they were riding through Durban with a police car on either side of their vehicle. Alan Paton was with them, and Ethel Kennedy asked the writer what he thought about their escort. "I'm not used to having them alongside me," Paton said. "I'm used to having them follow me." Others who have had encounters with the Security Police sometimes let their apprehensions carry them to flights of exaggerated fancy. One Cape Town man had the impression that the Special Branch was trying to harass him by putting iron filings in the gas tank of his car. He started off on a drive one day, heard a clanking noise, and exclaimed, "They've done it again!" It turned out that he had a loose exhaust pipe.

A journalist visiting South Africa is always conscious of the country's tensions. I was warned even before going there not to leave any notes lying around my hotel room, which, my informants added, would like as not be bugged. I was warned not to telephone certain individuals; their phones were probably tapped. Instead of calling one such person, I dropped in at his office unannounced. He said he was busy and would telephone me at my hotel, which he presently did, obviously being far less concerned about a tapped phone than I was. In all fairness, I am bound to say that never once in South Africa was I aware of being followed or listened in on or having my room searched or bugged. The only time I may have had any contact at all with the Security Police was when an appointment was canceled. The appointment was with the Prime Minister's daughter, who was then a university undergraduate and has since married a farmer. I had had a pleasant chat with her on the phone, and we had agreed to meet for tea. The night before our date I received a call from a man who did not identify himself but asked if I was the person who had an engagement with Miss Vorster. When I said I was, he said, "Well, she won't be coming." However, it might not have been the Special Branch at all but just her fiancé.

Since Africans are predominant in South Africa, it follows logically enough that they are the ones who most often get picked up by the Security Police. It was in June 1963 that Parliament authorized the Minister of Justice to detain for ninety days anyone he chose without any need to make a charge; in June 1965 Parliament made it a hundred and eighty days. One African I know spent three months in prison for no other apparent reason than that he happened to be attending a rugby-club meeting in one room of a building while a meeting of the African National Congress was concurrently being held in another room. But arrests under these two hard-boiled detention laws have not been quite as widespread as is perhaps commonly thought. In over a three-year stretch, according to Prime Minister Vorster—and there is no reason to doubt his statistics—1,095 individuals were detained. Five hundred twenty of them were never ultimately charged with anything and were released. Of the 575 charged, 272 were convicted, 210 were discharged, and 93 were still awaiting trial.

In defense of its detention laws, the government generally argues that South Africa is under constant pressure from enemies both outside and inside its borders, and that by locking up people it considers questionable it is merely doing the country a protective service. Most of South Africa's judges are men genuinely dedicated to justice, but when it comes to the detention laws they have remained uncommonly silent. "We're supposed to be nonpolitical, and the government tells us there is an emergency," one Supreme Court justice told me. "I once spoke to Mr. Vorster when he was Minister of Justice about the detention laws, and he told me that they had helped immensely in getting crimes solved. I couldn't say, 'You're wrong Mr. Vorster,' because I didn't have the facts. The basic question is, I guess: Are we in a state of emergency or are we not? Whenever our bar associations issue statements about encroachments on individual liberties, the government's standard answer is that the lawyers don't have the facts. The government may be right, it may be wrong; I don't know." He seemed a troubled man.

The South African version of involuntary detention is not pleasant. It is often featured by solitary confinement and interminable interrogations. Whole books have been written about its disagreeableness. Some who have been through the ordeal can now and then, retrospectively, be lighthearted about it. In ex-detainees' circles the story is told of one of them who had been in solitary confinement for weeks when a fly came into his cell. The insect was followed by a warden with a spray gun. Ah!, the detainee thought, finally someone to talk to! But the jailer just stalked the fly, silently, and as it was finally falling dead and the warden was walking out, he merely said, "When the Minister of

Justice says solitary confinement, he means solitary confinement."
When veterans of the experience get together, they are apt to debate matter-of-factly whether it is tougher to have to stand on
one's feet for twenty-four hours at a stretch or to be beaten.

Banning is another tactic that the government has come up
with in alleged insurance of its security. A banned person leads a
sort of half life. At the time of his death, Chief Albert Luthuli, the
nation's only Nobel Prize winner, was all but unknown to many
young South Africans. A banned person's writings, no matter how
renowned internationally, may not be circulated. He may not go to
any social gathering; a dinner for three is considered a social gathering. He may not attend a meeting; playing billiards has been con-
strued as attending a meeting. South Africa having no television,
banned people get very fond of books and phonograph records.
As a rule, they are allowed to hold jobs, but here there are restrictions on that, too. They may not work in a building that houses
any tenant—a trade union, say—that might be directly or indirectly involved in political activity. A banned person may not
communicate with another banned person. If a husband and wife
are both banned, however, they can usually get permission to
speak to one another.

Some banned people are also under house arrest. They are ordinarily required to be in their homes by six in the evening and to
stay there until morning. They may not go out on weekends or
holidays. One woman who lived in an apartment that had a swimming pool was refused permission to use it even though she had
gone to the trouble of making sure that none of the other tenants
would go swimming at the time she requested. Another banned
woman, after getting special permission to attend her own daughter's wedding, had to ask for further permission to have her dress
fitted; her couturier happened to be in a building where a political
party also had an office. Banned people are supposed to have no
truck with journalists. One of them nonetheless took the risk of
inviting me to his office. He wouldn't talk there; he figured the
place was bugged. We rode down on an elevator together, acting,
at his direction, like strangers. We went to a coffee shop, he walking half a block ahead of me. We departed separately by different
entrances. Conversation was difficult, because my companion

spent most of his time looking over his shoulder, or over mine, to see if anyone was on to us.

Banned people may not travel more than a limited distance from their homes, and are required to report to the police at least once a week. The artistic child of one forgetful parent who is banned has done his filial best to ameliorate the situation by decorating their home with gaily painted signs saying "Don't Forget to Report."

One African, reporting in to the police, found the officer on duty dozing, and roused him by putting his hand on his shoulder. The policeman awoke with a start. "Don't worry," the African said, "the time hasn't come for me to get you yet." It is the kind of talk that makes South Africans laugh, but nervously.

Of the South Africans who have been banned, only a few dozen have been white, but their cases generate fierce discussion. The banning in the summer of 1967 of Dr. Raymond Hoffenberg, a Cape Town endrocrinologist, had all of the country's liberals and some of its physicians and educators in an uproar. And of the country's average daily prison population of over seventy thousand, only thirty or so individuals are whites convicted of political crimes, perhaps a smaller number than is commonly thought. Apartheid is the rule in prison, too. Whites and non-Whites have separate jails (there are no Whites at Robben Island, the celebrated stockade off Cape Town), and the different races are assigned different tasks. Whites make mailbags. Blacks break rocks.

Most prisoners, whether political or nonpolitical, are sentenced by judges. South Africa has a jury system, but its use is optional, and it has been all but abrogated by disuse. The twenty-two Supreme Court judges in the Transvaal preside among them over only half a dozen jury trials a year. The unpopularity of jury trials is understandable. Most South Africans accused of crimes are black, and all juries are white. Non-Whites would rather take their chances with a judge. Most South African judges, especially those on a higher-than-magisterial level, have a reputation for fairness. A black man may have his day in court. It is quite possible, for instance, for a servant involved in a legal wrangle with his employers to suggest to the court that Master or Madam may not be telling the truth. And there are judges perfectly willing to believe that a black plaintiff is an honest man and a white used-

100

car dealer say, is a scoundrel, or that three white witnesses may have conspired to lie about a single nonwhite adversary.

Some Supreme Court justices, however, are concerned about the caliber of some of the lower courts, particularly those known as Bantu Commissioners' Courts, where Africans accused of pass offenses are arraigned. Some of the commissioners who sit in these courts are not lawyers but civil servants. If they sentence anyone to three months or more in prison or fine him upward of seventy-five dollars, his case is automatically reviewed by a Supreme Court judge. The twenty-two Transvaal judges handle a thousand such cases apiece a year. But lesser sentences are not automatically reviewed, and some Supreme Court justices feel that serious miscarriages of justice occur in this area. "Many poor men accused of pass violations plead guilty when they haven't a clue to what's going on," one Supreme Court judge told me. "The explanation always is that the magistrates are always overworked. But in the administration of justice that's no excuse."

A South African cabinet minister said not long ago, "Dealing with human beings is a very personal thing." He can hardly have been thinking of the Bantu Commissioners' Courts, the impersonality of whose proceedings is their most striking quality. The chances are he had never been to one. These courtrooms have accommodations, more or less, for both black and white spectators, but few Whites ever bother to go there and see how they function. (The ladies of the Black Sash used to, but they hardly turn up any more.) There are such courts in all the big South African cities, and among them they process a thousand cases a day. The magistrate in charge of a court I visited one morning in Johannesburg disposed of some of the people brought before him in less than a minute.

His courtroom, a small, drab chamber, was conveniently situated right alongside an open-air cage in which stood or squatted or sat a hundred or so alleged wrongdoers who had been rounded up the night before. Assisting the judge in his assembly-line proceedings were a prosecutor, a clerk, a couple of uniformed African policemen, and an interpreter. There were no defense lawyers. The interpreter, whose English was poor, was an elderly Uncle Tom-ish African who was clearly hamming it up for his white visitor. It was hard for me to comprehend just what the charges

101

were against some of the accused men, and, judging from their facial expressions, they were equally confused. To keep things moving at a fast clip, three or four of them were always in line just outside the courtroom door, so that as soon as one case was finished another could begin. Now and then an accused man would be pushed inside while his predecessor was still pleading his case.

Some of the prisoners seemed very young. One said he was sixteen. The judge asked him when he was born, and the young man did not know, or at any rate the interpreter said he did not. The judge gave him short shrift. Another man had come to town for his mother's funeral, but he had got picked up before he found his family and wasn't sure whether or not the funeral had yet taken place; in this instance the judge said he would have the police investigate the circumstances further before passing sentence. When he did pass sentence, it was usually "Guilty." The usual punishment was seven days in jail or a fine of seven rand—about ten dollars. A few men turned out to be not South Africans at all but natives of neighboring countries; the judge directed that they be sent to something called "A" Court. A guard inside the courtroom instructed the departing foreigner to proceed in one direction, but while the judge and his assistants at once took up the next case I could see the fellow being shoved by an African policeman outside in the opposite direction from the one the guard had told him to take. I wondered if he would ever make it to "A" Court. Half the time the judge and the prosecutor were so busy conferring with one another or shuffling papers that they scarcely paid any attention to the people to whom the papers related. Through it all, the clerk went thump-thump with a rubber stamp —like the accompaniment of a muffled, arhythmic tribal drum.

There is much concern among contemporary white South Africans as to whether tourists visiting their country will find their justly celebrated game reserves plentifully stocked with a suitable variety of animals. When I happened to be discussing this one day with a South African non-White, he told me with a wry smile that visitors to the Bantu Commissioners' Courts need have no worry; the cages are always full.

102

V

At any given time, there are probably close to a quarter of a million Africans in and around Johannesburg who have no legal business being there. According to a long-range plan brought out in 1955 and embraced by the late Dr. Hendrik F. Voerwoerd, the apostle of apartheid, most of these Africans, and many others, will end up in homelands that they will some day govern, just as Whites will govern their own areas. In Verwoerd's vision, there would ultimately be seven quasi-independent black territories, called Bantustans, one for each major tribe or group of tribes. Altogether, the Africans would control 13 per cent of the area of South Africa. The other 87 per cent would go to the white minority.

South Africa has been stuck with the Bantustan concept ever

since Dr. Verwoerd advocated it. The government has had to defend Bantustans stoutly because they represent the one big argument it has to justify its separatist attitudes and actions. It argues in their favor even though many of its own supporters doubt that they could ever work, on the grounds of impracticality. Its opponents often denounce them as a farce or a fraud. There are more than a few black South Africans, though, who have lately seemed to be abating their criticism of Bantustans.

Not too long ago, the African editor of one newspaper esteemed by many of his race made a survey of African leaders ("We don't have many now; they're all behind bars," he says) to ascertain their viewpoint. They had all been solidly opposed to Bantustans, and he was surprised to find a change of attitude. "The majority of them seemed to feel that there wasn't much sense in opposing the government's Bantustan policy any longer," he told me. "They seem to be saying, 'Let's accept it and see if it'll work.' It's put us in something of a quandary—having a majority of our people apparently think that there might be something after all in something the government favors."

To date, there is one Bantustan—the Transkei. It has been more or less semi-independent since 1963. It is the homeland of the nearly million and a half members of the Xhosa tribe. It is a land of rolling hills and sparkling streams and myriad round huts, or *rondavels,* perched on the high ground. Crossing the border that separates it from the rest of South Africa one sees a sign, "Beware of Stray Animals." Cattle and sheep are abundant, on and off the highways. The Xhosa, like many other tribal Africans, often measure their wealth in livestock. Many Africans, even those who have been thoroughly urbanized, still faithfully cling to the custom of paying a dowry, called a *lobola,* for a bride. It is traditionally paid in cattle, but a city boy who doesn't have any may give the equivalent in cash at the going exchange rate. In the Transkei the Africans who do have cattle are often to be seen on horseback counting, or at any rate looking after, their wealth. Even on warm days they are apt to be bundled in blankets or, more incongruously, clad in suit coats and neckties.

When the weather is good and the rains have fallen, much of the Transkei is lovely to look at. Some of its agriculturally most

104

promising acreage, however, is off limits to the Africans for whom the state has been theoretically set aside. The one real seaport the Transkei has is Port St. Johns, on the Indian Ocean. Just inland from Port St. Johns there is so much rainfall that tropical crops like bananas, avocados, and papayas can easily be grown. But this lush land has been decreed a Whites-only area. Dr. Verwoerd laid down that law, and while he was at it said Port St. Johns would always be white. The reason was obvious enough; if the Transkei were ever to become *really* independent and if it were to decide to welcome an anti-South African invasion force, Port St. Johns would make a nice port of entry.

The rest of the Transkeian ocean front is called the Wild Coast. There are a few seashore resorts in this black territory, but they are all owned by Whites and cater to white patrons. When it comes to that, the capital of the Transkei, Umtata, is just about as all-white as any other South African city. The all-black Transkeian Legislative Assembly, about which the South African government has done a good deal of self-satisfied crowing, has its meeting hall in Umtata, but until recently none of its members could have a meal or a drink in any hotel in their own capital city (they had a cafeteria at the Assembly so they could legislate without starving), and Umtata's one municipal swimming pool—or swimming bath, in the South African terminology—does not admit non-Whites. There are some all-black smaller towns in the Transkei, but there are still other towns in this Bantustan where the only bar bars Blacks. When the African editor of one of South Africa's principal nonwhite newspapers, a man of cultivated and cosmopolitan tastes, went to the Transkei for three weeks to inspect the much-touted Bantustan, he had to live four miles outside of Umtata, and he could only buy a meal there by going around to the kitchen doors of hotels and having food passed to him outside.

The Transkeian legislature has a hundred and nine members. Forty-five are elected. The other sixty-four hold their seats by virtue of their hereditary chiefdom. Many of the chiefs are flattered by being thus honored and are reasonably friendly toward the South African government. Even so, the legislature has now and then crossed Pretoria; when the South African government tried

105

to impose one educational system on the Transkei, the legislature balked and voted to adopt another. Whatever the future of the Transkei, nearly everyone is agreed that because African society remains in so many respects a tribal one the chiefs are going to continue to be influential. To train their sons to become even more astute legislators than some of the current crop have shown themselves to be, the government has set up a specal school thirty miles east of Umtata called Jongilizwe College, and its student body is restricted to sons of chiefs and headmen. According to the school's prospectus, one of its chief aims is "to instill in the student the functualities of Responsibility, Dedication to Duty, Recognition of an authority higher than himself, and dedication to his people."

Jongilizwe, which has been operating since 1959, offers a high-school program, but only two of its graduates have gone on to college. At present it has eighty-eight students and a library of about twice that many books. The main course is called Bantu Administration and Law, and this embraces instruction in world affairs and diplomacy. I asked the principal, an Afrikaner whose contact with his students is limited because he speaks no Xhosa, what world affairs were being discussed. He said the boys were considering the independence of Botswana—formerly Bechuanaland. I asked what they would be taking up next. "If we have time, we'll go beyond Botswana to the rest of the world," he said. As for diplomacy, he said emphasis was placcd on general etiquette and how to conduct a meeting. I asked if the Jongilizwe boys were introduced to Robert's Rules of Order. He had never heard of them. There may be more hope for the Transkei than some of us suspect.

The Chief Minister of the Transkei is an articulate, university-educated Xhosa named Kaiser Matanzima. In the legislature most of the hereditary chiefs vote with him; most of the elected members don't. His opposition favors an eventual multiracial state in the area; Matanzima seems to be a black-power advocate. At the same time, he usually gets along fairly well with the South African government. His present power, after all, depends on his maintaining good relations with Pretoria. He has a handsome, clean-cut face, not unlike Cassius Clay's. In self-esteem he also sometimes seems Clay's peer; not long ago Matanzima declared that people were coming to realize "that in me there are indications of a future statesman equal to any in the world." Some South Africans, both black and white, think that he is little more than a stooge of the Republic, and their feelings were reinforced when, after Verwoerd's assassination, Matanzima called *him* South Africa's "greatest statesman of all time."

Chief Matanzima's right-hand man, who serves as acting chief minister when Matanzima is absent or indisposed, is his brother George. He has a law degree and was the first Minister of Justice in the Transkeian cabinet, but after he was stricken from the legal rolls because of some professional chicanery he became Minister of Education. It is one of six government departments—the others are Finance, Interior, Agriculture and Forestry, Justice, and Roads and Work—that South Africa has ostensibly let the Transkeian government run on its own. I made an appointment to see George Matanzima at his Umtata office one day, and he seemed surprised when I arrived without an escort from the South African Ministry of Information. "Why did you come alone?" he asked. "An Information man always comes along." He told me several things about education in the Transkei. The local government, for instance, was planning to build two hundred new classrooms a year, but even those would barely accommodate all the children whose parents wanted them to be educated. He said further, interestingly, that after Transkeian communities had finished giving their younger children instruction in their mother tongue, they had the option of then continuing their education in either English or Afrikaans, and that not a single community had yet chosen Afrikaans.

But for the minister of an independent department, he seemed at times oddly unauthoritative. We got to discussing a technical school—for mechanics, engineers, surveyors, bookkeepers, and accountants—which the Transkeian cabinet hoped would be in operation in 1968. When I inquired how large it would be or how many students it would have or what it might look like, he had no idea. "They haven't informed me yet," said the Minister of Education. A week or so after I left the Transkei, I came upon a publicity handout issued by the Information Service of South Africa,

107

which quoted George Matanzima at length about the true state of affairs in the Transkei, in purported contrast to the United Nations' version of that state of affairs. The handout had him saying that the Transkei was "a self-governing state, developing to total stable and enduring independence. It is in full control of the Departments of State handed over to it by the Republican Government."

On a nongovernmental, hereditary level, Chief Minister Kaiser Matanzima is a paramount chief. Also resident in the Transkei is a white South African named J. H. Abraham, who holds the title of Commissioner-General of the Xhosa National Unit. If both leaders were to attend a formal dinner, the Commissioner-General, who calls his headquarters "Abraham's Kraal," would be at the hostess' right, except that no such dinner would take place. Matanzima and Abraham do meet and chat at occasional social functions—the installation, say, of some Xhosa chieftain—but when refreshments are served they repair to separate areas.

The Commissioner-General is forever tilting with people who he says do not care as much about the welfare of Blacks as he does. He once compared the liberal *Daily Dispatch*, in nearby East London, to a witch doctor. Mr. Abraham said the paper was doing a devilish disservice to Whites like himself who had the Blacks' real welfare at heart. "Let us put the matter to the test, and let the Africans themselves decide who they prefer," a *Daily Dispatch* editorial retorted. "We hereby invite the Commissioner-General to answer the following questions in the knowledge that the African people of the Border will be awaiting his answers with interest." Among seventeen questions asked (but never publicly answered by Mr. Abraham) were:

Is the Commissioner-General opposed to all forms of racial discrimination? We are.

Is he in favor of making merit, not color, the test of full citizenship? We are.

Would he admit Africans to South Africa's best universities? We would.

Would he like to see the Transkei Government chosen by a majority of Transkei voters? We would.

If the best man for the Prime Ministership of South Africa were Black, would he serve under him? We would.

Would he admit Africans of his own standard of living into restaurants and hotels? We would.

Is he in favor of Africans getting the same opportunities for advancement as Whites—throughout South Africa? We are.

At last count there were some five hundred white civil servants in the Transkei administration. In theory, they will all be replaced, sooner or later, by Africans. Many of the Whites will be missed when they leave. Some of them are lackluster, but there are quite a few—as there are working elsewhere for Bantu Affairs and Development—who are earnestly devoted to doing whatever they can to improve the lot of Africans. In any event, it will apparently be years before enough qualified Africans will be available to take over. I spent an evening in Umtata with a white doctor who'd been practicing there for years. He liked the place, but he was about to pull up stakes, as were four others of the eight white doctors then in the capital. There were also three African doctors.

The white exodus had nothing to do with Transkeian independence. The trouble was, my host told me, that the Umtata hospital, with which all eleven physicians were affiliated, was the central hospital for a population group of more than a hundred and fifty thousand people, and that it was terribly shorthanded. Young white doctors were uninterested in doing interneships there; they were afraid of being stuck out in the sticks, and they were also afraid to settle in an enclave surrounded by a sea of black men who were getting a taste of power—not, my host added hastily, that he perceived any justification whatever for the latter fears. The five white physicians were getting out simply because they were tired of having to do internes' work on top of their normal practices. Recruiting African doctors wasn't a practical solution; there just weren't enough of them around.

When it came to that, my man didn't have too high a professional opinion of some of the black doctors who'd served in Umtata; with one or two exceptions, he said, they were unpredictable and undependable. And their lapses could result in aggravating side effects: African nurses admired African doctors, and if the nurses' heroes didn't seem to care too much about asepsis, then neither would the nurses themselves. "The government keeps talking about giving doctors here a kind of hardship allowance to keep us from pulling out," my informant said. "We don't want more money. I've never made so much money in my life as I've made here. We want help."

Nobody expects medical services in the Transkei to wither away. The government in Pretoria has a national public-health service, and it can always deploy some of its doctors to the Transkei. Or it can try to recruit private physicians from, say, western Europe, who might be looking for adventure and challenge. In any case, the Republic does not seem especially worried about this seeming threat to the orderly evolution of Transkeian life. In Pretoria I asked one government official what plans there were to cope with the looming Transkei medical crisis. "We shall not let the Transkei down," he replied.

Chief Kaiser Matanzima has prophesied that the Transkei will be completely independent by the year 2000, but optimism is a universal characteristic of politicians. Some reflective South Africans think that, no matter how piously the central government may preach its dedication to real self-government for Bantustans, in practice it is in no hurry to make that come true. One historian, in that connection, has alluded to the "theory of indefinite postponement." When I asked a responsible government official what kind of a timetable had been drawn up, he said, "That's in the hands of the people concerned."

It's not entirely in their hands. Still operative in the Transkei is a 1960 law making it a criminal offense to hold a meeting of more than ten persons without a permit or to treat any tribal chief or headman with disrespect. Moreover, any chief, whether or not he thinks his dignity has been abused, may arbitrarily order the removal of any individual from one section of his bailiwick to another. Insofar as freedom of assembly or expression or movement are essential to independence, the people of the Transkei are not yet much better off than any other South African non-Whites, although they do have some small advantages. In the Transkei, its indigenous legislature has proclaimed, one may not, with impunity, address a male nonwhite adult as "boy."

Whenever, if ever, the Transkei becomes a bona fide nation, that is unlikely to occur before the region attains that state of grace called economic viability. The Transkei is a largely agricultural region, but even though the central government says its food supply is "adequate," it has had to import more than a million bags of mealies a year to meet the demand for its staple foodstuff. There is no question but that the productivity of the area's arable land could be vastly improved if its farmers tilled their soil more efficiently. Near Jongilizwe, the government now has an agricultural college, where a hundred men a year are instructed in subjects like crop rotation and the proper use of fertilizers. There is a long way to go. The same Transkeian land that now yields two and a half million bags of maize a year could be made to yield eighteen million bags if it were properly farmed, according to the head of the agricultural college.

Transkeians, furthermore, think of their livestock quantitatively; it is usually most or all of their wealth. But if they could be brought to think of it qualitatively, and to go in for improved breeding methods, controlled grazing, and the like, they'd have better animals and would probably end up richer. There is very little industry in the Transkei. A South African government commission said in 1955 that for the Transkei to become economically self-sufficient, fifty thousand new jobs would have to be created for its people every year. In the twelve years since then, the new-job figure has been closer to a thousand a year. As things stand now, there are about three hundred thousand Transkeian males of employable age, and at least half of them, to earn a living, have to work away from their homes and usually much farther away than any border industry. "I like the Transkei best, but my stomach is here," is the way one urbanized Xhosa put it to me in Johannesburg.

What this means is that a good many men from the Transkei are lucky if they can be with their families more than a few weeks a year, and that the permanent male population of the Transkei consists in large part of boys too young to work and men too old to. That is hardly an ideal resident framework on which to build a

111

fledgling nation. And the longer that Transkeians, or any other rural Africans, work away from their country homes and in the quite different atmosphere of big cities, the less likely they are ever to be satisfied with their traditional tribal existence. White South Africans keep saying that outsiders simply do not understand their policy of separate development and that the Transkei and the other Bantustans supposedly to be created in its image represent an equitable and workable solution to some of their racial problems. And indeed it *is* difficult for a visitor to make much sense of a so-called independent state that can sustain so few of its potentially productive citizens within its boundaries, and a state, moreover, whose own chief minister is not allowed to cool off in his capital's public swimming pool.

The Transkei has an unusually high number of one kind of business establishment. This is the native recruiting office. There are three hundred and ninety-five licensed labor agents in the Transkei, all but twenty-two of them white. Many of them are storekeepers who recruit as a sideline and who get what is called a "capitation fee" for each worker they send to the Republic's mines, farms, or industries. In the case of miners, the fee is a bit higher for men found fit for underground duty, so it is to the labor agent's advantage to sign up the healthiest men possible. Of late the agents have had some frustrations. In the last six years there has been a drop of 26.8 per cent in the number of Transkeian men who've agreed to work in the mines. A South African government report issued in 1966 sounded unhappy about what it called "the 'choosiness' of work-seekers regarding certain types of employment."

South Africa's mines still nonetheless attract four hundred thousand nonwhite migrant workers every year. The front of one document typical of the kinds of agreements they sign has space for an affidavit from an attesting officer saying, "The Contract of Employment on the reverse hereof was read aloud, interpreted and fully explained to the above-named Employee who acknowledged that he understood the same and voluntarily affixed his signature (or mark) thereto in my presence . . ." The contract on the reverse thereof comprises nearly two thousand legalistic

112

words, in small type. Eighty-five per cent of all novice African mine workers in South Africa are illiterate. If indeed every word is read aloud, interpreted, and fully explained nearly four hundred thousand times a year, it's a wonder that one does not encounter more hoarse South Africans.

An African en route from his home to a mine goes through a processing experience much like that of a tyro soldier between his induction and the battlefield. The mineworker moves along faster. His first principal stopping-off place, where he stays less than a day, is apt to be a Johannesburg encampment run by the Witwatersland Native Labor Association, known for short as Winela. Six days a week, week in and out, Winela receives, processes, and passes along a thousand new mineworkers. Every day it handles an equal number going home from the mines. The place has its own railway spur, known as "The Mineral Line." Winela is so important to the South African economy that the Bantu Affairs and Development ministry maintains a full-time office there. So does Portugal; a good many miners hail from the Portuguese colonies of Angola and Mozambique.

In the main courtyard of Winela there are a few of the distorting mirrors one associates with amusement parks; they give the transient miners a chance to look at themselves and laugh. Otherwise, the atmosphere is bleak and businesslike and terribly efficient. Most of the men who arrive have not been physically examined beyond the ascertainment by the labor agents who recruited them that they had two arms and two legs. At Winela they are more thoroughly checked, and because the average length of their stay is only twelve hours, no time is wasted. There is a Multiple Mass Miniature Radiography Department that can do twelve chest X-rays a minute. About five of every thousand men are sent back home as unfit; about twenty in each thousand are declared qualified only for surface, nondusty work. This means that when they get to a mine their starting rate of pay is thirty-five cents per eight-hour shift; underground miners start at forty-nine.

That sounds low, and it is low, but not, paradoxically, as low as it sounds. For mineworkers get free lodgings and board and beer and medical treatment (their employers say the average annual weight gain for Africans in the mines is fourteen pounds),

113

and if they decide to work for a year at a stretch, as many of them do, they can end up with what for a rural African is a tidy sum of cash. They usually have time, during their demobilization, to shop in downtown Johannesburg, and after they tire of looking at themselves in the comical mirrors many of them do go on buying sprees. They return to Winela happily laden with stylish hats, blankets, umbrellas, sewing machines, and briefcases. The blankets aside, most of these purchases can have little utilitarian value at home, but they are all status symbols, and the kind of status symbol an African can buy is very often, in southern Africa, the principal kind of status he can attain.

Despite the mineworkers' high illiteracy rate, more than half of South Africa's Africans are now literate—for urban Africans, the figure is probably close to 90 per cent—and of the younger black people, between the ages of seven, say, and twenty, perhaps 80 per cent can read and write a bit. (Statistics, however, can be misleading. Some Africans are taught to read and write at school, but drop out early, have little occasion to practice their skills, and forget most of them. Some African adults, accordingly, are classed as lapsed semiliterates.) Since 1947 an organization now called the Bureau of Literacy and Literature has brought literacy to about a hundred and seventy-five thousand African adults. Much of the outfit's early work was done with mineworkers. It began as an offshoot of the South African Institute of Race Relations, and the Bureau's sparkplug has been the wife of Quintin Whyte, the Institute's director. The Bureau began in the mines because their workers lived on the premises and the teachers, accordingly, had a sort of captive audience. When Mrs. Whyte was getting started, she used to put on boots and a helmet and go down into the mines at 3:00 A.M. to find out what kinds of situations the workers faced and what kinds of words might therefore be most useful to them.

Today the Bureau, aided by twenty-six primers in nine languages that it has compiled over the years, conducts voluntary literacy courses at fifty mining compounds. (Currently it has its eye also on prisons, where there is another kind of captive audience.) Inasmuch as most Africans have a chance to learn to read and write in conventional schools, the Bureau takes no students under sixteen. (It has had some considerably older. Once, when it was conducting classes for African women in a native township, a taxi driver came into a classroom and dumped on the floor what seemed at first to be a bundle of rags. Then the bundle quivered, and turned into a crippled old woman. "She's come to learn," the driver said. She did.) Now, under the Bureau's auspices, ten thousand adult Africans take a course each year on completion of which they attain a degree of proficiency called "just literacy."

From the start of the literacy program, the mineowners have been cooperative. Their attitude is not entirely altruistic: the easier it is to communicate with a worker, the more productive he is likely to be. Now and then they try to communicate graphically. Safety is much on the proprietors' minds, and they try to instill respect for it with posters that do not require words. These are sometimes misunderstood. To deter employees from putting their hands inside moving machines, they were shown some meshed gears with a crocodile's yawning mouth above them. When one worker was asked what he thought of it, he said it seemed ridiculous to him, because there were no crocodiles in Johannesburg. Another picture portrayed a matador with a cape, a bull, and a cannon. This was supposed to convey the idea that it's safer to shoot a bull than to tease it. An African who was asked what it meant to him replied, after brief reflection, "Boss selling his blanket."

The African miners, coming as they do from many tribes in many regions, speak many tongues. A single shaft compound may harbor men with as many as fifty home languages or dialects. To expedite communal communication on the job, a kind of lingua franca called Fanakalo has evolved, and it was with this expedient language that Mrs. Whyte and her associates first worked. Fanakalo is a descriptive language, its own name being a native word that in English means "like this." Its vocabulary is limited: two hundred and twenty nouns, two hundred and fifty verbs, and a few dozen adjectives. It can be learned in five days, and now in the mines it is taught not only to the African workers but to all white employees as well. The Africans find Fanakalo useful when they go home, too. They employ it there as a secret language among themselves. They can speak it in front of their exasperated

115

womenfolk when they don't want to be understood.

Ninety per cent of all South African mineworkers are non-Whites, but few of this majority have good jobs. Some of them work above ground, on a permanent basis, as personnel assistants, but the government has imposed limitations on the numbers who may be thus employed. In 1950, for instance, the giant Anglo-American Corporation tried to embark on a program that, had it gone through, would have resulted in a permanent non-white group of employees amounting to 10 per cent of its entire labor force. The government—Dr. Verwoerd was then Minister of Native Affairs and the principal official concerned—vetoed the scheme. It could also have resulted in an increase of the urban African population, and that was something the government was, and still is, dead set against.

Underground, at the mines, the highest rank an African can achieve is that of boss boy. Periodically the mineowners try to give Africans greater responsibilities. Not only would this increase efficiency, since many semiskilled jobs that Africans could easily perform are now held by white-skinned incompetents, but it would also save money, since the African wage scale is always lower than the white. But many white mineworkers—whose trade union is one of the most reactionary groups in South Africa—have implacably resisted such moves. They have insisted over the years, for instance, that only they may handle dynamite. (In a recent court case a notably lazy white mineworker was sentenced to a sixty-rand fine or sixty days in jail after being caught reading a book while one of his black assistants put dynamite sticks in holes.) African mineworkers' wages have gone up 40 per cent in the last five years, but the average white mineworker earns almost as much in a month as the average black one does in a year.

One would be mistaken, though, to equate working in the mines with slavery. The fact is that many Africans keep coming back to the mines voluntarily. In some tribal circles, indeed, members are not considered to have attained manhood until they've done a tour in the mines. "It's like getting a scalp used to be," a visiting American trade-union official said after touring some mines himself. The minimum age for employment in the mines is supposed to be eighteen, but some of the African workers look younger and they probably are; they fake their age to get to the mines early and thus demonstrate premature manliness.

Nothing infuriates white South Africans more than some of the stories that have been published about conditions in their mines. In one mine I visited, my white guide showed me a safety device called a lifeline. It is a metal chain hooked to a rubber belt worn around the waist of certain workers while they are clearing rubble from chutes down which ore is dumped. Some years back, the guide said, an American photographer had taken a picture of a man on a lifeline and had published it with a caption saying the worker was chained to his job. "This is a rough, tough industry," my escort said, "but we don't go around hitting people. Why, if I hammered away at anybody I'd be up before a magistrate in no time at all. I've been in the mines for nineteen years, and if in all that time I've hit three people that's about it."

Different mining operations have different customs. In the diamond industry, for instance, the African workers, by tradition, buy and cook their own food. Because of the enormous value of the product they work with, moreover, they also agree to remain locked into their compounds for four months at a stretch. When they go out, they are X-rayed. Even so, they manage to spirit away enough diamonds so that in South Africa everybody knows what "I.D.B." means—"illegal diamond buying." My introduction to I.D.B. was at a crèche of the African Self Help Association. The black woman in charge asked a visiting white woman if they could have a private chat. I assumed that one of the children had some special problem. Later, the white woman told me that the African woman had a friend who had a few diamonds he wanted to sell, and had hoped that maybe her visitor had some I.D.B. connections.

Gold miners live in compounds, too, but they are free to go out after work. Most of South Africa's gold used to come from reefs in the Transvaal province. After the Second World War the mining industry began to exploit the gold resources of the Orange Free State, where some ten billion dollars' worth of the metal was entombed. The hub of the Free State's mining activity is a city called Welkom, which didn't exist before the war. Now a modern oasis in a desert, it is a community with a resident population of

117

thirty-five thousand Whites and fifty-seven thousand non-Whites, plus another sixty thousand transient African mineworkers. There are seven big mines around Welkom, six of them now working; among them they produce nearly five hundred million dollars' worth of gold a year.

In some gold mines the temperature underground gets up to 115 degrees Fahrenheit. Heatstroke used to be a major problem. In 1930, when all the country's gold mines together employed a hundred and seventy thousand Africans, there were twenty-six deaths from heatstroke. In 1966, with more than twice as many employed, there was one such death. This change is attributable in large part to the researches of an organization in Johannesburg called the Human Resources Laboratory of the Chamber of Mines. It has conducted numerous tests to determine how human beings function at varying temperatures. (The average tennis player, it has found, runs a fever of 101 at the height of a spirited match; squash players hit 103.) For one experiment, having to do with measurements of the radiation effects of heat, the scientists found it useful to paint white men black. (South Africa being South Africa, they used a paint that would wash off fast.) Genuine black men have been borrowed from the mines to undergo tests calculated to measure human horsepower. (Baboons are used too; they can be kept at temperatures of 110 degrees for an hour without collapsing.) The Laboratory has been able to assert authoritatively that with an air temperature of 84 degrees and a shoveling rate of six shovel loads per minute, two average Africans can fill five three-quarter-ton cars with ore in an hour. At the mines themselves, new workers go through a twelve-day acclimatization process. They spend up to four hours a day in an artificially heated room, with thermometers in their mouths, doing controlled exercises. It's possible thus to determine which of them can't take underground work, and to prepare those who can for some of the conditions they'll meet below ground.

A generation ago, the biggest and toughest-looking Africans who showed up at the mines were arbitrarily designated boss boys. Now the selection process is somewhat less capricious. All incoming mineworkers are put through a series of aptitude and leadership tests (some of these, because of language problems,

118

involving the use of silent films), and a better class of boss boy has evolved. It is in part to this that the mineowners attribute a gratifying rise in their re-enlistment rate. Whereas in 1954 only 3 per cent of the African labor force signed up for more than one hitch in the mines, now 72 per cent come back at least once.

Boss boys themselves get special instruction. At Welkom a white mining official took me into a room where seven of them were seated at desks. "Ask them a question," my escort said. "Ask them anything you like." It was a liberal offer, but with a white boss there, and having furthermore to operate through an interpreter, I was stumped. Should I ask them whether they thought Prime Minister Vorster was better or worse than Verwoerd? Should I ask what they thought about the latest United Nations resolution on South West Africa? Finally I asked how old they were. The first man, a native of Malawi, said he was twenty-eight. "He's a liar," the white boss said. The second man, from Mozambique, said he didn't know his age. "A lot of them don't," said the boss. The next, from Lesotho, said he was thirty-four. "Damned near." The other four were South Africans. One said *he* was thirty-four. "He's saying it because the other said it," said the boss. One said he was twenty-five, and his statement went unchallenged. The third said thirty-four. "Another repeater." The last said he was twenty-eight. The white man snorted with disbelief. "But make no mistake," he then said. "These boys know their jobs. Some of them are as intelligent as you or I are. I may not like that, but it's the truth."

There was time for one more question. I asked the men what they wanted to do when they left the mine. One wanted to use the money he had earned to buy cattle so he'd have *lobola* for a wife. Another said he'd give his money to his family. The first repeater said he wanted cattle for *lobola*. Not a single one of the men, to my surprise, expressed any interest in becoming urbanized. They all wanted to go back home.

Among South Africa's natural resources are just about every kind of mineral there is. South Africa produces more than a billion dollars' worth of gold a year—72 per cent of the free world's output—and nothing would make South Africans happier than if the price of gold, which at present accounts for 40 per cent of

119

their country's foreign-exchange earnings, were unpegged. This would happen most quickly if the United States dollar were to be devaluated. An American banker who had been in South Africa for eight years told me, "They asked me how soon the dollar would be devaluated when I got here, and they're still asking."

South Africans do not exactly worship gold, on the whole putting God ahead of mammon, but a statue of Moneta, an ancient goddess of gold, is on prominent display at the Johannesburg stock exchange. The statue honors the memory of Sir Ernest Oppenheimer, and was given by his son Harry F. Oppenheimer, who is chairman of De Beers Consolidated, which controls most of the country's diamonds, and also of the Anglo-American Corporation, which controls 40 per cent of its gold. Anglo-American alone is a four-hundred-million-dollar enterprise; Oppenheimer calls it "a big business for a small country." De Beers is even bigger. Oppenheimer, a small-statured, gentle, soft-spoken giant, used to be in Parliament, and is now the principal financial backer of the powerless but pesky Progressive Party. He is frequently assailed in South Africa for his comparative liberalism; one right-wing editor not long ago called him "the deadliest enemy of our national survival."

National survival is much on most South Africans' minds these days, particularly with so much of the rest of the world muttering about sanctions. The only natural resource generally considered basic for survival in a modern world that has not yet been produced in the country is oil. (There's oil around—possibly more of it offshore than underground—but it has not yet been exploited; in any event, the country has lately increased its reservoirs of the precious commodity by setting up huge new storage tanks and establishing a refinery in the Johannesburg area that will be handling Iranian oil imported in a new fleet of South African tankers.) With or without its own oil, South Africa has become far and away the biggest industrial nation on its continent. It generates 57 per cent of all the electricity used in Africa, although it has only eighteen million people as opposed to three hundred million to its north. (It sometimes seems to generate 57 per cent of the continent's agitation, too.) Between 1960 and 1964 its annual industrial growth rate was 8 per cent, a pace surpassed only by Japan.

The South African economy has slowed down a bit since, but it is still moving along at what most countries would consider a nice clip.

South Africa's economic success is the result in no small part of white managerial ability. It is the result in even larger part of the availability of cheap nonwhite labor. As Olive Schreiner put it nearly forty years ago, "The dark man is here to stay. . . . Not only can we not exterminate him—but we cannot even transport him, because we want him! We desire him as thirsty oxen in an arid plain desire water, or miners hunger for the sheen of gold. We want more and always more of him—to labor in our mines, to build our railways, to work in our fields, to perform our domestic labors, and to buy our goods. . . . They are the makers of our wealth, the great basic rock on which our State is founded—our vast laboring class."

The class is still big, and getting bigger. A white farmer who wants an extra hand can procure one through an employment agency for three dollars a week plus food and shelter. Hotels can easily provide 'round-the-clock room service. Parking lots can hire enough attendants so that instead of having one driver move a car in and out of spaces, two or three nondrivers push them around. Outside of parking lots, too, two or three Africans can often be found doing what in other areas would be considered one man's work.

It has long been a conventional white South African belief that many, if not most, black men are lazy and shiftless and have innately second-rate capabilities. But nowadays more and more thoughtful white South Africans are beginning to wonder if perhaps they have ever really understood their dark compatriots. Several of the English-language papers carry tricky, British-style crossword puzzles. After the *Johannesburg Star* disclosed that one of its puzzles had been solved by an African woman in a local township, a white reader wrote in—using the signature "Heartbroken"—to say, "Tussling with a language that was not her own, and brushing aside the scientifically demonstrated fact that she is a member of an intellectually inferior race, she has done it. Excuse me a moment while I go and jump in the river."

"We have been inclined to underestimate Bantu ability simply

121

because we have been accustomed to see him doing unskilled work," the director of the Bantu Wage & Productivity Association said not long ago. The Association, a nonprofit organization that was founded in 1959, has three hundred corporate members, to whom it sends material calculated to make them better understand their African employees. It informs employers that African workers who don't say "Good morning" to their bosses are not necessarily being surly; it is simply not the practice of most Africans to initiate such pleasantries. The Association often relies, as do other South African groups, on the studies of the psychologist Dr. Simon Biesheuvel. After the Second World War, as director of the National Institute of Personnel Research, Dr. Biesheuvel developed the aptitude tests that the mines are using today. Now he is personnel director for South African Breweries, but he still devotes much of his time to independent research. In one publication, called "Study of African Ability," he wrote:

The only scientifically valid standpoint, which does not outrun the known facts, and which neither prejudices nor prejudges future findings, we hold to be the following:

That observed African abilities are different from, in some respects superior, in others inferior to those of Western man; that environmental, more particularly cultural, circumstances have greatly contributed to bring about these differences, which are sometimes artifacts of the method of measurement, sometimes the result of social conditioning; that it is not known at present from what genetic origins the manifest mental attributes of Africans have developed, nor whether this development would have equalled that of the average European if environmental circumstances had been comparable; that a new orientation in research and the utilization of different experimental and control techniques will be necessary, in order to provide conclusive answers.

People generally think as effectively as their cultural environment demands. If its requirements are low, this does not mean that the capacity to think at a more advanced level is equally low.

There are quite a few South Africans who believe that if the grip of apartheid on their country is ever going to be broken this

122

will come about not from external force or internal revolution but from the inexorable pressure of economic factors; it is a view held by some Africans as well as Whites. Most South African Whites —whose views, of course, are presently the determining ones —are realizing more and more how utterly dependent they are, economically, on non-Whites. White industrialists are beginning to grumble about the inadequacies of the Bantu education system. The employers say that its graduates learn so little that when they come into a factory time has to be wasted teaching them things that are matter of fact to graduates of the white system. The employers grumble about the Group-Areas laws that in effect require most non-Whites to live at a considerable distance from their jobs; a man who has to travel three hours to work and three hours back home each day, the employers say, is too tired to be efficient. And, above all, employers are aware that there simply aren't enough Whites available to fill the jobs they have to offer; non-Whites—in the mines and elsewhere—will sooner or later have to be pushed ahead. As an official of the country's garment workers' union has put it, "A country as vast and rich as South Africa cannot be sustained forever by the efforts of a quarter of its population."

It has been estimated that by 1970 there will be a shortage of thirty thousand white workers to fill jobs for which non-Whites cannot now apply. What has held back the non-Whites is a government policy called job reservation. Perhaps as many as 25 per cent of South Africa's Whites are unfit for anything more than semiskilled labor. They get the better jobs notwithstanding, because the government says these have to be reserved for men of their skin color. Non-Whites can become eligible for many categories of work only by special exemption. Employers who are more interested in efficiency and profits than in the spirit of the law have found ways of getting around the letter of it. There are many nonwhite clerks and administrative assistants today who are called "tea boys" or "messengers" although they neither brew nor tote. In the building-construction trades black men are supposed to be mere assistants to white artisans, but contractors who can't find enough white artisans are using black ones, too, though they often tuck them off in corners where they can't readily be seen by passersby. The Whites who work alongside them are comforted

123

by the reflection that a substantial wage differential still exists between the two groups. The average monthly pay for white construction workers is more than three hundred dollars. The average for Africans is fifty-nine, even though the government itself has said that sixty-seven dollars is the minimum monthly subsistence figure for an African family of five.

Most postmen's jobs are reserved for Whites. Some of the mailmen around Johannesburg were so incompetent—they were suspected of burning or burying letters when they didn't want to be bothered delivering them—that two years ago the government gave ninety postal jobs to non-Whites. People began to get their mail. When the engineering industry got permission for non-Whites to operate such equipment as fork lifts, there was a notable increase in efficiency and decrease in absenteeism. Five years ago the engineering industry had two hundred thousand employees, of whom fifty thousand were Whites. Today the total is two hundred and sixty thousand, of which there are still only fifty thousand Whites. The sixty thousand additional nonwhite jobs can't all possibly be at the lowest level. At some automobile-assembly plants, practically all the engine operations are now being performed by non-Whites. According to the job-reservation laws governing that industry, 45 per cent of all employees are supposed to be white. A trade-union man who was walking around one plant not long ago estimated that not more than 15 per cent of the workers he saw were white, and he asked a manager how he was adhering to the 45 per cent minimum. "We have some trouble," the manager said, "but we do get an exemption at times." The government is usually quite willing to grant exceptions when they will benefit the national economy. When one clothing manufacturer told me that nearly all his factory employees were nonwhite, and I asked him if he wasn't affected by job reservations, he replied blandly, "I have a blanket exemption."

VI

The chinks that have lately appeared in the wall of resistance to Africans' economic progress are the result partly of the increasingly active economic role being played by those white South Africans who have traditionally been wariest of the blacks and thus readiest to keep them submissive—the Afrikaners. It used to be the pattern of South African life for Afrikaners to let the other white-skinned South Africans, the English-speaking ones, attend to most business affairs, while they themselves concentrated on agriculture, government, and the church. Not being businessmen, the Afrikaners didn't have to take a dollar-and-cents approach to race relations. Now, however, more and more Afrikaners are involved in the nation's economy. When the economic shoe pinches, they, too, hurt.

There is an Afrikaans word that characterizes many of the people who speak principally that language: *kragdadigheid*. It means toughness. It is exemplified in many ways. An English-speaking woman I know, for instance, told me of a fleeting encounter she'd had with an Afrikaner street-gang foreman. She was working in her garden one afternoon, at the edge of a road, when one of her African servants brought her a cup of tea. She said, "Thank you." A few minutes later the foreman came over and upbraided her. She should never be polite to an African, he said. "If you treat them nicely," he told her, "they'll sooner or later take advantage of you and"—here, in recounting the incident, she ran a finger across her neck—"cut your throat."

I found it hard to believe that much of that sort of talk existed until I happened to spend the better part of a week with an Afrikaner who hardly talked any other way. Since he was, in his peculiar fashion, a decent chap, and since he was quite civil to me (my skin is white), let us disguise his identity and call him Botha. It is a fine old Afrikaner name, and he did in fact come from a fine old Afrikaner family. This can make a lot of difference to some Afrikaners, as to oligarchs everywhere. Botha, who was fiftyish, had finished high school and put in some years as a civil servant. Now he had a middling job in private industry. He was married but was childless, which may have made him, as a loyal adherent of Afrikanerdom, feel guilty.

Botha and I took a drive of several days together, and exactly twenty-nine hours and fourteen minutes after we met he asked me if I'd want my daughter to marry a black man. I said I only had sons. "Well, your sons?" I said that would be their business. He pointed out that I'd be the grandfather of the unhappy children of such a union. The thought of being a grandfather at all was so depressing that I tried to change the subject. He soon drew us back to it. If God meant everybody to be the same, he said, why wouldn't he have created them that way? "God didn't mix up all the animals," Botha argued. "He didn't let goats mate with those sheep over there." Botha couldn't have picked a worse analogy for his case. The sheep to which he was directing my attention had black heads and white bodies.

Botha had never been outside of South Africa, but he had some

126

mild curiosity about the United States. At one hotel we stayed at overnight, he was shocked to see women sitting at the bar. Did they do that in America? "Too much," I said. Botha seemed pleased at this evidence of American depravity. At another point he suddenly said, "Tell me, are our roads better than yours?" I said that it was a hard comparison to make, but that I thought his were excellent, as indeed they are. Later, discussing road markings, specifically single and double lines, which he adored but ignored, he suggested that maybe a South African had invented them before an American did. South Africans sometimes sound very much like Russians.

Botha's favorite reading matter, aside from the Afrikaans-language newspapers, was the *Reader's Digest*. Once, while we were driving through some farm country, he said that he had read and been much taken with a *Digest* article about how to get paid for not working; could I figure that one out? I couldn't. "Make your job your hobby!" he exclaimed. "My job is my hobby!" He had grown up on a farm, and would explain nature to me as if I'd never heard of it before. (We passed a good many tall, thick-trunked, spiky-leaved, cactuslike growths called aloes. I had never seen *them* before except in crossword puzzles, where they grow like weeds, and I asked Botha whether an aloe was a tree or a bush. "I don't know," he said. "Is a tomato a fruit or a vegetable?" He had me there.) Pointing to some fields of grain, he said to me, "Corn." I said it didn't look like corn to me. "Sure —you had bread made from it at breakfast this morning," he said. "Unless you had dark, made from rye." "Oh," I said, "you meant 'wheat.' " "Corn—wheat, same thing," he said, and lapsed into silence. A few miles later we passed a similar stand of grain. "Wheat area," he told me.

So he was not untractable. But in most matters his mind was made up. His views of nonwhite persons, for instance. He often seemed to act as though they did not exist. When he had to communicate with them, he never talked to them. Instead he barked *at* them. "You can never make human beings out of these people," he said to me once. I will forget many of the ludicrous things that were said to me in South Africa, but I will never forget that. Now and then he would casually refer to Africans as "goril-

127

las," but sometimes he was kinder. As we rode along in an air-conditioned car, we passed many of them on foot. "Here they walk along for miles, happy as the day is long, perfectly unspoiled," he remarked. "Children of nature. All the Bantu needs to make him happy is a full belly and his wife dropping a child each year."

Many African children would wave at us as we passed them, but only once did Botha wave back—at a teen-age girl. "She's practically naked," he said. "You might see some naked women on the other side of those mountains—from the waist up, that is." I figured he meant African women; he would never have talked that way about white women. I said I had seen thousands of bare-breasted women on Pacific islands, and was quite used to the sight. "Indians?" he said. "No, not exactly," I said. "What color?" "Dark," I said. He seemed relieved.

Driving through one town, Botha didn't slow up when he saw an old African woman crossing the road with her back toward us. Instead, he bore down on her and honked his horn. She jumped out of the way, and he laughed. It was really a very disagreeable sound. He was much more solicitous about not running down a little dog—a black dog at that. He ignored Africans even to the extent of almost driving our car off the front of a ferry one time, apparently because the hand that was raised to halt him from disaster was a black hand. Or it may have been simply that Botha was an incredibly inept driver—fast, reckless, often on the wrong side of the road and always complaining that others were on the wrong side. It was, in a way, an attitude typical of many Afrikaners, even when they are standing still.

Botha really had no use for any Africans, except to the extent that they could tend to his needs. Many unenlightened Afrikaners like him don't want to see the African get ahead economically because whatever advances the Blacks make will diminish the reassuring gap that separates them from the Whites. These Afrikaners meditate that people who are prospering economically are apt to get fancy social and political ideas as well. (Many Africans would gladly settle for economic equality.) Other, more intelligent and more compassionate Afrikaners—though, alas, they often seem to be the minority segment of their own group—reason that if Afri-

128

cans prosper they, too, will prosper. (Many English-speaking white South Africans prefer to avoid thinking about the problem at all and to play golf or lawn bowls instead.) "We Afrikaners are so motivated by self-interest we'd even be *liberal* if we thought it would help us," one of their principal intellectuals told me. Many Africans wish there were enough Afrikaners who thought it would.

Most Afrikaners are ruefully aware that among South African Whites they represent 60 per cent of the population but have only 40 per cent of the income. This state of affairs, however, represents a big step forward for them. And that particular gap is diminishing. More and more Afrikaners are going into finance and commerce. There are big Afrikaner banks and insurance companies, Afrikaner mining houses and brokerage firms. Afrikaners are even turning up these days in the members' enclosures of the South African race courses, which used to be as alien territory for them as the august precincts of the Rand Club in Johannesburg. The Afrikaners have crossed its portals, too, by now, though in modest numbers.

Some Afrikaner businessmen have taken prodigious strides. Perhaps the most celebrated of these, and certainly the most successful, is a fifty-year-old industrialist and philanthropist named Anton Rupert. He started off his adult life as a lecturer in chemistry at the University of Pretoria, where he also took law courses. He went into the wine business for a while, and in 1948 began making cigarettes. Now he is head of the Rembrandt Corporation, which controls various brands, among them Rothman's, and accounts for about one-tenth of all cigarette sales on earth. Rupert is very international-minded. He says he has spent one out of every five days since 1953 on an airplane going somewhere. At his corporate headquarters in the old Cape Dutch city of Stellenbosch, an hour's drive from Cape Town, stands a column of flagpoles for displaying the national colors of foreign visitors. Sometimes there are seven different flags flying at once.

Rupert is a dedicated exponent of corporate culture. His offices are full of paintings and sculpture, and his companies have two foundations—one domestic and one international—which sponsor art exhibits and concerts all over the world. He has sent a Rodin exhibit to Zambia and the London Symphony Orchestra to Australia. He is converting an old Lutheran church in Stellenbosch into a museum to serve as a permanent home for his art collection. He has cigarette factories in, among other places, the Sudan, Uganda, and Malaysia, and he insists that 50 per cent of any company he establishes in a foreign location be owned by natives of that area, whatever their color.

Not long ago, when he opened a plant in Kenya, the vice-president of that country quit his job to work for Rupert. When a businessman in Nairobi issued a statement saying that all this indicated that Rupert was antiapartheid, Rupert, who is basically a supporter of the South African government, replied that he was in favor of peoples' choosing their way of life wherever they were, and that being for apartheid in South Africa and for cooperation between the races outside South Africa were not necessarily incompatible. "We recognize their right to choose freely and to determine themselves their own way of life, exactly as we defend those rights in South Africa," he said. (He didn't bother to add that in South Africa non-Whites have no self-determination.) When one of South Africa's immediate neighbors, Lesotho, became independent at the end of 1966 its government invited Rupert to become its chief economic adviser. Lesotho, one of the most poverty-stricken sovereign states on earth, gravely needed such advice, and Rupert was glad to give it. It is his contention that Africans should be helped to become people of property; the better off they are materialistically, he believes, the less revolutionary they are apt to be. His favorite summary of his own philosophy is, "If they don't eat, we don't sleep."

Another of the new breed of consequential Afrikaner businessmen is Albert Jan Jurie Wessels, now fifty-nine, whose forebears were sheep farmers in the Orange Free State. His brother still farms. In 1940 Wessels was a junior clerk at a bank that had an interest in an insolvent clothing firm. The bank put him in charge of it because its situation seemed hopeless and because Wessels was young and expendable. Now he is chairman of the clothing company, a notably thriving one, and of the bank as well. As one of several profitable sidelines, he deals in foreign cars. He introduced Japanese cars to South Africa. He has had traffic with Japanese textile houses, too, and in 1961, with their cooperation, he achieved a South African breakthrough. He brought blazers to Africans.

One does not have to be long in South Africa to become aware of the ubiquitousness of blazers. They are a British heritage, of course, but white South Africans seem enamored of them to a degree beyond the dreams of Albion. To wear a Springbok blazer—a green jacket with gold piping given to sportsmen of national prominence—is the highest honor a South African athlete can attain. Each of South Africa's many clubs has its own blazer, and for years each white school has had its own. (Matching ties and hatbands are commonplace.) To avoid duplications in design and the misunderstanding that might ensue, the government has a blazer registry in its Department of Heraldry. Some South African men who have led rich, full lives have a closet's worth of blazers—one for each club, an old-boys' one from a boarding school, a university-undergraduate one, a university-alumnus one, and so on. There are joke blazers: young blades in Johannesburg give out blazers to anyone who can consume four pints of beer in four minutes. The successful imbiber gets a "Dorstal Old Boys' Club" blazer, decorated with crossed pistols and a skull and crossbones.

The mania for group identification has spilled over into neckties. Articled clerks have a tie with an inkwell and quill-pen motif. The South African Institute of Chartered Secretaries has a secretary bird on its tie. One man I checked with said he had two dozen ties, but only six of them were ordinary; all the others signified something. Some organizations have special tie-wearing days, and a member can be fined if another member catches him not wearing the appropriate tie at the appropriate time. It can be tough on a gregarious man who has two competing Wednesday ties.

Before Wessels, however, the nonwhite community had scarcely shared in all the fun. He made a survey of the African market in 1959, and concluded that Africans considered clothing a status symbol. He deduced further that since African parents wanted nothing but the best for their children, and since there were then eight thousand schools for Africans, blazers were the answer—or at least his answer. It took a while to come up with enough differ-

131

ent color combinations, but within two years he was in production. Now Wessels' company is the largest manufacturer of striped blazers on earth. (The prospectus for the Transkeian school for sons of chiefs and headmen lists a prescribed school uniform; the first two items are a Jongilizwe College Blazer and a Jongilizwe College Tie.) There are over two million African students in South African schools today, and not long ago Wessels happily declared, "It gives me infinite pleasure to daydream and castle build about the day that my company will supply blazers to 10 per cent or 20 per cent of these children."

When it comes to education, blazers are just about all that the white and nonwhite students have in common. White schools are relatively decentralized and are run by provincial authorities. Nonwhite schools, since 1954, have been very much centralized and have been run by the Bantu Education Department in Pretoria. (A number of nonwhite schools used to be administered by missionaries, who got government subsidies. The subsidies were stopped in 1958, and only two of forty-four mission schools have managed to hang on.) The government has forty-two teachers' colleges for Africans and a current corps of thirty thousand African teachers. Even so, the teacher-pupil ratio in African schools is one to fifty-two, as compared with one to thirty-three for white public schools.

Many of the African teachers are incompetent by any standard, and are miserably paid. Some of them who could probably earn a hundred and sixty dollars a month in industry get ninety a month for teaching. I visited one African school with a young white woman who had no university degree and was receiving a hundred and twelve dollars a month as a typist. She fell into conversation with an African woman teacher who had a graduate degree, and asked her what *she* was getting. Sixty-two dollars a month, the teacher said. "I feel like hanging my head in shame," said the stenographer. White public-school teachers have a pension plan; Africans don't. Moreover, they have a special morale problem; they are regarded as traitors by other, militantly anti-apartheid Africans who deplore their working for the government.

The Bantu Education statistics look good. Of two million two

132

hundred thousand nonwhite children in South Africa, one million seven hundred thousand are in school, and this despite education's not being compulsory for them. The government insists that Africans aren't ready for compulsory education, and that rural Africans in particular want their children to work as soon as they can, so that if a compulsory system were instituted innumerable parents would have to be prosecuted for violating it. Maybe so, but many urban Africans feel quite differently. One African mother put it to me bluntly. "If my children aren't forced to go to school, like the Europeans, there's no hope for them," she told me. In any event, the statistics are deceptive. A lot of very young African children who go to school don't stay there long. Ninety-seven per cent of African pupils don't get beyond primary school, and only one-tenth of 1 per cent of those Africans regarded as economically active finish high school. Up to the sixth grade, African education is supposed to be conducted in the vernacular, so that those who drop out before then learn neither English nor Afrikaans, the languages they will need to get anywhere.

Of course, one of the objectives of the Bantu Education program is that Africans *shouldn't* get too far ahead. An official government syllabus spells out one of the chief aims of social studies for Africans: "To give the pupil a clear conception of his social and economic environment, taking into account that he must of necessity adapt himself to the environment in which he will have to live as an adult." One of the points that the syllabus says teachers of vocational-guidance courses should stress is loyalty to the employer. As things stand now, moreover, a lot of older children who would like to go to school simply can't because there aren't enough classrooms. In the Transvaal province in 1967, fifty thousand Africans had to be turned away from high schools for lack of space. The government is reluctant to put up more schools in the urban areas because that would be an admission that its plan to steer Africans back to their tribal homelands isn't working very well. African teachers are supposed to inculcate in their students, along with the right kind of loyalty, a yearning for the rural life. "I tell them about the homelands because I have to," one teacher in an urban school said, "but the part about yearning I leave out."

133

The government often brags that there are twenty-eight hundred Africans with college degrees in South Africa. It tends to be more reticent about the fact that it spends only a little over eighteen million dollars a year on Bantu education and ten times that on education for Whites, though there are far fewer of them. This averages out to two hundred and sixty-six dollars for each white child, and eleven dollars and twenty cents for each black one. Some African educators are understandably gloomy. One high school principal told me that the equipment the government had given him for his science laboratory the year before consisted of one beaker and one test tube. His teachers didn't like to let the students touch the laboratory equipment lest it get broken. Other African educators, though, are more cheerful. When a white woman not long ago visited another high school, its principal took her around and as they entered one classroom he said, "Look, you kaffirs, here's a nice English lady come to pick out a slave." Everybody laughed uproariously.

Some white South Africans argue that there are limits to what an African can learn. "There are lots of white engineers today who would be grateful if they could be replaced by black engineers," an official at Pretoria told me. "Any number of Bantu can be absorbed in their own development programs. We find, though, that it is extremely difficult for Bantu to master pure sciences, as well as engineering, surveying, and civil engineering. As their communities develop, their innate abilities will help them, because there are no genetic deficiencies. The trouble is with their associations and their background. As a student and friend of these people, I'd be dishonest if I didn't pinpoint this problem." There is a vocational school for Africans just outside Johannesburg, however, which trains carpenters, plumbers, and electricians, and its students have shown themselves remarkably adept at mathematics and mechanical drawing. The school once had a motor-mechanics course, but had to abandon it under pressure from white motor mechanics, who were leery of prospective competition. It is astonishing that Africans in any kind of educational institution learn as much as they do.

A recent visitor to South Africa was Dr. Robert Birley, a former headmaster of Eton, who for three years was a Visiting Professor of Education at the University of Witwatersrand in Johannesburg. Dropping in at one African township school, he invited a class to ask him questions. "I was amazed when one boy asked, 'How did Mussolini set up a totalitarian dictatorship?' " Dr. Birley told me. "Ninety-nine per cent of white South Africans would never think that an African boy would or could ask a question like that." Birley would frequently play hookey from the university and go out to an African township. Whites are supposed to get a permit before making such a trip; Birley refused to, as a matter of pride. He is a gentle, stooped, white-haired man of impressive bearing. He was assumed to be protected in his transgressions by the armor of his invulnerable respectability.

Sometimes Dr. Birley would take over a class, which is not the sort of thing the Bantu Education Department condones. He was teaching one day when a subinspector from the Department came around and caught him. A member of the school's authorized staff told Birley not to worry: the inspector would be too frightened to report him, because the inspector himself had no business being there that day, the only purpose of his visit being to collect a bribe from an African teacher who wanted some kind of permit. "It was such a charming incident," Birley said later. Some months after that, he went to a Bantu Education office and bumped into the man who had flushed him. They looked at each other and then the inspector said, "Professor, you and I have met before," and they shook hands and that was that.

The Department puts out a *Bantu Education Journal,* a monthly that all teachers under its jurisdiction are required to sign, by way of testifying that they've read it. It was Birley's impish habit to sign it, too. Just before Christmas in 1966, a few months after Balthazar John Vorster became prime minister, Birley drifted out to a township schoolroom and was invited to tell the students a holiday story. He chose the tale of the three biblical wise men who came to Bethlehem and shared a single bed—one of them, Birley emphasized, being a European, one an African, and one an Indian. He glided over Gaspar and Melchior, but to make sure that the children remembered the name of the third member of the interracial trio, he had them write "Balthazar" on a blackboard. (It may have confused some of them, for Vorster prefers

135

to call himself plain "John.") Birley has left South Africa now, probably somewhat to the relief of the government, but he has left behind a legacy. Almost singlehandedly he raised money for the construction and furnishing of a new library for one African high school which had a thousand students but prior to his beneficence had a library that measured only ten by fifteen feet.

As in practically all other phases of their lives, Africans have little say about their education. They are now being permitted to elect some members of local school boards, but the big decisions are made in Pretoria, and everybody there who counts is white. No African can rise higher in the school system than deputy inspector, and no African can ever get into a position where he would be superior to any White. At the University of Fort Hare, one of three colleges for Africans, there are no white students, but of the thirty professors on the staff only two are nonwhite. The African professors may join their colleagues for tea in the common room, but—even though this is an institution for Africans—they may not attend a staff cocktail party. One of the white professors there used to ask all his students to his home for tea from time to time, but he gave up the practice when the Security Police stopped by uninvited and took down the names of his guests. The Fort Hare faculty is discouraged from any contact with the student body outside of the classroom.

In the old, preapartheid days there were quite a few nonwhite students at white universities, and a few non-Whites can still get permission to attend them. Witwatersrand used to have so many nonwhite students that it had a dean for them. He was called the Black Dean. Contemporary Wits students would find all but incomprehensible an experience he had a generation ago. He was crossing the campus with his young daughter when a student greeted him. The girl asked who that was. The Dean said he didn't know. "It can't be a student," his daughter said. "Why not?" said the Dean. "He isn't black," his daughter said.

Most of the nonwhite universities are located out in the country, at a considerable distance from the major population centers. This can make it difficult for prospective students to get to them. For some non-Whites it is all but impossible to get to *any* university. In the province of Natal there is a colored population of forty thousand. English is the primary language of the Coloreds of Natal. The only South African university for Coloreds is the one in the Cape province, where the primary language for Coloreds is Afrikaans. The handful of colored students from Natal who have entered the Cape institution have soon come back home because they couldn't understand the lectures.

The three African colleges have excellent facilities, but among them have a total of only 1,160 students. Fort Hare had five hundred students in 1959, the year before the government took over nonwhite university education; now it has four hundred. Fort Hare began in 1916, and it is the oldest nonwhite university south of Khartoum, but nowadays its campus does not exactly seem to throb. It offers no courses in engineering or fine arts. It used to have a thriving divinity school, but the syllabus laid down for it by the government satisfies only the Dutch Reformed Church, and most Africans do not belong to the Dutch Reformed Church. Six years ago Fort Hare asked the Bantu Education Department to appoint a commission to re-evaluate its theological curriculum, but nothing has happened yet. There is no other place in South Africa where a non-White can get a degree in theology, but there is not a single nonwhite theologian on the Fort Hare staff. In the card catalogue of the university's library there is no entry at all under "Apartheid" and only four entries under "Race."

The syllabuses for all South African universities are controlled by an unusual educational institution called the University of South Africa. It has twenty thousand students. (Considering South Africa's population, a comparable university in the United States would have over two hundred thousand.) U.S.A., as the place is sometimes known for short, has no conventional campus. All its students take correspondence courses. More than half of them are over twenty-seven, and a quarter are over thirty-four. Most have full-time jobs; four thousand of them are teachers themselves. Its exams are given at five hundred different locations. Some of its science courses are restricted to students with access to laboratories; most of its chemistry students, accordingly, work for chemical companies. (The university has laboratories of its own, but they are for staff research; without them, it wouldn't be able to attract qualified professors.) The University of South Africa is thoroughly interracial, but only because its students are not there. When some of them do come in for summer-vacation seminars, they are taught separately. The only non-Whites on its academic staff teach Bantu languages, and whereas their colleagues are called professors or senior lecturers or lecturers or junior lecturers, they are senior language assistants or language assistants.

South Africa has sixty thousand students at the university level, fifty-three thousand of whom are white. Several of its universities were mixed, or "open," until the passage of a 1959 law called the Extension of Universities Education Act. Since then the quality of teaching has gone downhill. Quite a few good instructors have left the country or left education. Many of those who stay on have deemed prudence the better part of tenure. "You use the few liberal acts you perform as a test of how far you've gone down the drain," one academician told me. The students don't seem to do too well. Seventy per cent of B.S. candidates and 50 per cent of B.A. candidates either don't finish or take from one to three extra years to get their degrees.

There is little dialogue between white and nonwhite undergraduates, and not too much between the two main white factions. The major educational institutions in the Cape province, for instance, are the universities of Cape Town and Stellenbosch. They are only thirty-five miles apart, but their students hardly mingle nowadays except at a joint singsong and dance before their annual rugby game. Stellenbosch is the undergraduate citadel of South African rugby. For night games its rugby stadium is illuminated by the brightest arena lights in the country. "For rugby we'll do anything," one Stellenbosch student told me.

Stellenbosch students are called Maties, a nickname that is said to derive either from the tomato-red shirts their rugby players wear or from the Afrikaans word *mat,* meaning friend. Stellenbosch is the elite university for Afrikaners; all of South Africa's prime ministers have gone there. The University of Cape Town is largely English-speaking and is a traditional center of South African liberalism. (Harry Oppenheimer was recently elected its chancelor.) It still has four hundred and twenty nonwhite students

138

—7 per cent of its enrollment—who eat at their own end of the dining hall. The entire student body has taken a stand of sorts on their behalf; in 1965, it decided that if the university could not hold mixed dances, it would hold no dances at all.

The U.C.T. students are called Ikeys, because the place used to have a large Jewish enrollment. Matie boys allegedly go for Ikey girls because they are supposed to be uninhibited. By contrast, an Ikey boy once said to a Matie boy, "You know why so many telephone poles in Stellenbosch are crooked? It's because your Matie girls run against them to strengthen their shoulders for rugby." Actually, Matie girls care more for field hockey. Stellenbosch is fairly strict; its girls can't wear shorts or slacks outside their dormitories. Non-Afrikaners sometimes say critically of Stellenbosch that it's not really a university at all but a training college for Afrikanerdom, and that everybody there has to toe the line. It is specifically charged that Stellenbosch students are bewildered when they can't just take notes and instead have to think.

At that, Stellenbosch is generally regarded as the least straightlaced of all the Afrikaans-language universities. For one thing, among its six thousand students are a leavening minority of seven hundred English-speaking students. The Afrikaners, who for the most part are reasonably tolerant of the others, are typical offsprings of National Party adherents: insecure, naïve, devout, and anti-American. Most of them have never talked to a nonwhite student. They have an almost Pavlovian reaction to anything that smacks of liberalism. There is little revolt, little ferment on the campus. When one student leader mentioned to some fellow Maties that a few years earlier, while in high school, he had experimentally tried marijuana, the others were shocked. It was as if he'd confessed he was mentally retarded. A good guess would be that if Stellenbosch students were asked what "LSD" stood for, a majority would reply, "Pounds, shillings, and pence."

The other principal Afrikaans-language universities have fewer, if any, English-speaking students, and are more rigid. At the University of Pretoria, the Students Representative Congress passed a resolution against folk singing. At the University of Potchefstroom, which has twenty-five hundred students and calls itself "the largest Afrikaans Christian Nationalist university in the

139

world," dancing is forbidden, and the girls may not smoke on campus.

It was a Potchefstroom professor of logic and ethics—he was, incidentally, the son of the country's Minister of Education—who in 1966 caused a stir by preparing a speech in which he criticized both enlightened, or *verligte,* Afrikaners and *verkrampte,* or "narrow-visioned," ones, and then before delivering the paper deleted the rebuke to the *verkrampte* faction. One South African young man who happened to live in Potchefstroom did his undergraduate work in economics at the University of Witwatersrand. Then he thought he might try for a Master's degree at his hometown university, but when he asked about the courses involved he learned that he had already done all the required graduate work. He asked what in the world they taught their economics *undergraduates* at Potchefstroom. "Christian economics," he was told.

When Senator Robert F. Kennedy went to South Africa to talk to students, he was not formally invited to any of the Afrikaans-language universities, though he did make a brief appearance at Stellenbosch. For those students who did get to see or hear him, it was one of the biggest things that had happened to them in a long time. He was *theirs.* Nobody else had asked him to come, their government had ignored him, they had an eye-opening and thought-provoking exclusive. And they got an unexpected bonus when the very student who'd personally invited him, Ian Robertson, the president of the National Union of South African Students, got banned. NUSAS itself hasn't been banned yet, except by individual institutions, but it has its problems, because it is determinedly interracial. As long ago as 1961 Mr. Vorster called it "a red cancer which should be cut out."

NUSAS began in the early 1920s. A decade later, Afrikaner students judged it too British for their tastes and formed the Afrikanse Studente Bond—an organization open only to individuals whose primary language was Afrikaans and who belonged to the Dutch Reformed Church. NUSAS is generally oriented toward the rest of the Western world; the A.S.B. is oriented toward South African Christian Nationalist philosophy. In 1957 there was talk of some sort of affiliation between the two organizations, but when NUSAS insisted that nonwhite students be included, that was the end of that. NUSAS does have a branch at Stellenbosch, but it is a small one, with probably no more than sixty members, and it is not recognized by the university administration. Afrikaner students, no matter how comparatively open-minded they may be, realize that Stellenbosch is the spawning ground of national leaders and that anyone with the remotest political aspirations has nothing to gain and everything to lose by being connected with an interracial group. "Choosing NUSAS as a base from which to launch a political career in South Africa today would be suicidal," its penultimate president said. The president, unusual for a patriarchal land, was a young woman, a twenty-two-year-old graduate of Witwatersrand named Margaret Marshall, a History of Art major. NUSAS is weak, but it is perhaps the largest multiracial opposition group in South Africa. Nobody pays much attention to students in South Africa, however. Miss Marshall, soon after assuming office, announced that she would like to meet the Prime Minister and talk things over. Mr. Vorster said he didn't talk to kids.

However well educated or well employed an African may become, his residential prospects are bleak. He may have a much more expensive and comfortable house than his neighbors, but in nearly every circumstance it will have to be located in a homeland or in one of the sprawling urban townships that fringe each South African metropolis. The principal township at Port Elizabeth, where the majority of South African automobiles are assembled, is informally called Kwa Ford, because quite a few of its residents still live in houses made from large green packing cases in which Ford parts were shipped to that city twenty-five years ago. The most imposing of all the nonwhite residential areas is Soweto—an abbreviation for South West Townships—a thirty-eight-square-mile tract southwest of Johannesburg. Here live somewhere between six hundred thousand and a million Africans. Few white South Africans ever get there. They have no occasion to. (How many white Americans, when it comes to that, ever visit a Negro's home?) There have been districts, or ghettos, for non-Whites in South Africa for many years, but the modern concept of the township probably can be traced back to 1951, when on

141

the government's behalf the Council for Scientific and Industrial Research made a survey. After ascertaining the monthly income of urban Africans, it deducted what was spent on transport, fuel, food, and clothing, and allocated the remainder to rent. It came up with a brick house—suitable for a family of five—that could be built at that time for seven hundred and fifty dollars. Actually, there were three kinds of houses, known as economic (detached), subeconomic (semidetached), and subsubeconomic (terraced), the differences being based on size of income and size of family. (It must be tough for anybody to go through life being classified as subsubeconomic.) In theory, every house of every category would have electricity and running water. At the start, interior doors were provided, but then the government decided that too often these were being used for firewood. After that, people who wanted houses with doors between their rooms had to pay extra rent, presumably to deter them from burning the partitions.

Some houses were put up not only without doors, but without floors and, though they were roofed, without interior ceilings. But housing was, and is, cheap. It is possible today to rent a four-room house in Soweto for about twelve dollars a month. The rub is that Africans may not own the land on which their houses rest. In the slums from which they were forcibly removed they had freehold rights. Furthermore, the Africans insist, the slums, unhygienic though they were, had a soul. Probably the most celebrated of them all was Sophiatown, a dreadful and lovely and vital place in Johannesburg that has now been proclaimed a white area and—the Africans are not unaware of the irony involved—is known as Triomphe.

When the township-building program began, the government figured on putting up thirty-five thousand houses a year for non-Whites over a ten-year period. It has not missed that target by too much, and has, for a small country, done a big job. Nearly three hundred thousand new houses have been built, at a cost of more than two hundred million dollars. But the areas in which they stand are dreary. Soweto has one movie theater for all its hundreds of thousands of people, and one swimming pool. There are, to be sure, other amenities—sports fields, community halls, a golf course, and a sward for lawn bowls, so that the Africans can, if

142

they like, emulate the English-speaking Whites. Everybody who moves into a new house is supposed to get a fruit tree or two, but these rarely survive the tenants' lack of interest in agriculture or the depradations of the neighbors' children.

The Soweto townships come under the jurisdiction of the Non-European Affairs Department of the city of Johannesburg. A booklet that the Department puts out, called "Happy Living," says, *inter alia,* "The endless stream of personal trouble is dealt with expeditiously and with understanding." It is not all that good in Soweto. The on-the-spot authorities are white superintendents, each of whom has five thousand homes under his jurisdiction. The superintendents are mostly concerned with collecting rent. The area is depressingly full of neglected children, emaciated dogs, and unemployed men.

At night, Soweto is dark and dangerous. The *Rand Daily Mail* has called it "the bloodiest place on earth." It is roamed with abandon by predatory fellows called *tsotsis,* who do not hold anyone's life dear, including presumably their own. The residents who have jobs—mostly in Johannesburg—have a long way to go to get there, usually on crowded and rickety trains called "matchwood trains." The Non-European Affairs Department nonetheless runs guided, daylight tours of the Soweto area, and usually fills its buses with white sight-seers, at twenty-five South African cents—thirty-five American cents—a head. The buses naturally travel through the best parts of the townships, where the wealthier Africans have their homes, some of them—though on tiny plots—boasting two-car garages. One of these places, when I took a tour, had a printed sign in its window saying "This is it"; perhaps the tenant knew that the lady who was guiding us would point the place out. Our guide, a woman, drew our attention to several crêches, but somehow gave the impression that the government was responsible for them. She pointed out Soweto's only swimming pool and let us infer that that, too, was government-sponsored; actually, it would not be there were it not for the Anglican missionary Father Trevor Huddleston, who is now persona non grata in South Africa. (Our guide added that "in due course" four more such pools would be built in Soweto.) We were taken to something called a Sheltered Employment Work

143

Shop, where handicapped Africans are employed, though we did seem to spend an inordinate amount of time there, considering that only eighty-five disabled Africans were involved. They make three kinds of nets: camouflage nets for defense purposes, luggage-rack nets for railway cars, and tennis nets. I saw just one tennis court in Soweto, on one of my unconducted tours through the area; it had no net and the playing surface was covered with litter.

An Afrikaner woman in charge of the Work Shop joined us and said she would anticipate our questions, since she knew which ones would always be asked. " 'Are they grateful?' They don't seem so, but they are; sometimes they bring us vegetables to show that. And they don't always say what they mean anyhow. Not that they're liars; they'll give you the answer they think you want to hear." She was warming up. "A lot of South Africans don't understand the working of the Bantu mind," she said. It was clear that she thought she did. A woman sitting next to me said, "They seem happy, you know." I couldn't tell: it is as hard for me to understand the Bantu's mien as his mind. We drove on to a replica of the Zimbabali Tower in Rhodesia. The building materials came from demolished slums. From the summit we had a good view of Soweto. "There must be thousands of people living here," an American tourist said. "Millions," said a German. Our guide had not ascended and could not correct either of them.

We went on to a municipal hall, where the guide said symphonies were performed. "Bantu are beginning to appreciate serious music," she said. (There are not too many Africans who will go out at night to hear even frivolous music; the risks to their lives are too great.) There were a number of school-age children hanging around the main door when we emerged. They had their palms outstretched, and some of the women on our bus began digging in their purses. Our driver told them not to. "It starts a fight," he said. "The big ones smash up the little ones and take the money away from them." One American passed out some coins anyway. Within seconds, a small child was lying on the ground, bawling, while the driver stood there purse-lipped, with a well-I-warned-you expression. When we got back to Johannesburg, our guide asked the woman sitting next to me how she'd liked the tour. "Lovely, lovely," the woman said. "I really enjoyed it." The guide moved on down the aisle, and the woman said to me, "And only two and six!" As we started to get off, I offered to help her on with her jacket. "No thanks," she said. "We're not spoiled in South Africa; we've got to do things ourselves."

The African women who live in the townships don't consider themselves spoiled, either. I talked at length to one of them. She had moved to Soweto from Sophiatown, where life had certainly not been easy. Ordinarily the residents there got their water from wells, but the wells often ran dry, and they had to buy water at exorbitant prices. Still, she wished she was back there. In Soweto, she could see through the walls of her house, and the roof wasn't snug. She had no electricity. She said she might be able to get some, but there would be the expense of the fittings, and a hook-up cable, and a gratuity to an inspector. She had no husband. She had had one, but he was run over by a negligent African bus driver. She had had ten children, and was still supporting five, one of whom was an eight-year-old cardiac case. The child had to go often to a nonwhite hospital where she was treated by white doctors who never charged a cent and who the mother thought were wonderful. "You must never get sick," she said. "If your rent payment is late, you get a summons, and you are fined one rand. If you can't pay it, you go to jail for three months, and when you come out you still owe the one rand. And if you buy a house, the superintendent can sell it out from under you if you're late with your payments."

She herself was just barely making ends meet. She usually got up at four each morning, she said, to hang the wash she'd done the night before. Six days a week she left her house at five-thirty would get back home, like as not fighting off pickpockets on the matchwood train, at about seven, in time to do dinner before tackling the laundry. I asked her how much help she got from her children, and she said, "Your children are no help to you any more. Anyway, you can't send a daughter to a store after dark in Soweto. She'd be lucky to get off only getting raped." I asked her

145

if she ever went to any of the cultural affairs that the lady guide on the bus had told us about. "Are you kidding? Who goes out after dark?" the African woman said. "Life is not happy," she concluded. "You just do the best you can."

VII

Individuals who assassinate heads of government, as Americans hardly need to be reminded, do not always live to have their day in court. It was thus a considerable event when, at a little past ten o'clock on the morning of October 17, 1966, Demitrio Tsafendas, a vague-eyed, paunchy man of forty-eight, was ushered into a Cape Town courtroom to answer a charge that he "did wrongfully, unlawfully, and maliciously kill and murder Dr. the Honourable Hendrik Frensch Verwoerd, Prime Minister of the Republic of South Africa." Throughout South Africa there was obvious pride that, no matter how the rest of the world might handle these affairs, the slayer of the nation's leader would receive full democratic justice. The case of the State vs. Demitrio Tsafendas naturally provoked almost incessant talk in the days immediately following the assassination, on September 6. But when I got to South Africa, only three weeks after the slaying, Dr. Verwoerd, though he was still much mourned by his compatriots—most of the white ones, anyway—seemed to be less deeply mourned than was John F. Kennedy in the United States three years after his death. In behind-the-times South Africa, "knock-knock" jokes are still bandied about. The very first night I was there I heard one, and a surprising one, considering how recently the country had been bereaved: "Knock, knock." "Who's there?" "Hendrik." "Hendrik who?" "Have you forgotten already?"

Dim as Dr. Verwoerd's image had already become to at least some of his people, the assassination itself, which took place at the Prime Minister's front bench in Parliament, was still being vividly discussed, especially by those M.P.s who were eyewitnesses or who looked up, unable to believe their eyes, a moment after Tsafendas, who had begun working as a Parliamentary messenger on August 1, plunged a six-inch dagger into Dr. Verwoerd's body. Another of the questionable jokes that were circulating had Saint Peter saying to his newest arrival, "How did you get here?" and the Doctor replying, "A messenger sent me." (The only American known to have been present was a young man attached to the local consulate, who, as he saw Tsafendas being pummeled and dragged from the scene of his assault, vaguely remembered having seen the man somewhere; the American later recalled that Tsafendas had come around to the consulate not long before to announce that he planned to sue our country for a hundred thousand dollars—damages that he somehow thought he had coming for having been deported from the United States twenty years earlier.) It was not the first time that Dr. Verwoerd had been attacked. A farmer named David Pratt had shot him six years earlier, had been declared mentally ill, had been confined, and had subsequently hanged himself. Mrs. Verwoerd is said to have observed after that near miss that the only times she felt unworried about her husband's physical safety were when he was sitting in Parliament.

By the time Tsafendas got to court, most South Africans had learned a good deal about him, though they are unlikely ever to understand this mixed-up man. He had always been a loner, a

148

misfit, and an outsider. He was born, apparently illegitimately, in 1918 at Lourenço Marques, capital of the nearby Portuguese colony of Mozambique. His father was from Crete—the explanation of the Greek name. (A newspaper columnist in Cape Town who had referred to the assassin as a Greek felt constrained to apologize to the local Greek community for the identification.) His mother was a Colored—half White, evidently, and half Swazi. Tsafendas never knew her. He was a youth of better-than-average intelligence, but at thirteen, after a childhood with an uncongenial stepmother and an education that stopped at the equivalent of the American seventh grade, he embarked on a life—an existence, rather—characterized by odd jobs and even odder deportment. He traveled rootlessly over three continents, pausing from time to time at mental institutions, most of which agreed that he was suffering from schizophrenia. Occasionally he would write letters, usually incoherent, to such people as a President of the United States (Harry Truman), a prime minister (of England), and a queen (of Greece). Like Lee Oswald, he apparently resented people who were successful and authoritative. A relatively liberal South African newspaper editor, in talking to an acquaintance about a militant right-wing editor there, described him as "an ideological Tsafendas," adding, "He's always trying to stab at success."

To a country where racial classification is all-important, one of the most embarrassing aspects of the assassination was that a careful racial assessment of Tsafendas had never been made. Messengers' jobs in Parliament do not go to known non-Whites. Tsafendas, on applying and being interviewed by the legislature's chief messenger, had said he was white, and had produced an unemployment card certifying that he was. On being asked for his identity card, he had said he didn't have it, and nobody had bothered to follow up on that. They evidently hadn't even paid much attention, as many a South African would have, to his hair, which was gray and short and kinky. The reason Tsafendas didn't have the telltale card, ironically, was that he had sent it in to the government more than a year earlier, along with a request to be reclassified as colored. South African bureaucrats, though, are as slow as any. His request, it was to turn out, had never been acted

149

on, but it had precipitated some action: the government had decided to throw him out of the country. Indeed, four weeks before the assassination, the Minister of the Interior had signed a deportation order against him. But nobody had ever got around to sending it to the police so they could carry it out.

Tsafendas, however, hadn't consistently thought of himself, it appeared, as colored. For much of his stay in South Africa he lived in indisputably colored homes, but even then he sometimes seemed to align himself with the white community. At one point, he was supposed to have said that he was mad at Dr. Verwoerd because the Prime Minister paid more attention to helping non-Whites than to helping needy Whites—a category in which at that moment Tsafendas included himself. But it was hard to know what to make of the thoughts or opinions of a man as clearly irrational as Tsafendas. One of the witnesses in the court proceedings, for instance—the foreman of a power station where Tsafendas had worked briefly—had the impression that the accused was, if anything, more bigoted racially than most South Africans. One day, it seemed, the foreman and Tsafendas had been doing some chores in a dark, dank, dungeonlike area where water flowed beneath the plant. The foreman recalled that he had remarked to the accused—and it was in this curious fashion that the name of Dr. Verwoerd's successor was first mentioned in the courtroom—that "this would be a good place for Mr. Vorster to keep his political prisoners." And Tsafendas had replied, "Yes, they should put them all down here. In fact, they should put all the Coloreds down here, open the doors, and drown the lot."

Color aside, it seemed ridiculous that a man with Tsafendas' uncertain and unstable past should have been given a job that would put him in close contact with the leaders of a state. It didn't take the Houses of Parliament long, after the murder, to tighten their security procedures. People who had been around there for years were required to fill out long personal questionnaires, setting forth such things as their mothers-in-law's birth dates and answering the familiar question "Are you or have you ever been a member of the Communist Party?" (Tsafendas apparently had been, briefly, but that didn't come out until much later, and anyway his connection with the party, whatever it was,

150

had evidently ended twenty-five years before the stabbing.)

Security was supposed to be tight at the Tsafendas trial, too. It was announced in advance that the police had, and might exercise, the right to search all who entered the premises. Newspapers ran photographs of police perched on the courthouse roof. (The papers didn't have many other photographs to run, because no cameras were allowed in the courtroom, and Tsafendas was kept under such tight wraps that nobody even got a picture of him being transferred to or from court—in a police van with curtains over its wire-mesh windows.) Actually, it was quite easy to get in and out of the courtroom, and nobody ever asked me for any identification, conceivably because I was white. In any case, I saw no one, of any color, searched. The seat to which I was assigned was ten feet from the presiding judge and ten feet from the accused, and had I been armed and possessed of homicidal inclinations it would not have been difficult for me to shoot either one. Security didn't seem to be too good anywhere. I was told by a man who was in an excellent position to know that while Tsafendas was in custody awaiting his day in court, the policemen guarding his cell would now and then let their girl friends have a peek at the celebrated captive.

The premises of the Supreme Court of the province of the Cape of Good Hope are only a few blocks from the premises of Parliament, and although Parliament, with a swatch of new green carpet concealing the bloodstained Curly Wilton pattern next to the Prime Minister's seat, was finishing up a session when the Tsafendas case was heard, its activities were all but ignored, for all eyes were on the courtroom—a small, carpetless one, which could accommodate, at most, a couple of hundred spectators. A few determined citizens started lining up for seats a day in advance. The morning the trial got under way the streets outside the court were jammed with colored hopefuls, but most of the people subsequently admitted were white. The police later announced that fifty Coloreds had been admitted that first day, but police everywhere have a way of exaggerating crowd numbers. The courtroom was an English-looking chamber, its dark-paneled walls bare, with one peculiar exception—a calendar tacked up behind the jury box. Nobody had torn a page from it since the previous January. The

151

prisoner's dock was in the center of the chamber, and when Tsafendas, with half a dozen policemen escorting him, first materialized there, the general public had had no glimpse of him since he was hauled, bruised and bleeding, from Parliament on September 6. He had suffered several facial injuries then, at the hands of outraged and enraged M.P.s who had rushed up to Dr. Verwoerd's bench, but now he bore no sign of any wounds. He looked fit and calm. He was wearing a rumpled gray double-breasted suit with broad lapels, a white shirt, and a dark red tie. During the three and a half days of the court proceedings his costume did not change, though it is possible he put another shirt on. A policeman sat on either side of him, but he didn't talk to his guards, and only once did he hold a colloquy, in whispers, with one of a number of lawyers whom the state had appointed to defend him. Not that it would probably have mattered much, one gathered, if he had communicated more freely with the lawyers; as the proceedings went on, it became more and more apparent how confusing conversation with him could be. A man who had known him testified during the trial that, in talking with Tsafendas, "You're on various levels all at once. It's like peeling an onion."

According to South African law, an attorney general—in this instance, the one for the Cape province, Willem Martin van den Berg, who also served as prosecutor—may call for a nonjury trial in a murder case, the verdict being left up to the presiding judge, and Mr. van den Berg did so. (Twelve more seats thereupon became available in the courtroom; they were assigned to the press.) If the judge chooses, he may designate two assessors to assist and advise him, and two such men were duly named—a lawyer and, since it was taken for granted that the only defense Tsafendas' counsel could make was that he was out of his mind, a psychiatrist. (There are only about a dozen psychiatrists in the vicinity of Cape Town, and most of them figured in the proceedings at one point or another.) The assessors, quiet and drab in business suits, sat on either side of the judge, who, in keeping with the custom followed in criminal cases, wore a red gown with a black collar and black cuffs, but he did not wear a wig. The South African climate is not conducive to the wearing of

152

wigs.

The judge—Andrew Brink Beyers, Judge-President of the Cape Division of the Supreme Court of South Africa—is a colorful figure even in mufti. An earthy, no-nonsense man who was raised on a farm outside Cape Town, he professes to be nonplussed by highfalutin city talk, and I learned that during an earlier trial he had said, among other things, "I don't want to hear any more argument. It would just confuse me." He has crinkly, leathery, sundarkened skin, and during another trial he was heard to remark, "I defy anyone to distinguish in half-light between the Judge-President when he goes fishing and a colored wharf boy." Subsequent to the Tsafendas proceedings, the judge sat in on a review of a decision of the Race Classification Appeals Board, which, interpreting a federal law about racial determination, had decreed that two women formerly called white would henceforth be colored, because, among other things, they seemed to be on familiar social terms with other Coloreds. Mr. Justice Beyers said that if social behavior were a criterion, he'd be in trouble himself, inasmuch as he had a colored friend whose name was "Baas" and whom he frequently addressed by name. "The chairman of the Board just had to hear that and it would be finished with me," remarked the Judge. As for the law itself, he said, "I suppose we have to assume that the Members of Parliament know what they were doing. I am swallowing hard to make that assumption. But I am doing my best."

Mr. Justice Beyers, who is addressed as "My Lord" while he is on the bench, is admired by many South African Coloreds, who fondly refer to him as "Big Boy." They like him partly because he does not insist upon complete apartheid in his courtroom; to his left, alongside the jury box, two nonwhite male reporters sat throughout the trial, chatting away with a white female reporter, a Nordic blond type who looked like a German Olympic athlete. Among his compatriots Mr. Justice Beyers is sometimes thought to be too informal; they deplore the lighthearted, sometimes even vulgar quips with which it pleases him to regale his courtroom. Unusual he certainly is, but in an earlier trial he said, "The sanctity of human life is the absolute cornerstone of any ordered society," and after one watched him in action one came to respect his devotion to justice, however unorthodox his comportment. At the start of the Tsafendas proceedings he made a short speech to the spectators and the press—alternating, as many South Africans do on official occasions, between Afrikaans and English. "We believe that justice should be done in public, and should be seen to be done," he said, in the old British tradition. He reminded us that we were in a court of law, not a beer garden, and that he expected us all to behave properly, because "a man is on trial for his life."

But in a sense Tsafendas never went on trial. Before he even had a chance to plead guilty or not guilty to the charge of murder, his lawyers asked that the Mental Disorders Act of 1916 be invoked. According to that statute, if a judge finds that an arraigned person is incapable of managing himself or his affairs, the judge may just order that he be placed in custody. This was what Tsafendas' lawyers clearly hoped that Mr. Justice Beyers would do. Indeed, the principal advocate for the accused, Wilfred E. Cooper, conceded right off that there was no argument about whether or not his client had killed Dr. Verwoerd. "That is not an issue," Cooper said.

Tsafendas had two batteries of defense lawyers, divided—roughly according to the British distinction between solicitors and barristers—among attorneys and advocates. All of them had accepted, at the Judge-President's request, what may well have been an unwelcome assignment and what was bound to be an unremunerative one. The principal defense attorney was David Bloomberg, a young Cape Town lawyer whose sideline is the legitimate theater; he was then involved in a production of Dürrenmatt's *The Visit*. The principal defense advocate, Mr. Cooper, was one of relatively few lawyers who are qualified to appear before South Africa's Supreme Court. By coincidence, he once served briefly as a Parliamentary messenger himself. Though he was only forty, he had had considerable courtroom experience; another judge, who admired his trial tactics, once bestowed on him the nickname Tiger, but most of his friends continued to call him Wilfred. One of his sidelines is literature, and he can quote large chunks of James Joyce; he is also the co-author of an 865-page book called *South African Motor Law*.

Cooper, very gently for a tiger, began to tell the judge about his

154

client—"a nomadic, drifting person" who had "a delusional pre-occupation with his health." It was hard to tell how much Tsa-fendas was taking in, or even whether he was listening. Sometimes he held his head up and let his eyes move around the room; some-times he looked down at his feet, and all one could see was the grayish top of his head, bobbing slightly. What his chief delusion was emerged a few moments later, when Cooper called his first witness, a psychiatrist—also named Cooper but unrelated to the advocate. Dr. Cooper began to tell how he had examined Tsa-fendas, and Mr. Justice Beyers began to indicate that he was going to be as informal as ever—serious business or no serious business. Dr. Cooper said that Tsafendas often lost the trend of his thinking. "I have that difficulty with counsel quite often," the judge said, smiling. None of us knew whether to laugh or not. The doctor said that Tsafendas got lost when he tried to deal with ab-stractions. The judge grumbled that 99.9 per cent of all criminals did, and he slumped down in his chair, as if to indicate that he didn't have a much higher estimate of psychiatrists. "Judge obvi-ously hostile," a reporter next to me scribbled.

But then the judge sat up, and so did all of us, for now Dr. Cooper was telling us about the accused's delusion: For the past thirty years, Tsafendas had been under the impression that he carried an enormous tapeworm inside him and that its demands were responsible for all of his irrational behavior. Dr. Cooper quoted Tsafendas as saying, "If I did not have the tapeworm, I would not have killed Dr. Verwoerd," and went on to say that Tsafendas thought his worm was a devil, a dragon, a snake. He paused.

"A demon?" advocate Cooper asked.

"A demon," said Dr. Cooper.

The doctor went on to say that Tsafendas, with his "tactile hallucinations," had wandered all over the world, to at least twenty-five countries—a number that seemed above average, the doctor said, even for a globe-trotter. The judge broke in. Twenty-five countries didn't seem like an awful lot to *him,* he said, and, when it came to that, what did the doctor—or, for that matter, the judge himself—know about globe-trotting? There were further acerbic interchanges. (The two men couldn't even agree on the

155

pronunciation of schizophrenia; the judge took to calling it "skyzophrenia.") At one point Mr. Justice Beyers, evidently feeling that Dr. Cooper was being evasive about the extent to which the accused could comprehend the proceedings, said in exasperation, "Does he know that he's being tried for a crime of murder and does he know that for murder he can swing? Well, what else does he have to know?"

For the remainder of that first day Dr. Cooper stayed on the stand, with the advocate Cooper leading him on softly and the tart-tongued judge badgering both Coopers. When, for instance, the advocate asked his witness whether it could be considered a rational act for a man to walk into Parliament, seemingly with no hope of escape, and kill another man, the judge didn't wait for the doctor's answer but interjected, "Is murder ever rational?" Soon after that, with the observation that "this is heavy material," the judge adjourned court for the day.

The following morning, while we were waiting for court to reconvene, a clerk confided to one of the reporters that late the previous afternoon, while the stenographers were in the courtroom working on a transcript for the judge and the lawyers to read, they had suddenly become aware of a woman sitting in the dock that Tsafendas had vacated not long before; she had been praying softly for the accused. The second day fewer spectators turned up; whereas the streets outside the court had previously been jammed with onlookers, there were now hardly a dozen. This morning, also, the judge seemed to be in a different mood. The day before, except when he was cracking jokes, he had been stern-faced. Now a smile flickered across his creased face more often than not. When the advocate Cooper started to cite the qualifications of another witness—a nonpsychiatric doctor—Mr. Justice Beyers said, "They're very high. I've been through the doctor's hands." That doctor had also examined Tsafendas; he had found no trace of a real tapeworm, but he had heard a good deal about the imaginary one. (Just about the only indication that any doctor ever found any kind of worm inside Tsafendas came from a diagnosis made on him at a hospital for tropical medicine in Portugal, in 1952; he was reported then to be suffering, along with manic-depressive psychosis, from intestinal parasitosis.)

156

Still another doctor followed, and he was a blockbuster of a witness. He was the district surgeon of Cape Town, and nearly three months before the assassination he had by chance examined Tsafendas, who, referred by the Department of Social Welfare, had come around to his office to seek medical certification for a disability grant. And what had the district surgeon, who could have had no possible inkling of what the lawyers would seek to prove in October, put down about Tsafendas on his June report? "I put down 'schizophrenic,'" he said. The judge seemed impressed, and the Attorney General, who had cross-examined the earlier defense witnesses with some verve, hardly asked the district surgeon the time of day.

And now came a curious interlude. Four witnesses in a row— two men and their wives—were presented to the court. They all knew Tsafendas well. He had lived with them, for weeks or months. He had come to know them by corresponding with members of a sort of nameless religious sect to which they all rigorously adhered. They called themselves, nontitularly, "followers of Jesus Christ." They were all colored. The first of them, Peter Daniels, who was a foreman in the inspection department of a furniture factory, seemed to receive special attention from Mr. Justice Beyers. "I'm interested in the reactions of an ordinary man," the judge said.

Daniels had had a lot to react to. It was through his family that Tsafendas had turned up at Cape Town in the first place. The drifter, who had had little success with women all his life, had received a proposal of marriage from a sister of this witness. She belonged to the followers, and one of them had sent her a photograph of Tsafendas that had prompted her offer. If it was a good likeness, she could not have been having too much success with men. As soon as Tsafendas arrived, she'd looked at him in the flesh and changed her mind about matrimony, but he moved in with the Daniels family notwithstanding. According to her brother's testimony, Tsafendas would keep his hat on at the table and liked to spray chickens with water on hot days to cool them off. The judge said he sometimes did that himself. (Laughter.) Once, said Daniels, Tsafendas prepared a huge meal of steak, eggs, onions, and tomatoes, and gobbled it, like a dog, without benefit

157

of utensils. Daniels said he had concluded then that Tsafendas was mad, and his wife, in her turn, said she had decided that he "wasn't all there." Among other things, she said, he used to keep his boots on in bed.

The other "followers of Jesus Christ" had similar unsettling experiences to recount. A schoolteacher named O'Ryan said that at *his* house Tsafendas had sometimes stayed in bed all day, and that when his host remonstrated with him, the guest had said his tapeworm sapped his energy. As for Mrs. O'Ryan, it seemed that she was often called upon at night to give Tsafendas a hunk of bread to soothe the hungry worm. One could not help wondering about the people who had so long played willing host to this queer man, who kept his hat and boots on at the wrong times and was himself the alleged involuntary host of so sinister a creature. During a recess, some of us talked to Daniels outside the courtroom. What, we asked, did he think the worm really was? "We believe that the evil in this man came from Satan" was the answer. Did Tsafendas talk politics? "Only in that he thought it was laughable that all over the world people were free to marry anyone of any color they chose but here you were told whom you could marry and whom you couldn't." Daniels added that the "followers of Jesus Christ" believed that there were only two kinds of people on earth—sheep and goats—and that on Judgment Day everybody would find out which kind he was, and his color wouldn't matter.

That afternoon Mr. Justice Beyers, who had hardly stopped smiling all morning, began to look grim again when the defense came up with yet another psychiatrist. But this one, a youngish-looking doctor named Sakinofsky, was so self-assured and so knowledgeable that when he told the judge firmly that Tsafendas was schizophrenic and that the prognosis for his recovery was hopeless, the judge nodded.

By the third day of the trial, or sanity hearing, or whatever one chose to call it, a biographical picture of Tsafendas had begun to emerge. Most of the details of his life had, to be sure, come from interviews with doctors, but while all the doctors agreed that he was delusional, they all seemed to agree also that he was probably fairly accurate in his account of his past. Between 1936, when he first became obsessed with his tapeworm, and 1966, when he stabbed Dr. Verwoerd, he had been extraordinarily peripatetic, though nobody explained satisfactorily where either the funds or the travel documents had come from that made his roaming possible. He first set foot on South African soil, it seemed probable, in 1927, as a schoolboy. A decade later he had applied for admission as a permanent resident. When the response was negative, he came anyway, and was not apprehended. He had first been in Cape Town in 1941, when he'd joined the merchant marine. He'd gone to Canada, and late in 1942, it appeared, he had entered the United States illegally by walking across a frozen border river. For the next four years, until the United States finally deported him to Greece (presumably because of his name, since it is not certain that he ever held Greek citizenship and is more probable that legally he is a citizen of Portugal), he was in and out of American mental hospitals; he escaped from one of them, and later escaped from one in Germany. His travels also took in France, Spain, Portugal, Denmark, Sweden, England, Belgium, Turkey, Lebanon, Egypt, and—always carrying the heavy burden of his delusionary tapeworm with him—he finally, early in 1965, migrated back to South Africa. He knew a lot of languages by then—English, Portuguese, Spanish, and Greek were his best ones, but he could get by also in Afrikaans, French, Italian, Arabic, Swedish, and a couple of African dialects—but his linguistic prowess had done him little good. He had spent a quarter of a century going everywhere and getting nowhere.

The witnesses during the third day pretty much reiterated what had been said before. A clinical psychologist who had given Tsafendas a white-adult test after his arrest (in South Africa there are separate psychological tests for colored adults) testified that he had found the nomadic assassin a man of better-than-average intelligence but one lacking in "meaningful interpersonal contacts." That was almost bound to make the judge react, and it did; he asked for clarification of the fancy talk. The tapeworm, inevitably, came in for considerable discussion. A neurologist who had talked to the defendant in prison told of trying without success to get Tsafendas off the subject of the worm. "It did not take

159

long [for me] to realize that this worm was the central theme of his thoughts," the neurologist said. The worm had "disorganized his real personality and his relationship with the real world," the witness noted, and went on, "When I asked him what he would want if he could have one wish granted, I expected him to say he would want to be free. To my surprise, he said it would be to get rid of the worm."

By the fourth day the defense had no more witnesses, and it was the prosecution's turn. To the spectator who had been in the courtroom thus far, it seemed likely that Mr. Justice Beyers had been persuaded that the man before him was not fit to stand trial. Whatever it was that afflicted the fellow, he clearly had a bad case of it. The prosecution did not challenge this notion. It produced only two witnesses, and they both agreed with the defense. Indeed, when one of the two gave it as his conclusion that Tsafendas could be characterized by "thought-blocking" and "a lack of contact with his surroundings," the judicial question that followed showed how far Mr. Justice Beyers had swung around in his thinking. "Are these not textbook descriptions of schizophrenia?" asked the judge. How Tsafendas felt about the prospect of escaping the noose, or whether he had any feelings about it, was unknown.

The court had been in session only half an hour that fourth morning when the Attorney General suggested that His Lordship had heard enough to make a decision. It is part of the Mr. Justice Beyers legend that he never takes a note. He had not quite lived up to that reputation, but while his assessors had been furiously scrawling away on either side of him, he had set pen to paper only desultorily, and some of the time he had obviously been doodling. It is not often that any individual has the responsibility for passing judgment on the slayer of his country's chief executive, and it would surely seem to be a time for measured words. Probably the judge had thought hard overnight about what he planned to say; in any event, after a mere fifteen-minute adjournment he returned to the bench and delivered himself of a fifty-five-minute, seemingly off-the-cuff address that won him new admiration. "This court is no less conscious of the momentous background to this case than anyone else in this country," he said.

160

"Once, however, the case is brought in a court of law, these considerations of the immensity of this crime and the effects it has on the people of this country—they really disappear." He had quite a few points to cover. He knew, he said, that many South Africans —particularly those among whom Dr. Verwoerd was most cherished—were rugged men who believed in rugged retribution. "This is a civilized and, if I may proudly say, a highly civilized country," he said, and continued, after a bit, "The principle is centuries old that men are not tried if they are found to be insane. The question I have to ask is: Is the man before me a man that can be tried by a court of law, irrespective entirely of his mental condition at the time he committed the crime?"

Now the judge harked back to the first day, when he had hectored Dr. Cooper. "At that stage it was obvious that the court was prepared to resist as far as it could suggestions that Tsafendas was not responsible for his actions. If Dr. Cooper got it, that was what the first man over the top could expect. It became clear, however, that there can be no doubt whatever that the man before me is a schizophrenic. . . . If this man were to pay with his life for what he has done, that would do nothing for us. It would make no difference to our loss. . . . To tell the truth, people come and go, but if this nation should lose its trust in its legal institutions and the bench, we would indeed have brought about humiliation and shame which would be an irreparable blot on this country. One of my assessors said that a great statesman such as Dr. Verwoerd, without any doubt, would have wished it no other way. I can expect a certain amount of shock and dissatisfaction among certain people, but I am sure that they will realize it could not be otherwise and that it is not humane, or Christian, to condemn mentally ill people. When the law says he is not responsible for his actions, it is not only legally right but humanly right, too. You cannot have a feeling of revenge against sick people, and I cannot do other than come to the conclusion that the accused is a deeply, tremendously sick disturbed person and his actions do not spring from a rational state of mind. It is my duty to order that this person, Demitrio Tsafendas, be taken from here to a jail and be held there at the State President's pleasure."

The outcome may have been a disappointment to the proprietors of a waxworks exhibit at the Durban amusement park. John F. Kennedy, Lee Oswald, and Jack Ruby are all on exhibit there. But according to South African law, no resident of that country may be displayed in effigy unless he has been convicted of a crime. That, of course, made Dr. Verwoerd ineligible, and his would-be assassin of 1960 and successful assassin of 1966 both escaped this particular memorialization by not being brought to trial. The outcome, at the same time, gave most South Africans cause for satisfaction. Aware that their detention laws and their disregard of habeas corpus have put them in a bad light abroad (not that some of them much cared; they bask in their own self-generated light), they were generally pleased that this grubby, scruffy man who meanly infiltrated their holiest sanctum and who deserved so little at their hands had been accorded such civilized justice. And from Tsafendas' being certifiably insane, they could readily infer that no sane person would have attempted to do bodily harm to their Prime Minister.

Tsafendas quickly disappeared from view, and few people aside from his guards have had a glimpse of him since. (The story goes that a short time after the court proceedings ended, Cooper, the advocate, went to see how his client was reacting to his escape from the gallows and found him fast asleep.) One man who did get to talk to him was a judge of the Appellate Division of the Supreme Court, the Hon. Jacques Theodore van Wyk, who within days of the assassination was designated a one-man Warren Commission.

There are South Africans who will always believe that Tsafendas did not act alone but was part of a plot (some think he was a C.I.A. man), and the public disclosure, after Judge Beyers' decision, that he had once—however long before—had communistic leanings has tended to fortify their misgivings. Judge van Wyk did not see it that way. Yes, he said, he knew about the rumor that Tsafendas had been to Russia, possibly in 1961 or 1962; and he did have some silver fillings in his teeth. But there was no proof of any such visit, and Tsafendas had said he'd had the dental work done in Turkey.

The van Wyk report, which was issued in December 1966, was hardly exhaustive by Warren Commission standards. It covered

162

only thirty pages, though they were big, double-column pages. The hiring procedures for Parliamentary messengers got a stiff going-over. The Judge dwelt at length on the inadequacy of the government functionaries who were supposed to keep undesirables out of South Africa. As far back as 1959, it was revealed, Tsafendas' name had appeared on a "stop list" issued by the Department of the Interior, but at least twice, traveling once by car and once by ship, he had been waved across the border by officials armed with that very list. One of the men involved said that he couldn't remember what had happened but that when he heard the name of the arrival he might have taken it as "Stafendas" and looked at the entries under "S" instead of "T." Judge van Wyk did not think that much of an excuse.

The van Wyk Commission had searched in vain for an indisputable motive. Shortly before committing the deed, Tsafendas had spent some time, it came out, with the crew of a Greek ship that put in at Cape Town. The seamen were in a surly mood. Because of apartheid, they'd been refused permission to bring nonwhite women aboard while in port, and they'd told Tsafendas that men who made laws like that ought to be killed. Tsafendas himself had long resented the immorality laws, and the sailors' frustration could have intensified his own indignation. A few days before the assassination, Tsafendas had paid one of the Greeks thirty dollars for a gun, with which he presumably meant to carry out his plans; the seaman had fobbed a gas pistol off on him instead, and when Tsafendas had demanded his money back he'd been told to go packing. That could have made him even more indignant.

Judge van Wyk had appealed for any and all information about Tsafendas' shadowy past. He was favored with a number of allegations that, in sum, made the stodgy messenger sound like a man with a formidable criminal record—attempted murder in South Africa, actual murder in Mozambique, rape in Montreal, rape of a white woman in Ontario, rape and murder in Greece and Portugal, plural murders in Germany, dynamiting a ship in Boston, trying to blow up another in New York, and so on and on. But there seemed to be no hard evidence to back up any of these charges. Tsafendas had had a few fights, but he had been on the whole a harmless enough fellow—"a maladjusted, rejected, frustrated, feckless rolling-stone," the Judge summcd up. And he had done his wicked deed, the Judge felt obliged to conclude, all alone.

Demitrio Tsafendas may never be seen alive by the outside world again—though should he ever be declared sane, he could still be made to stand trial for his murder—but the addled linguist may have made one permanent contribution to the language of the nation whose history he so violently altered. Since Dr. Verwoerd's death, the young, knife-wielding toughs who prowl around South Africa's townships have been snarling at one another, as they go into action, "I'll demitrio you!" or "I'll tsafendas you!"

VIII

In the memoirs of Theodor Leutwein, a German army officer who served at the end of the nineteenth century as colonial governor of German South West Africa, there are two diverting photographs. One, taken in 1900, shows the Governor and some military aides drinking around a table, while black servants wait on them. Then the officers rearranged everybody present—one can almost hear the hearty Teutonic laughter that must have accompanied the transposition—for a gag shot: the African retainers lolled in the Germans' chairs, and the officers served *them*. The second picture, the Governor said in his book, represented what life in South West Africa might be like in the year 2000. Today, two-thirds of the chronological way toward Leutwein's prophetic date, no administrator of that much disputed area would pose for such a study in black and white, nor would he think that anyone who suggested that he do so was being very funny.

South West Africa, known to many South Africans simply as "South West," was one of two far-flung outposts that Germany lost after the First World War and that became Class C mandated territories under the League of Nations. The other was that group of islands in the northwest Pacific called Micronesia. "C" mandates were granted over territories that, according to Article 22 of the League Covenant, "are inhabited by people not yet able to stand by themselves under the strenuous conditions of the modern world," and their well-being and development, the Covenant went on, "form a sacred trust of civilization." South West Africa and Micronesia are the only two C-class mandates there have ever been. The British got the former and turned its administration over to the closest member of their Empire, the Union of South Africa. Japan got Micronesia, which after the *Second* World War—under the name of the Trust Territory of the Pacific Islands—became a United Nations responsibility and was given to the United States to administer.

The original League mandates for both backward areas stipulated that the nation in charge of them should "promote to its utmost the material and moral well-being and the social progress of the inhabitants of the territory" until they were ready to stand alone. Nowadays, the South African government, in answering charges that in forty-seven years it has been remiss in exercising its sacred trust, sometimes likes to argue that the twenty-year United States administration of Micronesia has been even more laggard. Early in 1967 the South African Broadcasting Corporation devoted an entire edition of its program *Current Affairs* to the United States and Micronesia, chiding America for its negligence there and concluding, "Was there ever such self-righteous, such nauseating hypocrisy?"

Now, it happens that I have been to both Micronesia and South West Africa. Indeed, I may be the only person on earth who holds that distinction, such as it is. The *Current Affairs* program made me blink. Many of the American deficiencies in Micronesia that it cited were, or once had been, real enough, but the program was so slanted it was preposterous. While it is true, for instance, that the United States has done nowhere near as much as it might have for Micronesia, the natives there *are* moving into the modern world. Of the ninety thousand Micronesians who live in the Trust Territory of the Pacific Islands, quite a few occupy responsible positions in the local government. Micronesia has its own legislature, and a large-scale accelerated educational program is under way. Discrimination because of race or color is outlawed. The attorney general is an American Negro.

The four hundred and fifty thousand non-Whites in South West Africa have had a few schools, hospitals, and clinics built for them, but their political progress has been negligible. The United States has introduced Micronesia to the Bill of Rights; South Africa has introduced its wards to apartheid, and imposed it on them. "In most of the twenty years of responsibility," the S.A.B.C. program said, "there has been virtually no schooling for the [Micronesian] natives beyond the elementary grades." No Micronesian did graduate from a four-year college until 1958, but today, with the encouragement and assistance of the United States, nearly two hundred Micronesians are getting degrees each year. Nonwhite South West Africans outnumber Micronesians by five to one, but only three or four of them go to college each year. In the Pacific territory a Micronesian who used to be the director of education for his district—it has a population of twenty thousand—is now the chief administrative officer of the district. No non-White holds any kind of administrative job above a clerical level in South West Africa. "If every single black man in South West Africa had a Ph.D. or an L.L.B.," one white man who has lived in South West nearly all his life told me, "you would then find out that the root of the whole thing is that the black man should never be the equal of the white man at the dinner table. South Africa will do a lot for the black man in South West, provided it does not conflict with the interests of the white man."

South West Africa, which measures some three hundred thousand square miles, is not a terribly prepossessing patch of the globe. It is perhaps not very important, really. And yet the United Nations has devoted endless hours to the territory, and in the spring of 1967 held a special General Assembly session mainly to discuss the area. (Prior to that the Assembly had passed seventy-

167

six resolutions about South West Africa.) Moreover, the International Court of Justice, the world's most elevated—though far from best known—judicial institution, has devoted more of *its* time to South West Africa than to any other portion of the earth.

South West is uncommonly desolate. Forty per cent of it is desert. Its bleak surface is dotted here and there with an outlandish plant called *Welwitschia mirabilis,* which attains an age of twenty-six hundred years, can survive for many months without a drop of water, and sprouts leaves eleven feet long, at the rate of a leaf a century. Within South West's borders lie only two surface lakes. Eons ago there was another huge one. Its dried-up bed now harbors the Etosha Game Park, one of the world's most splendid wild-animal reserves. Until recently the region had a golf course without a single blade of grass on it. By diligence and perseverance, its proprietors have managed to coax one authentic putting green from its surface, but until then two kinds of sand were used to differentiate so-called greens from so-called fairways. One writer has called South West "a strange world that appears never to have been completed—as if God had left it till the last in his creation and then got sick of it."

An African legend has it that long ago Fate stopped by at South West and threw a lump of clay upon the ground. The clay broke into pieces, and the pieces became native tribes, their numbers proportionate to the size of the lump from which they sprang. The biggest chunk became the Ovambos, who now number two hundred and forty thousand, or 40 per cent of the whole South West African population. They live in Ovamboland, in the northernmost part of the territory, and there are still other Ovambos to the immediate north of Ovamboland in the abutting Portuguese colony of Angola, where all Ovambos once dwelled. At any given time some forty or fifty thousand Ovambos are employed as contract workers in the central portion of South West Africa. This, covering more than half the territory and including the best of its soil, is white man's land, and it is called the Police Zone.

Actually, only two of South West's ten major nonwhite population groups are indigenous—the Damara and the Bushmen. The Bushmen are nomadic and quite primitive. They find it hard to cope with a civilized environment, and magistrates are reluctant to convict them of crimes because they have a tendency to pine away and die in jail. (There are odd aspects of the administration of justice in South West; a woman was not long ago acquitted of murdering a child when it developed that the main evidence was a confession that had been wrung from her by a tribal chief who'd had her head squeezed between two wooden blocks.) There are mixed-blood groups in the territory, principal among them the Rehoboth Basters, sometimes called Bastards. There are the Hereros, a proud and stubborn people originally from Bechuanaland (now Botswana), who raise cattle and whose womenfolk— still following a style set for them by nineteenth-century missionaries—wear turbans, layers of brightly colored shawls, and shoe-length skirts, and yet manage to look clean and cool and handsome in South West's often stifling heat.

There are close to seventy thousand Hereros in South West Africa, more than half of whom live and work in the vicinity of its capital city, Windhoek. For many years their chief has been Hosea Kutato, who was ninety-eight in 1967, and was living on a native reserve three hundred miles from Windhoek. By then he had pretty much turned over the conduct of tribal affairs to a forty-three-year-old deputy, an ex-teacher named Clemens Kapuuo, who was running a general store in a native township just outside Windhoek. Most of South West's non-Whites have been so docile over the years that South Africans, until recently, would sometimes call the territory "the perfect colony." The Hereros have been an exception. They are a constant source of irritation to South West's administrators. A training school for Herero teachers, founded by missionaries but now run by the South African government, has been disrupted by student strikes three times in twenty years; after the last strike, in 1960, half the student body left the school. "The Hereros resist *everything*," one official in Windhoek told me plaintively. In the spring of 1966 the chief administrator of the territory addressed an open letter to the Hereros, beseeching their cooperation and chiding them for their past intransigence. They had, he said, been "acting like a bull, standing against the hookthorn, and sweeping forward with his horns so that no one can come near to look after him." The He-

169

reros resisted the metaphorical language and ignored the letter.

As in the Republic of South Africa itself, the Whites of South West are a dominant minority. The South African government claims that there are ninety-six thousand of them; the real number is probably something less than that. Whatever the total, thirty-two thousand of them live in Windhoek, which lies just above the Tropic of Capricorn and sits snugly in a valley surrounded by hills. Windhoek is a unique metropolis, for Africa. Having only twenty-two thousand nonwhite residents, it is the only city on that continent with a white majority. Windhoek was founded in 1890, and according to one of its civic boosters, "has no subways, no trams, no skyscrapers, and no smog." It has plenty of affluence. When I was at a jeweler's there one day, two frumpish-looking farm women came in and bought six jewel boxes; a companion with me expressed the wry surmise that up to then they'd been storing their gems in a silo.

Thirteen thousand automobiles are registered in the names of Windhoek residents. (Cars wear out fast in South West; there were at last count a mere eight hundred and eighty-one miles of paved roads, though more were under construction.) Windhoek has a night club called the Pigalle, and a public swimming pool of Olympic dimensions, which is of course for Whites only. It has an estimable symphony orchestra and several bookmakers' establishments where bets are taken on horse races being run in South Africa and in England. One Windhoek man is celebrated for having recently been elected president of the World Council of Young Men's Service Clubs. In the Windhoek museum, above a glass-encased replica of *Welwitschia mirabilis,* is an enlarged photograph of South West Africa taken by an orbiting American astronaut. South Africans are sticklers for formalities; beneath the picture is the legend, "Copyright waived by U.S. Consul, Cape Town."

The average annual rainfall in Windhoek is thirteen inches. A Canadian woman who married a South West man while he was studying in Montreal came to Windhoek to live. Her mother-in-law met her at the airport, and the bride remarked that the countryside seemed terribly brown and depressing. "Don't you worry," said the mother-in-law. "In South West, after a nice good rain,

170

everything turns green overnight." The older woman was quite correct, but it took the younger one five years to find that out. Meanwhile, she had had a son, who was nearly five when the rains finally came. He had never experienced anything like it, and burst into frightened tears.

As in South Africa, non-Whites may work in any part of Windhoek, but except for domestic servants they must sleep in prescribed residential areas. Most Africans in Windhoek have lived for years in what is called the Old Location. It is a slum with unpaved streets. Its houses, made of oil drums, scrap lumber, and other improvised building materials, are huddled together. Rusty junked cars decorate its yards. According to the government, eight thousand Africans lived there at the start of 1967. According to Clemens Kapuuo, the Herero leader, whose store was in the Old Location, the number was fifteen thousand. Crowded as it is, the Old Location has a low crime rate. It is basic to the South African policy of separation of the races that different African tribesmen should live apart, but there have been Ovambos, Hereros, and Damaras all jumbled together in the Old Location, and they have seemed to get along all right. "Why, our women marry Ovambo men," Kapuuo told me.

The Old Location has communal toilets and inferior water sources, but for all its outward indifference to hygiene it has stayed remarkably free of epidemics; the hot, dry climate helps. To white eyes, for all that, it has been an eyesore. A decade ago, accordingly, the territorial administration created a new township for Africans. It has bigger, tidier, more sturdily constructed homes, each with running water and a backyard toilet. They rent for six dollars a month. It has schools and churches and medical facilities and playing fields and a tennis court. It has dormitories for Ovambo contract workers. (The dorms have been ringed by floodlights since the spring of 1966, when some Ovambos rioted in protest against what they said was too skimpy a meat ration in their mess hall.) When the new location was under construction the government invited some Africans to choose a name for the community. They picked "Katatura." The government men who were involved in the selection were evidently confused. They thought *"katatura"* was a Herero word meaning "this is the place where we will stay eventually." But the word for *that,* the authorities discovered too late, was *"ngatatura,"* and the name they'd been offered and had accepted for use actually meant "this is where we won't stay."

Katatura hasn't even been temporarily filled. Seventy-five hundred homes were built there. After ten years more than a thousand of them still remained vacant, while their prospective occupants clung to their jerry-built shanties in the Old Location. They liked it there for all its seeming disadvantages; it was their traditional residential quarter. The Katatura tennis court went to weed.

On November 30, 1966, the South African Bantu Affairs Department took a deep breath and announced that it was going to demolish the Old Location and that everybody would have to get out of it and move to Katatura. The Hereros said they wouldn't budge. One of their leaders said his people would die before they'd switch; he was soon imprisoned. Only a handful of families did move. South Africa doesn't relish violence, especially with the United Nations vigilantly watching South West Africa. There was a riot in the Old Location in 1959. Twelve Africans were killed and fifty were wounded. South Africa doesn't want to have to try to explain away a repetition of anything like *that.*

At last reports, as a sort of intermediary substitution for demolition, the government was planning to "deproclaim" Katatura. That would make it illegal for any nonwhite person to live there, and would also make it a crime for an employer to give work to any non-White who lived there. It all seemed to add up to a classic case of an irresistible force meeting an immovable object. The last time I drove through Katatura a movie theater there was showing *Hercules Against the Barbarians.* The title suggested all sorts of analogies. Meanwhile, at a theater for Whites in the center of Windhoek, audiences were laughing their heads off, apparently oblivious to the implications of *its* title, at *The Russians Are Coming! The Russians Are Coming!*

South West Africa is trilingual. English, Afrikaans, and German are all officially used in the administration of its affairs. (The resident administrator has no control over native affairs, which come directly under the supervision of the South African government, at Pretoria; the Republic does not delegate authority, either, in the areas of defense or foreign relations.) The post office entrance at Windhoek that non-Whites are supposed to use is identified by "Non-Europeans," "Nie-Blankes," and "Einge-borne." English is the primary tongue of merely 10 per cent of South West's white population, and in the whole territory there is just one English-language newspaper. An Afrikaans semiweekly, *Die Suidwes-Afrikaner,* is editorially opposed to the South African government, and as such is a wonder of the Afrikaner world. Sixty-seven per cent of the Whites are Afrikaans-speaking, and 23 per cent speak German. South West's most influential paper is the daily *Allgemeine Zeitung,* which thinks the South African government is *gemütlich.*

Until the First World War, South Africa never cared much about South West. The region's chief seaport today is Walvis Bay, a hundred miles west of Windhoek. In 1793, the Dutch East India Company outpost called the Cape of Good Hope staked a claim to Walvis Bay, and in 1878 the Cape, by then British, formally an-nexed an enclave around the port. The occupiers could probably have had all of South West if they'd wanted it, but the area seemed hardly worth acquiring. That land—four hundred and thirty-four square miles of it—has been recognized ever since as South Af-rican, not South West African, soil, and it did not come under the League of Nations mandate. German missionaries had gone to South West as early as 1812, and in 1883 a trader named Lüderitz, after whom a seaport was named, moved into the area. Two years later, to protect Lüderitz in a routine imperialistic colonial opera-tion, Bismarck began to take over the rest of South West Africa for Germany. The first resident commissioner was Hermann Goering's father.

Germans have been prominent in South West ever since. The hills of Windhoek support three heavy stone castles that could have flanked the Rhine. The territory has two breweries that make *echt* German beer, which South Westers consume copiously in *echt* German beer gardens; the *Financial Mail* of Johannesburg has said that life in South West was characterized by "an endless round of hearty, sober drinking." Unlike South Africa, where the Dutch Reformed Church has insisted on strict observance of the Sabbath, bars in South West may be open on Sunday. At the end

173

of 1966, while the rest of the world was wondering what the outcome would be of the impassioned U.N. debate about the future of South West and when one might logically have thought that in South West itself there would be endless talk about a crisis in the region's history, a leading Windhoek businessman told me that the only kind of crisis he could visualize would be a simultaneous shutdown of the breweries and a halt in whiskey imports. (South West Africa imports nearly everything it consumes except beer, meat, and dairy products; its cost of living is 10 to 15 per cent higher than that in South Africa.)

In the spring of 1915, with Germany and the Allies at war, the Union of South Africa sent its armed forces to South West and quickly seized it, although the Germans resisted. Among other tactics, they poisoned many of the local boreholes that were the major source of water. In 1924 all was forgiven, and all Germans living in South West were offered South African citizenship. By the Second World War a good many white South West Africans had become ardent Nazis, and half of the adult male Germans there were interned. In 1942 most of them were stripped of their South African citizenship, but by 1949, a year after the National Party assumed power in South Africa, the Germans once again became eligible for naturalization.

The Nats then had a fairly precarious majority in the South African Parliament. To fortify it, they created six new seats in its lower House for South West African legislators. This was very generous. In South Africa the average M.P. had ten thousand constituents; the ratio for South West came to one per twenty-five hundred. The Nats figured correctly that inasmuch as it had been their principal opposition, the United Party, that had interned the Germans of South West, the newly enfranchised group would be pro-National. The Germans did not disappoint their benefactors, although since then they have never become wholly absorbed into the mainstream of Afrikanerdom.

The urban areas of South West Africa are still markedly Teutonic. The main street of Windhoek, originally called Kaiser Wilhelm Street, is now plain Kaiser Street; the mayor of Windhoek is also called burgomeister. The main hotel of the town of Otjiwarongo is the Hamburger Hof. The most influential group in South

174

West doggy circles is the German Shepherd Club of South West Africa. At Christmas time the toy-store windows house Hansel-*und*-Gretel displays, everybody goes to hear *Weihnachtskonzerts,* and there are special holiday flights to the *Vaderland*. At any time of the year South African Airways has weekly scheduled service between Windhoek and Frankfurt. Near the Old Location there is a part of Windhoek called the Musical Area because its streets are named after, among others, Bach, Beethoven, Brahms, Schubert, and Strauss.

Germans have long been the sparkplugs of Windhoek culture and, aside from South Africa itself, West Germany is now South West's principal trading partner. West Germany is the only nation that has a full-time consul in South West Africa. With three official languages, the territory has three sets of schools for Whites alone. West Germany gave a million dollars toward the construction of Windhoek's new German high school building. In one of its lobbies is a plaque honoring the memory of forty-four graduates who died in the Second World War. There is no mention of which side they fought on, but an Iron Cross surmounts their names.

Most immigrants who venture to South West come from Germany. They do not amount to a human wave—perhaps a couple of hundred a year at most, some of whom don't tarry too long. In any event, they aren't exactly what South West needs. It needs doctors and engineers, but instead it has been getting footloose young men who hear of openings for clerks' jobs in South West African German delicatessens. South West Africa is so German that during the recent fuss about its eventual status a couple of cynics suggested that the whole problem could be resolved by just giving it back to Germany. There is no reason to believe, however, that either present-day German state wants it.

One of the most astonishing cities anywhere in the world must be the seaside town of Swakopmund, South West's main summer resort. Swakopmund rises from the Namib Desert twenty miles north of Walvis Bay. The territory's German governors traditionally went there in December and January, when Windhoek is unbearably hot; its South African governors have continued the refreshing custom. The Administrator's summer home is a tur-

175

reted edifice that looks as if it were made of gingerbread with white icing, like a turn-of-the-century Bavarian railroad station. Swakopmund's railroad station looks like that, too, and so does its jail.

Swakopmund is so German that if one asks a question there in English or Afrikaans, the answer is likely to come in German, and a local joke has it that there are four kinds of South West Africans—English, Afrikaner, German, and Swakopmunder. (The joke probably doesn't strike non-Whites as hilarious.) Swakopmunder elders walk their streets behind white mutton-chop whiskers, and the seals in the local museum were processed by a Bremen taxidermist. When I went there to cool off after a week in Windhoek, the big news was that the local Hansa brewery had just hired a new *braumeister,* direct from Germany, and everyone was busy sampling his output to see how it compared with his predecessor's.

There is never any measurable rainfall in either Swakopmund or Walvis Bay, and nobody in either place owns raincoats or umbrellas, except a few people who fancy the latter as sunshades. One can stand on a pier at Swakopmund with a hand line and no reel and catch a dozen or more presentable fish in twenty minutes. South West's waters offer a rich harvest. (Swakopmund, moreover, makes mountains of salt from evaporated sea water, and it has an offshore platform outside town from which tons of guano are profitably scooped each year; it also has a large resident colony of flamingos.) At Swakopmund and Walvis Bay there are no retail fish stores, as anybody who goes fishing is almost bound to catch so much more than he can use that he can fill his friends' refrigerators. Walvis Bay is the area's main commercial fishing port. Pilchards are its specialty (canned Del Monte sardines are Walvis Bay pilchards). Nearly a million tons of them are hauled in a year, and to accommodate just part of this catch Walvis Bay has a factory that makes two hundred million cans a year. Walvis Bay exports canned fish to Japan, and fishmeal and fish oil everywhere.

Until 1961 most of the fishing boats were owned and manned by South Africans or South West Africans. In the last few years the United Nations has had some difficulty getting foreign ob-

176

servers into South West Africa, but during the same period the docks and streets and shops and bars of Walvis Bay have been visited by seamen from all quarters of the earth. Attracted by South West's cornucopian waters, fishing boats from fifteen distant nations have converged on Walvis Bay to trawl just beyond a twelve-mile limit—boats flying the flags of Japan, South Korea, Taiwan, Ghana, Israel, Belgium, Spain, Italy, Iceland, Poland, Holland, Bulgaria, West Germany, East Germany, and the Soviet Union. The first Icelandic vessel to make the scene arrived in September 1966 the day after Prime Minister Verwoerd was assassinated, and its skipper, a resolutely antiapartheid man, made himself remembered by refusing to fly his flag at half mast.

Of all the foreign fleets, the Russians have had far and away the largest. There are usually around forty Soviet trawlers at a time operating off Walvis Bay, some of these substantial vessels with crews of a hundred. Three canning ships stand by to process their haul. Then there are four new Soviet factory ships built primarily to make fishmeal from South West African pilchards. One of them can handle a quarter of a million tons a year. Every week or so a Soviet supply ship routinely turns up off Walvis Bay to replenish the fishing boats' stores. The crews come ashore, too, but have little effect on the Walvis Bay economy; the Soviet Union and South Africa have no foreign-exchange agreements, and the Russian seamen rarely have much spending money. The Russian member of the fourteen-nation U.N. Ad Hoc Committee that tried ineffectually to solve the knotty South West problem in the winter of 1967 said at one meeting that "the Soviet Union had no economic or financial interests in South West Africa and was pursuing no selfish aims in that territory." As far as Walvis Bay is concerned, though, the Russians aren't coming. They're there.

Even without any big Soviet spenders, Walvis Bay has been booming. Late in 1966 its municipal administration announced plans for the area's first skyscraper. It was to be six stories high. Up to then Walvis Bay had had mostly low-rising buildings, a disproportionate number of them being churches and bottle stores. "The people here pray all Sunday and drink the rest of the week," one irreverent Walvis Bay matron told me. "Actually, I don't

177

think they really pray. They just go to church to show off their new hats." Walvis Bay has a weekly newspaper, the *Namib Times*, that interchangeably uses all three of South West's official languages and claims to be the world's only trilingual journal.

The port also has a few military installations. Mandated territories are not supposed to harbor military bases. When it suits South Africa's convenience, the Republic incorporates the Walvis Bay enclave into South West, but when armed forces are involved South Africa is very careful. It likes to stress that what it has at Walvis Bay is *not* in South West Africa. Not that it appears to have much there. The Walvis Bay airstrip has bays for a dozen aircraft; not a single bay was occupied when I passed through. In Walvis Bay itself there were some army barracks, but they weren't very extensive, and I saw only a handful of soldiers and vehicles. However, it is reliably thought that twelve or thirteen thousand young South Africans undergoing military training each year get it in or around Walvis Bay. The barracks are near the town's golf course, and Walvis Bay civilians sometimes complain that the military carelessly uses the eleventh and twelfth greens as a thoroughfare. The beefs are not too loud, for the greens, made of sand and used diesel oil, have to be raked and smoothed before each putt under the best of circumstances.

The South West African economy is sometimes said to rest on a tripod; the legs are fish, copper, and diamonds. Bare as is much of the territory's surface, beneath it lies a wealth of minerals. As one flies low over the desert—like as not, with a pilot who will sportingly change his course to buzz a stray ostrich or gemsbok —one can see the excavations and tire tracks of bygone prospectors. South West has so many different kinds of minerals that it has been called "the sample box of the world." Semiprecious stones—beryl, amethyst, tourmaline, and so forth—are especially abundant. There is one whole hill made of rose quartz. The northeastern city of Tsumeb is the site of a huge copper-mining operation (most of its capital is American), and in the southwest of South West, where the desert meets the sea, a hundred million dollars' worth of diamonds are sifted from the sand and silt each year.

The territory has other resources. Most South African rock

178

lobster is South West African rock lobster. (An African posted to the U.N. once insisted, as an antiapartheid gesture, that South African rock lobster tails be removed from the menu in the delegates' dining room. Now that the U.N. has formally, if not physically, taken South West away from the Republic, perhaps the delicacy will be restored and more explicitly labeled.) The sparse vegetation that covers a good deal of the territory won't support cattle, but it is fodder enough for karakul. South West African Persian lamb—bred from stock originally imported from Astrakhan by Germans and now sometimes called "Swakara"—is a substantial export product. One Windhoek furrier advertises that he corresponds in English, Afrikaans, German, French, and Portuguese. At a Windhoek auction in the spring of 1967 a world's record was set when a South African farmer paid $1,582 for an eight-year-old South West African karakul ewe.

For many years the biggest businessman in South West has been the proprietor of South West Commercial Holdings, Ltd., Sam Cohen. Born in Russia and raised in England, Cohen first visited Walvis Bay in 1906, when he was sixteen. He settled in Windhoek ten years later. He was South West's first automobile dealer and became its largest, having the General Motors franchise for the entire territory. "Cohen for Cars" has been one of his slogans. At last count, he was the exclusive South West African representative of eighty-two American companies, and of almost as many more from other nations. He has lately installed a computer to help him keep track of all his commercial holdings.

Cohen's name appears in multicolored lights on a circular tower surmounting his headquarters on Kaiser Street, much as if he were a Tokyo night club. He maintains a permanent suite at the best hotel in Swakopmund. In that resort's museum, in a gallery of its benefactors, Sam Cohen's photograph is displayed above and is larger than that of Harry F. Oppenheimer, who in South Africa is usually the foremost benefactor of everything. Cohen is sometimes called the Uncrowned King of South West Africa, an unofficial title the use of which he himself has assiduously promoted. He has been amiably disposed toward the South African government—indeed, though Jewish, he has professed never to have had any run-ins with South West's Nazis—and he

179

sometimes archly refers to the Administrator of the territory, who rides around in a Cadillac-from-Cohen, as his senior partner. The incumbent administrator, for his part, declared in 1966 at the unveiling of an extension to Cohen's Caterpillar-tractor division, "I sometimes wonder whether we shouldn't have told the United Nations, 'Look, call off all this business about a trust territory for South West Africa and the one-man one-vote propaganda. The place doesn't belong to us anyway—it's Sam Cohen's, and what is more he isn't going to give the vote to anybody except to people in the Cohen organization and then they had better show him how they vote if and when they vote.' "

IX

To just whom South West Africa does belong has been an eloquently debated international topic for more than two decades. In the summer of 1966 Judge Luis Padilla Nervo, a member of the International Court of Justice, unreservedly called the South West African situation—Vietnam or no Vietnam—"the most explosive issue of the postwar world." The judge's assessment was understandable. For nearly six years the World Court, sitting in isolated majesty at The Hague, had done little but meditate upon the issue, following which it had in solemn absurdity reversed a solemn decision it had made in 1962 and had proclaimed that Ethiopia and Liberia, the plaintiffs—or Applicants—in what was formally called the South West Africa Cases, did not have the legal right to call into account South Africa's performance as a mandatory power.

The Court had been asked by the Applicants to resolve two basic issues: Had the United Nations fully succeeded to the supervisory powers of the League of Nations, which had granted South Africa its mandate over South West in 1920?; and had South Africa, by establishing apartheid within the territory, abused the mandate? On very few matters of either fact or law were the disputants, during their lengthy confrontation, able to see eye to eye, but the principal South African advocate did say, on March 30, 1965, that he concurred with a previous statement by counsel for the Applicants that "seldom in the history of judicial administration can there have been involved legal issues, the determination of which more profoundly will affect the 'material and moral well-being and the social progress' of a multitude of individual persons."

There were many extraordinary aspects of the case: pure-white South Africans rock-hard in their allegiance to apartheid found themselves addressing coal-black judges as "Sir"; one of the lengthier dialogues about apartheid in the Netherlands courtroom was conducted between two disputative Americans; and South Africa, a nation second to none in its anticommunism, invoked Andrei Gromyko, among others, in support of its righteousness. But apart from and above its uniqueness was the litigation's potential importance. For the first time in history, a grave social, moral, and political issue—what an Iraqi delegate to the U.N. once called "a hot and boiling subject"—had been brought before an international tribunal by whose verdict both sides were committed in advance to abide.

In a sense, the Court's 1966 disinclination to pass on the merits of the case made the whole litigation immaterial, but the record of the proceedings stands, like the record of a baseball game that is rained out after eleven deadlocked innings; and the documentation that piled up amounts probably to the most spirited assault upon and defense of apartheid that the world is likely to see for generations to come: thirty-six hundred printed pages of documents prepared for the Court's perusal; three hundred and sixty-six pages of verbatim transcripts of preliminary oral arguments; thirty-five hundred pages more for transcripts of ninety-

182

nine days of subsequent oral proceedings; and still another seven hundred pages of judges' reactions to it all. A phrase frequently used by the participants was *"inter alia"*; one shudders to think what might have happened had all the *alia* been spelled out. (When, at one point, the South African government got up a résumé of events that covered two hundred legal-size pages, it described this tome as "a brief insight into the crucial aspects of the case.") During the oral proceedings Ernest A. Gross, the former Deputy United States Representative to the U.N., who served as chief counsel for Ethiopia and Liberia, was trying to impeach the expertise of a witness for South Africa. When Gross asked whether the witness had studied the transcript of an earlier portion of the proceedings, he was interrupted by Sir Percy C. Spender, of Australia, the president of the Court. "Mr. Gross," said Sir Percy, "I should hope that the fact that he had not would not disqualify him from being an expert. If every expert had to read all that has taken place in this case he would have to take a couple of years off, I think."

Sir Percy is no longer on the World Court, his term having expired in February 1967. He is something of a hero in South Africa these days, and something of a villain to the rest of Africa. The Applicants lost their case by a vote of eight to seven, and as things worked out the Australian got to vote twice. Seventeen judges could have voted. One became ill, one was instructed by Sir Percy to disqualify himself, and another died. The balloting among the fourteen who were left produced a seven-to-seven tie. (Of the three others, two would most certainly have voted against South Africa had they been around on judgment day.) The Court's rules provide that in case of a deadlock its president may cast a second, tie-breaking vote. So Sir Percy, who had already voted once against the Applicants, cast another ballot. One of the ironic aspects of the complicated and interminable proceedings was that Ethiopia and Liberia and the Afro-Asian nations rooting for them should have been stymied by a contravention, in the world's loftiest tribunal, of the balloting formula so cherished in most of Africa today—one man, one vote.

The Versailles Conference of 1919 has been blamed for many earthly ills, and in a sense it can be held responsible for the furor

183

that has arisen over South West Africa. In 1917 the British had decided that if Germany was beaten the captured territory would be incorporated into the South African part of their realm. Woodrow Wilson, among others, demurred. He thought that former colonies of the Central Powers should become subordinate to the embryonic League of Nations, and at Versailles his views prevailed. When the British got a mandate over South West Africa, they turned it over to South Africa, whose man of that hour, Jan Smuts, had been a proponent of the mandates system in general —though not, when it came to specifics, of a mandate for South West Africa. South Africa would have preferred simply to take over the area. But it made the best of the situation and on December 17, 1920, formally assumed mandatory power over the territory, responsible to the League.

Article 2 of the mandate covering South West Africa contained two key paragraphs. One went:

> The Mandatory shall have full power of administration and legislation over the Territory subject to the present Mandate as an integral portion of the Union of South Africa, and may apply the laws of the Union of South Africa to the Territory, subject to such local modifications as circumstances may require.

That paragraph has ever since been interpreted by South Africa as giving it virtually carte blanche—the practice of apartheid included—in South West. The very next paragraph of Article 2, on the other hand, has been interpreted by many other nations to mean that apartheid—whatever its merits or demerits in South Africa—could not possibly be admissible in South *West*. It is in this paragraph that one finds:

> The Mandatory shall promote to the utmost the material and moral well-being and the social progress of the inhabitants of the Territory subject to the present Mandate.

The mandatory was required to report on its stewardship, periodically, to a League subsidiary located in Geneva called the Permanent Mandates Commission. There was a further obligation to pass along to the Commission written petitions that might be submitted on grievances by people in the mandated territory. "The Mandates Commission must be more than a group of experts and legal advisers studying problems at the seat of the League of Nations," one of the early Commission members said. "This Commission is not, in a sense, dealing with problems at all, at least it is not investigating them as abstract questions. It is concerned with human beings and—whatever else it may forget—this it must always remember." "History seemed to show," another commissioner was said by the P.M.C.'s minutes to have observed, "that, on every occasion in the past when whites and blacks have come into contact in territories equally inhabitable by both races, the blacks had gone to the wall. The mandate system represented a kind of protest against the continuation of this state of affairs."

But the Commission couldn't get much cooperation—about people or problems or anything else. When South Africa balked at answering a P.M.C. questionnaire about its activities in South West, one commissioner said:

It would seem to be the view of the mandatory powers that the P.M.C. should confine itself to seeing that no gross and general maladministration is taking place, and that questions should be asked only regarding matters on which the P.M.C. has cause for doubts. But it is by asking general questions that causes for doubt emerge. If the P.M.C. is to discharge only functions of the perfunctory nature indicated, it would hardly seem worthwhile for men who have many other demands on their time to devote themselves to the work. The South African delegate complained that the action of the P.M.C. "constituted an investigation of the policy of the Mandatory in its own country." Is not that precisely its function?

Whether or not it was, the question became academic with the outbreak of the Second World War; the last time that South Africa reported to the P.M.C. on South West Africa was March 31, 1939.

Toward the end of the war, the Allies had to start thinking about what was to be done with the spoils of conflict, and also about the mandates that were still more or less in effect after the

185

untidy aftermath of the war before. The United Nations organization provided for trusteeships to replace mandates, and for a Trusteeship Council to replace the P.M.C. Micronesia posed no problem. Japan, having lost the war, had nothing to say about its one-time dependency. South Africa, however, had been on the winning side (although some of its present-day government officials were then sympathetic to Nazism), and at the San Francisco Conference in the spring of 1945 had again suggested that outright annexation of South West was its answer to the world's question.

It was not a new idea. As far back as 1920 General Smuts had assured an audience at Windhoek that South West would always be "part and parcel" of South Africa. Periodically, South Africa had suggested to the Permanent Mandates Commission that it just absorb the territory, but the P.M.C. kept saying that "the time is not yet ripe." In 1934 South Africa had told the P.M.C. that its wards of South West were so eager to become fully affiliated with their guardian it was all the mandatory power could do to hold them back. At San Francisco Smuts said, "There is no prospect of the territory ever existing as a separate state, and the ultimate objective of the mandatory principle is therefore impossible of achievement. The delegation of the Union of South Africa therefore claims that the Mandate should be terminated and that the Territory should be incorporated as part of the Union of South Africa."

The recommendation was coolly received. When, in 1946, the League of Nations ceased formally to exist, the status of South West Africa was still up in the air. That year South Africa conducted a poll among the nonwhite inhabitants of South West—most Africans voted not as individuals but through their tribal chiefs, who were pleased with the responsibility and in some instances cast votes for newborn babes—and was happy to proclaim the results: 208,850 for incorporation, 33,520 opposed, and 56,790 unreachable.

One of the differences between the League of Nations and the United Nations is the status of the world organizations' judicial arms. The League had its Permanent Court of International Justice, which became operative in January 1922, in the Peace

186

Palace at the Hague. But the Permanent Court wasn't a part of the League. (It wasn't permanent, either.) A United States judge sat on it, but the United States Senate no more recognized its authority than it did that of the League itself. Between 1922 and 1936, the Permanent Court heard sixty-six cases, only one of which—it had to do with the commercial rights of a Greek businessman in Palestine—pertained to the administration of a mandate. (Some of the old Court's cases had beguiling names: the Lighthouses of Crete and Samos Case, the Panevezys-Saldutiskis Railway Case, the Polish Postal Service in Danzig Case, the Employment of Women During the Night Case.)

The present Court is quite different, though it occupies the same premises. (It is a thrifty court; a lawyer who not long ago held up to a light its official letterhead discovered that the paper bore the watermark of the old Permanent Court.) The incumbent and titularly nonpermanent World Court is an integral part of the United Nations. It derives its authority straight from the U.N. Charter. Every nation that signed that document subscribed to Article 94 of the Charter, which says, "Each Member of the United Nations undertakes to comply with the decision of the International Court of Justice in any case to which it is a party." The article further says that if a member state fails to comply with a judgment of the Court, the Security Council may step in.

Since the present Court began to function, in April 1946, there has been only one instance of noncompliance. Albania refused to pay the United Kingdom two and a half million dollars' damages awarded at The Hague after some British ships ran into a minefield in 1946 while cruising in the Corfu Channel, just off the Albanian coast. If Ethiopia and Liberia had secured a judgment against South Africa, and South Africa had balked at doing whatever it might have been ordered to, the Applicant nations would almost assuredly have gone to the Security Council. In the Corfu Channel Case, Britain made no such move because at the time of the judgment Albania and the Soviet Union were still on comradely terms, and there was every reason to suspect that the Russians would have used their veto to negate any proposed Council action.

At full strength, the Court has fifteen judges; nine of them constitute a quorum. They are elected by a curious voting system that calls for concurrent balloting on a slate of nominees in both the General Assembly and the Security Council. Each of the five original veto-holding members of the Council has a judge of its own nationality; every judge is supposed to be fluent in either English or French. The judges travel on diplomatic passports and are paid twenty-five thousand dollars a year each; the President and Vice-President get more. All the judges' credentials are impressive. Most of them have had many years' experience in international law or international relations or both. V. R. Wellington Koo, for instance, who was vice-president in 1966, had been a Chinese ambassador to the rest of the world for about as far back as anyone could remember. He was then seventy-eight; at thirty-two he had helped Walter Lippmann draft the terms of the League mandates.

Most of the judges have been involved in the League or the U.N. or both. Sir Muhammed Zafrulla Khan, who like Sir Percy Spender is a former president of the U.N. General Assembly, was Pakistan's representative to the U.N. in 1961; he was also leader of the *Indian* delegation to the League in 1939. As the composition of the U.N. has altered, so has that of the Court. Now it has two black African members. The first was Isaac Forster, who before that was the first president of the Supreme Court of Senegal. Judge Forster's language is French, and in his dissent from the 1966 majority opinion he had a final ringing word or two to say about the barriers that apartheid automatically imposes against men who share his color. Where did one find these barriers?, he demanded. *"Il s'en trouve à foison: barrière dans l'admission aux emplois, barrière dans l'accés à la formation professionelle, barrière dans la condition de résidence et de libre circulation; et . . . jusque dans le culte religieux se dresse la barrière de couleur dans l'église et à l'heure de la sainte communion!"*

While a case is in progress, each of the litigants is entitled to an additional ad hoc judge of its own choosing. Ad hoc judges get forty-five dollars a day. At the start, Ethiopia and Liberia had recruited Sir Muhammed Zafrulla Khan, who had not yet been elected to the Court. He had changed his mind before actually serving in the ad hoc capacity, but because he had briefly held the title, Sir Percy informed him that he should abstain from participation in the case. The Applicants ultimately picked a black African for their ad hoc judge, Sir Louis Nwachukwu Mbanefo, the chief justice of Eastern Nigeria. South Africa picked Judge van Wyk, who was later to conduct the inquiry into the Verwoerd assassination and who still later, *vice* Judge Beyers, became Acting Judge President of the Cape province.

The two extra judges sat at each of the slightly curved ends of a raised dais from which the World Court surveys its courtroom. A Cape Town paper said that the bench, in physical dimensions, resembled the horns of a Zulu impi. Sir Percy, as president, sat in the middle. He is a small man, but his chair was slightly elevated above the others. He dominated the courtroom in every respect. (When he took a week off, in June 1965, to go to San Francisco for ceremonies celebrating the twentieth anniversary of the birth of the U.N., the Court simply closed up shop.) Sir Percy oversaw the proceedings as if he were a trial judge and his fellow judges were a jury. Not all the judges asked questions. Judge Koo never opened his mouth. Neither did a former president of the Court, the eighty-three-year-old Bohdan Winiarski, who in 1966 celebrated the twentieth anniversary of his election to the tribunal. Judge Winiarski, a noncommunist Pole, was a delegate to the very first session of the League of Nations, and was subsequently on the staff of the Permanent Court of International Justice.

Some of the questions that Sir Percy asked were sharp, especially when he was engaged in colloquy with Ernest Gross. The advocate for Ethiopia and Liberia was not disturbed by this; he and the Australian were old friends from their U.N. days, and the American surmised that the President's acerbity was calculated to demonstrate that he was not going to let personal relationships affect his impartiality. During one session Gross was cross-examining a South African witness about the ceilings imposed by his government on Africans who sought economic advancement. At adjournment time Gross said to the President, "I am still at the ceiling, Sir."

"I do not think you have got beyond the first floor," was Sir Percy's tart reply. Maybe that exchange was prophetic.

At The Hague, one South African lawyer said that his country's foes in the United Nations regarded their antiapartheid efforts "as

189

something in the nature of a holy crusade of modern times." One South African M.P. has said in Parliament that apartheid, which U Thant has called "the most conspicuous and anachronistic mass violation of human rights on earth," is just about the only contemporary issue that the rest of the world *does* agree on. Over the years there have been U.N. committees on apartheid and on South West Africa; there have been visits by U.N. representatives to South Africa, though not yet to South West; there has been an abortive attempt by the U.N. to appoint its own Resident Representative for Technical Assistance to South West Africa.

On several occasions before Ethiopia and Liberia filed their suit, the U.N. had appealed to its judicial arm in the Netherlands to clarify one aspect or another of the muddled South West Africa situation. The International Court of Justice hands down both advisory opinions and compulsory judgments. The latter, which evolve from contentious proceedings like the South West case, consist ordinarily of a statement of law and an accompanying order obliging the nation receiving it to do something, or cease doing something. An advisory opinion imposes no enforceable obligations.

In 1950 the General Assembly asked the Court to advise it just what South West Africa *was,* now that the League no longer existed. The Court ruled unanimously (of the justices voting then, Judge Winiarski alone still sits on the Court), that South West Africa remained a mandated territory. At the dissolution of the League, the Court declared, the League's Assembly had "manifested its understanding that the Mandates were to continue in existence until 'other arrangements' were established," and although these arrangements hadn't been spelled out, some sort of supervision by the U.N. was clearly in order. However, said the Court in 1950, South Africa's mandate did not have to come under the U.N.'s trusteeship system. The Court further proclaimed itself the properly constituted successor to the Permanent Court for adjudicating disputes about mandates.

Five years later, the General Assembly asked the Court what voting procedures it should follow in dealing with the South West Africa mandate. The Court's advice this time was that a two-thirds vote should apply—i.e., that questions about South West

190

fell into that category considered by the U.N. to be "important questions." The then South African Minister for External Affairs, Eric Louw, remarked after that opinion, "We do not care tuppence whether the United Nations observes the two-thirds majority rule or the unanimity rule in dealing with South West African affairs, because we have consistently said the United Nations has no right to concern itself with the affairs of South West Africa."

The General Assembly's concern was nonetheless unflagging. In 1956 it had a further request of the Court. The 1950 advisory opinion had declared that the U.N.'s degree of supervision over territories should not exceed that of the League's. The League had never received oral petitions from South West Africans or others who had grievances to air—only written petitions. In the special, prickly case of South West Africa, the General Assembly now wanted to know, could petitioners come forth in person? The Court ruled that they could (the Anglican cleric Michael Scott became the most vociferous spokesman), provided that written petitions were submitted before anybody turned up in the flesh.

By 1959, many member states of the U.N., the black African nations understandably the most vociferous among *them,* were openly talking about somehow hailing South Africa into the World Court to account for its administration of South West. The General Assembly itself could not do this; by the Court's statute, only states can be parties to contentious cases. South Africa's position was that—whatever kind of action might be brought against it—its mandatory functions were simply not justiciable, and that the proposed proceedings had nothing to do with law but were rather part of the tiresome old political conspiracy, or holy crusade, or whatever one wished to call it, that had been going on for so long. After the proceedings got under way, the headline that one South African government propaganda sheet put over a story about them read, "COURT CASE AGAINST S.A. PART OF BLACK PLAN TO RULE AFRICA." And another government handout said, "As long as the Mandatory honestly attempts to achieve the result [of promoting to the utmost moral and material well-being and social progress], its conduct cannot be regarded as a violation of its obligation. Whether a court, or anybody else, agrees, or disagrees, with the methods and policies employed in the attempt, or

191

whether a court, or anybody else, likes those policies, or dislikes them, does not matter."

Some of the Afro-Asian states at the U.N. thought otherwise, and early in the winter of 1960 they besought an informal advisory opinion on their own. They wanted to know if they had reasonable legal grounds for instituting action against South Africa, and the man they approached was Ernest Gross, by then privately practicing law in New York as a partner of Curtis, Mallet-Provost, Colt & Mesle. Gross was a logical selection. His firm had done some work for the Republic of Liberia, and he himself had an impressive background: legal advisor to the State Department, Assistant Secretary of State for Congressional Relations, four-time member of the United States delegation to the U.N. General Assembly, Deputy U.S. Representative to the U.N. from 1949 to 1953, special counsel to Secretary Dag Hammerskjöld from 1953 on, trustee of the Carnegie Endowment for International Peace, chairman of the Department of International Affairs of the National Council of Churches of Christ. A conference of independent African states was to be held at Addis Ababa in the spring of 1960. In anticipation of it, the Liberian government invited Gross to draw up a memorandum of law for itself and the other participating countries—Ethiopia, Ghana, Guinea, Libya, Morocco, Sudan, Tunisia, and the United Arab Republic. Algeria, Cameroon, Nigeria, and Somalia sent observers.

Gross prepared his memorandum and took it to Liberia, where it was approved by that nation's perennial president, William V. S. Tubman. Gross went to Ethiopia, where, in the course of the conference itself, he got Emperor Haile Selassie's imprimatur. The African states assembled at Addis Ababa were aware of the risks involved in what they were contemplating. Litigation would be expensive (the costs to both sides eventually ran into millions of dollars), even as much as a moral victory was by no means certain, and there was the danger that the General Assembly might be disposed to relax its pressure on South Africa while a case was *sub judice*. (South Africa did subsequently take the position that the U.N. couldn't pass any more resolutions about South West Africa until the proceedings at The Hague were concluded; the General Assembly's response was to pass a resolution re-

192

affirming the U.N.'s right—nay, duty—to supervise the mandate, Court or no Court.)

On June 23, 1960, at Addis Ababa, after several days of discussion of the political as well as the legal implications of the matter, the conference delegates voted unanimously to take South Africa to court. By then, Ethiopia had decided to become a party to the case. Like Liberia, it had been a member of the League of Nations. Under the original mandate, any member nation of the League, if it had a non-negotiable dispute with a mandatory power "relating to the interpretation or the application of the provisions of the Mandate," could as a representative of all nations take the dispute to the Permanent Court of International Justice. *Actio popularis* is another term for it. Most Africans expected the successor Court's verdict to be a legal milestone as weighty, internationally, as was a comparable national verdict— that of the United States Supreme Court, in 1954, in the case called Brown v. Board of Education. That, of course, was the judgment that outlawed segregation in American public schools and set the stage for all the civil-rights battles that have ensued.

The countries gathered at Addis Ababa agreed further to underwrite the litigation and to set up a steering committee to help the litigants. And, finally, Ethiopia and Liberia asked Gross to be their principal advocate—or, in World Court terminology, their agent. He accepted at once. "I felt privileged," he said later. "I felt that it would be the most important undertaking of my life, in or out of the government." He soon began to recruit associates, among them Edward Moore, the Under Secretary of State of Liberia, Nathan Barnes, the Liberian Ambassador to the U.N., Tesfaye Gebre-Egzy, then the Ethiopian Ambassador to the U.N. and later his country's Foreign Minister, Neville Rubin, a South African émigré living in London; and a shifting crew of American lawyers, the longest-lasting of whom, Gilbert Keith MacInnes Highet, had some prior acquaintance with Africa, having spent a year in Ghana teaching constitutional law and a summer holiday in Johannesburg.

The statute of the International Court of Justice divides the contentious proceedings that come before it into two parts— written and oral. The written part involves the successive filing by an Applicant of a Memorial, by a Respondent of a Counter-Memorial, by an Applicant of a Reply, and by a Respondent of a Rejoinder. There are provisions, however, for an intermediate round of exchanges. If, following the submission of a Memorial, the Respondent elects to raise some jurisdictional arguments, it may submit Objections, which in turn are answerable by Observations. The party that starts off this round robin of written pleadings has some problems. Should the Respondent choose not to answer a Memorial at all, the Court may issue a judgment on the basis of whatever facts are presented in that document, so a Memorial must contain enough of a prima facie case to give the judges something to mull over.

Ethiopia and Liberia made their intentions known to the Court on November 4, 1960, and the following April 15th Gross handed the Court two identical Memorials, one for each of his clients. Because there were twin briefs, the proceedings were formally and plurally named the South West Africa Cases. However, on May 20, 1961—just eleven days before South Africa changed *its* name, becoming a republic instead of a union—the Court joined the proceedings; thereafter the two Applicant nations were considered as one, which mainly meant, aside from the saving in duplication of documents, that they were entitled to but a single ad hoc judge between them.

For more than five years after the Memorials were filed, the Peace Palace—a somber agglomeration of marble floors, crystal chandeliers, stained-glass windows, and imperturbable judges—became a familiar setting, on and off, to all hands involved. When the Court is in session it sits for two and a half hours each morning. At ten o'clock sharp a tall usher marches in and cries *"La Cour!"* The judges emerge from their chambers, in solemn single file, and mount their impi-horn roost. They wear black robes and fancy lace bibs. The lawyers who appear before them are expected to wear the costume that would be suitable in the highest courts of their own countries. Thus the South African lawyers, a dozen strong, wore long black gowns and starched white bibs. Ernest Gross wore a morning coat and striped trousers. He also wore a vest; the Peace Palace is drafty, and while its radiators kept knocking promisingly, they rarely seemed to generate much heat. The whole atmosphere of the Court is old-worldly; when the oral proceedings came along, the verbatim transcript of each day's session would be delivered to the participants that evening by an elderly Dutchman on a motor scooter.

The courtroom can accommodate two hundred spectators, but it was rarely crowded. Japanese tourists would now and then stop by; when they did, they would exchange grave bows with their compatriot on the bench, Judge Kotaro Tanaka, who had formerly been Chief Justice of their Supreme Court. American Fulbright scholars in beards and sweatshirts were occasionally on hand, and from time to time a South West African exile would come and sit in rapt attention. The most faithful auditors, as the case went on, were the wives of the chief participants. The South African wives, who showed a strong partiality for Deanna Durbin-like turbans, gave the American wives the impression that they were shocked by the chatty rapport between Mrs. Highet, a very blonde American, and Mrs. Moore, a very dark Liberian.

A handful of journalists was likely to be present, but little of what they saw and heard ever reached print. The Applicants put out no press releases; the Respondent churned them out. Some of South Africa's handouts were nine legal-size pages long and read like briefs. They bore titles like "International Court Told of Calamitous Results of Alternative Policies in Africa," "South West Africa's Century of Bloodshed; How South Africa Brought Peace to War-Torn Territory"; "Alternative to Migratory Labour System is Misery and Chaos"; and "Motives Behind International Campaign Against South Africa; Communists Have Interest in Destruction of Bastion of Order and Security." Many of the releases hammered away at what South Africa deemed the low state of life in Ethiopia and Liberia. After dwelling on the high illiteracy rate of Liberia, for instance, one South African handout went on:

In the case of South West Africa, however, Liberia and Ethiopia take up the attitude that no account should be taken of factors which elsewhere have been considered of sufficient weight to affect the question of compulsory education. And, wonderful to relate, they see fit to offer solutions which they

195

themselves have not yet managed to solve and which, as South Africa has shown, are common and not easily solved in underdeveloped African countries having no tradition in modern education.

By the standards of this peculiar case, the Applicants' Memorials were fairly succinct; each ran to a mere hundred and sixty-nine printed pages. They concentrated on apartheid—"a deliberate and systematic process by which the Mandatory excludes the 'Natives' of the Territory from any significant participation in the life of the Territory except insofar as the Mandatory finds it necessary to use the 'Natives' as an indispensable source of common labor or menial service." There was much more:

The factual record of the Mandatory's conduct, as hereinafter more particularly set forth, has a desolate but remarkable consistency. Whatever segment or sector of the life of the Territory may be examined, the import of the facts is identical. Each part of the record supports and confirms every other part. The record as a whole supports and confirms the record in detail. Indeed, the record taken as a whole has an impact greater than that of a mere arithmetical sum of the several parts. The record as a whole reveals the deliberate design that pervades the several parts. . . .

Under apartheid, the status, rights, duties, opportunities and burdens of the population are fixed and allocated arbitrarily on the basis of race, color and tribe, without any regard for the actual needs and capacities of the groups and individuals affected. Under apartheid, the rights and interests of the great majority of the people of the Territory are subordinated to the desires and conveniences of a minority. . . .

It is an understatement to say that the Mandatory has violated its obligations. In its administration of the Mandate over the Territory of South West Africa, the Union, as Mandatory, has knowingly and deliberately violated the letter and spirit of the second paragraph of Article 2 of the Mandate and of Article 22 of the Covenant upon which Article 2 of the Mandate was based. In respect of its obligations thereunder, there is a polar disparity between the duties of the Union under the foregoing provision of the Mandate and its conduct in the administration thereof.

Nobody knew for seven months how South Africa would react to all that. Then, in November 1961, came enlightenment. The Respondent had chosen, as was its right, not to submit a Counter-Memorial at that time but instead to file Objections of a jurisdictional nature—two hundred and seven pages' worth of them. There were four principal arguments: First, the mandate had lapsed. Second, even if it hadn't there couldn't be any legal proceedings over it among members of the League of Nations, since there was no League of Nations. Third, the Court was supposed to adjudicate disputes, but there was no dispute about the South West Africa mandate, assuming that it still existed, that had anything to do with any Ethiopians or Liberians. Fourth, and finally, if there was a dispute it wasn't one that couldn't have been settled by negotiation before it came within the Court's purview.

It was at this stage that South Africa invoked Andrei Gromyko. Both litigants, before they were through, delved exhaustively into and quoted extensively from just about every available source that had the faintest conceivable relevance to the controversy; one of the minor gems later unearthed by the South Africans, who liked to twit the Applicants by describing them as "self-appointed protectors" of South West Africa, was a citation from a publication called *African Field Reports* that attributed to President Tubman of Liberia a fondness for the kind of two-level society that apartheid dictates. According to the quotation, the Liberian leader was reported to have "pointed to the necessity of having two sets of law, civil law taken from duress, and tribal law, and he cited arguments heard elsewhere in Africa, including South African reserves, concerning the benefit to all of this dual code . . ." When it came to Mr. Gromyko, South African research disclosed that in 1947, while the Security Council was debating a Polish amendment to a resolution about the one-time Japanese mandate over Micronesia, the Soviet diplomat had said, "There is no continuity, legal or otherwise, between the mandatory system of the League of Nations and the Trusteeship System laid down in the United Nations Charter. There is therefore nothing which might entitle the Security Council to discuss this question, let alone take any decisions on it. The mandatory system of the League of Nations is distinct from the Trusteeship System, which the United Nations is now trying to establish."

Mr. Gromyko's remarks were not especially germane to anything, the Court itself having ruled eleven years before the words were resurrected that South West Africa did not have to be administered within the Trusteeship system; but perhaps the Respondent wanted to give Judge Vladimir Koretsky, the Soviet member of the tribunal, some special food for private thought. Whatever profit South Africa may have reaped from the allusion to Mr. Gromyko may have been nullified when a witness for the Respondent subsequently blurted out, during cross-examination, that there were modern societies other than the one under discussion without political freedom. "Can you name one?" demanded Gross. The witness glanced toward Judge Koretsky on the bench and said, "No, I would prefer not to."

It took only four more months for the Applicants to prepare their Observations on the Respondent's Objections. The Observations said, *inter alia:*

Respondent's basic contention is the same as that submitted to the Court in 1950, and it suffers from the same fundamental defect: the inherently illogical and inequitable thesis that the Mandate lapsed with the dissolution of the League of Nations, relieving Respondent of its obligations under the Mandate instrument, yet at the same time leaving Respondent with all its rights and powers over the mandated territory, free of international accountability. . . .

Far from bestowing the right of annexation, the Mandate affirmatively imposes the duty to guide the people of the mandated territory toward political maturity which will enable them to determine their own political destiny. Such a duty is the very *raison d'être* of the Mandates System. As the Court stated in the Advisory Opinion, in regard to South West Africa, the principle of non-annexation was one of the two principles considered to be of "paramount importance"

198

in establishing the Mandates System. . . .
Either mandatories were permitted to annex mandated territories, or they were not. There was no provision for annexing the mandated territories just a little bit.

The stage was thus set for the Court's first formal ruling. It came on December 21, 1962, and it was one of those teeter-totter eight-to-seven verdicts (though that time fifteen individuals were involved) to which the Court is seemingly so partial. The majority ruled that South Africa's objections were "not well-founded." But several dissents were filed, one of them jointly written by Sir Percy Spender—who became president two years later—and by a British judge, Sir Gerald Gray Fitzmaurice, a veteran of international jurisprudence who had earlier helped draft the statute under which the International Court of Justice now operates.

The Spender-Fitzmaurice dissent of 1962 was ninety-eight prosy pages long, and it said, in part, that the co-signers didn't believe the Court should be getting into the South West Africa situation because this was a political rather than a legal matter. This was the same argument Sir Percy would be making in 1966: that, however members of the Court might feel about the moral issues involved, it was not their responsibility to usurp legislative functions and to make law, but rather merely to interpret law.

Only a year before the 1962 joint dissent, Sir Gerald Fitzmaurice, writing on his own, had contributed an article to the *British Yearbook of International Law* in which he said:

In the international field there is at present nothing comparable to a legislature, and the operation of the so-called law-making treaty is both uncertain and leaves many lose ends. The international community is therefore peculiarly dependent on its international tribunals for the development and clarification of the law . . .

Notwithstanding Sir Gerald's apparent divergence, in 1961, from Sir Percy's view of the situation in 1966, in 1962 the two of them were able to say together:

What the Court will principally be asked to decide on the merits is whether, in a number of different respects, the Re-

199

spondent State, as Mandatory, is in breach of its obligation under Article 2 of the Mandate to "promote to its utmost the material and moral well-being and the social progress of the inhabitants of the territory . . ." There is hardly a word in this sentence which has not now become loaded with a variety of overtones and associations. There is hardly a term which would not require prior objective definition, or redefinition, before it could justifiably be applied to the determination of a concrete legal issue. There is hardly a term which could not be applied in widely different ways to the same situation or set of facts, according to differing subjective views as to what it meant, or ought to mean in the context; and it is a foregone conclusion that, in the absence of objective criteria, a large element of subjectivity must enter into any attempt to apply these terms to the facts of a given case. They involve questions of appreciation rather than of objective determination. As at present advised we have serious misgivings as to the legal basis on which the necessary objective criteria can be founded.

The lawyers for Ethiopia and Liberia considered that dissenting paragraph critical, and much of their effort for the next three years was to be directed toward overcoming Sir Percy's and Sir Gerald's misgivings and to furnish them satisfactory objective criteria. At that time, though, what seemed far more important than the minority viewpoint was the outright dismissal, by the eight-judge majority, of all four of South Africa's jurisdictional arguments. There *was* a case, the majority ruled, and the case would continue, and—or so all concerned thought and continued to think for nearly four more years—would be resolved by the Court on its merits. Ethiopia and Liberia rejoiced at having scored an early tactical victory. On the other hand, an official of the South African government, which had been saying all along that the Court had no right to consider moral problems, acclaimed the interim defeat of his country as a moral victory for it.

Early in 1963 a South African legal staff one hundred and twenty strong began putting together the Counter-Memorial, which was to be the Respondent's major documentary exposition

200

of how it was promoting to the utmost the well-being and progress of the inhabitants of South West Africa. Concurrently, the
South African government appointed a five-man Commission of
Enquiry Into South West Africa Affairs. The group was directed
to inquire "into further promoting [the "further" must have
struck its author as a neat touch] the material and moral welfare
and social progress of the inhabitants of South West Africa, and
more particularly its non-White inhabitants."

The chairman of the Commission, all of whose members were
white, was the administrator of the Transvaal province, F. H.
Odendaal, who has died since, and the findings of the Commission that were published in the winter of 1964 became known as
the Odendaal Report. It was another massive tome—more than
six hundred large pages of small type—and it recommended the
expenditure of two hundred million dollars over a five-year period
to develop South West. Rivers were to be dammed to provide
power and irrigation, roads and airfields were to be built, and
bold agricultural reforms were to be instituted. But there was to
be no diminution of apartheid:

Where there are no significant differences between co-exist-
ing groups or nations, it might be sound and desirable to apply a policy calculated to wipe out the differences between
the groups, i.e. a policy of assimilation or complete socio-
economic integration. However, where, owing to fundamental differences in socio-economic orientation, stages of general development and ethnic classification, the differences between the groups concerned are of so profound a nature that
they cannot be wiped out, a policy of integration is unrealis-
tic, unsound, and undesirable, and cannot but result in con-
tinual social discrimination, discontent and frustration, friction and violence—a climate in which no socio-economic
progress can be expected to take place. Under such conditions the social cost in non-economic terms must outweigh
any possible economic advantages. In the circumstances it is
therefore desirable to accept the position as it is and not to
put idealism before realism. A policy of differentiation must
therefore be followed here, under which the various groups

201

are recognized and respected as the basic units of development, that is to say, a policy of protection and advancement of each population group.

Of the Odendaal Report's many recommendations, the principal one had to do with the redistribution of land. About half the usable acreage in South West belonged to white farmers; only a quarter of it had been allocated to Africans (and none of them individually owned a handful of dirt). The report proposed that Africans in the territory be segregated by ethnic groups, as they are officially destined to be within the Republic. To create these homelands, nearly a third of the hundred and sixty thousand non-Whites within the Police Zone were to be shunted to new areas. Some Whites would lose some land in the process; they were to end up with only 40 per cent of the usable soil, and the non-Whites with 44 per cent.

The proposal was not too burdensome on the Whites who would be displaced. Many of them had acquired their land very cheaply from the government in the first place, and now they were to be paid handsomely for it and, what was more, to be allowed to continue occupying it as tenants, at nominal rentals, until such time as non-Whites might be moved in. And there was no great rush about *that;* South Africa had no intention of implementing that section of the Odendaal Report while the South West Africa case was *sub judice.* (If it had tried, Ethiopia and Liberia were prepared to ask the Court for an injunction to halt it.) The non-Whites were to have no say in the matter; presumably some of them, had their views been solicited, would have demurred, inasmuch as a few of the homelands that were earmarked for them consisted almost exclusively of desert. Clemens Kapuuo told me in Windhoek that the Africans' reaction to the report was quite simple. "We reject it in its entirety," he said.

X

In May 1964 Prime Minister Verwoerd presented the Odendaal Report to the South African House of Assembly. "I issue this warning that anyone who tries to prevent the Government of South Africa from doing for South West what it wishes to do for all the people there," he said, "is playing into the hands of those who have their eyes and designs on Africa and on Southern Africa for the obvious reason of combating the West." One United Party M.P. expressed apprehension at Dr. Verwoerd's apparent determination to act unilaterally. "The matter we are dealing with here is the most delicate matter that we in this House will have to deal with while this Parliament is alive," he said.

Then the M.P. asked a National Party legislator, who was Deputy Minister for South West Africa Affairs, if he felt that the territory was already a *de facto* part of South Africa. When the Nat said, "Yes, I say it," the U.P. man came back with, "Well, Sir, I do not want to press the Deputy Minister on that. I shudder to think what repercussions such an irresponsible statement could have upon us, coming from the level from which it did come—deputy ministerial level—and the Honorable Prime Minister remains silent while it is made . . ." Parliament, to no one's surprise, approved the Odendaal Report, and over the next two years South Africa paid white farmers nearly $30,000,000 for 2,500,000 acres.

Meanwhile, on January 10, 1964, South Africa had submitted its Counter-Memorial to the Court. It comprised ten printed volumes totaling seventeen hundred pages and was accompanied by so many supporting documents that a furniture van was needed to deliver them all at once to the Peace Palace. One theme that the Counter-Memorial stressed was that the Applicants had accused South Africa of bad faith in exercising its mandate, and that unless bad faith could be proven, Ethiopia and Liberia would have failed in their suit. And the Court itself, the Counter-Memorial went on, was being dragged into the same old political plot that had so long roiled the chambers of the United Nations. As the South African advocate, David de Villiers, a Cape Town judge, would later enunciate that point (there was scarcely a point raised by either side that was not reiterated interminably), the Applicants were assigning to the Court

a most unworthy role . . . that of a revolutionary tribunal to aid and abet, and to rubber-stamp, the usurpation by the political majorities in international tribunals of legislative powers which have not been granted to them in the constitutive instruments or by the consent of the states who have created them.

The Counter-Memorial presented so much factual detail about South West Africa that in one agricultural section it included a statistical table showing the amounts of cream sold by Africans to creameries in the Police Zone from 1956 to 1959. Almost everyone who had ever had anything nice to say about South Africa's

204

administrative conduct was quoted. Among them was Allen Ellender, who was identified as a United States Senator, but not—although the biographical detail would have been pertinent—as a Senator from Louisiana. And there was a good deal of plain old-fashioned soapbox declamation in justification of the mandatory's policies:

If, without preconceived ideas about any policy, slogan, creed, dogma or philosophy, a solution is sought for the specific problem of South West Africa, what answers present themselves? Are the aims to be set at self-determination for the peoples of the Territory as a first priority, regardless of real ability on the part of some of them to "stand by themselves under the strenuous conditions of the modern world"? If so, would that not involve abandonment of one of the basic premises and objectives of the Mandate System? Could self-determination, in any just and equitable sense, be obtained by the expedient of artificially regarding the peoples of South West Africa as a unit, the majority of which must determine the future of the whole Territory and all its inhabitants? . . . Must the past and present contributions of the White population group in regard to economic and other development of the Territory, under circumstances where their presence for such purposes was necessary and encouraged, count for nothing in a form of "self-determination" which could flood their wishes and interests in a sea of African nationalism? Must the sacred trust, the protection of which will still be needed for a considerable time to come by the most primitive groups like the Bushmen, the Himba and the Tjimba, be abandoned and such groups left to their fate in what would amount to an experiment with, at best, an uncertain outcome? Such questions can be multiplied, but for present purposes the above should suffice. They illustrate how extremely complicated the problem is in the specific circumstances of South West Africa, and how utterly inappropriate the type of solutions found suitable in respect of other African territories.

"Constructive evolution," de Villiers would later say, was what South Africa was espousing; the alternative proposed by his country's antagonists was "disastrous revolution."

The Court gave the Applicants five months to prepare their answer to the Counter-Memorial. It must have taken them a fair amount of that time just to read it thoroughly. The Reply that Gross and his associates came up with, on June 20, 1964, was by comparison a slim production, only three hundred and ninety-six pages long. The Applicants had quickly perceived that it might be dangerous for them to have to try to prove bad faith. It is the sort of charge that does not readily lend itself to evidential substantiation. "Respondent's violations of the Mandate . . . do not turn upon the question of 'good or bad faith,' " Gross was thus at pains to declare, "or subjective motivation. Respondent," he went on,

is presumed to intend the reasonably predictable consequences of its acts. In this sense, intention is implicit in Respondent's conduct and Respondent has conducted itself with regard to the Territory in a manner consistent only with a Mandate the terms of which would be utterly incompatible with those of the Mandate in issue.

Nor should the Court be impressed, the Applicants argued, by South Africa's statements about education in South West Africa, as set forth in one 229-page volume of the Counter-Memorial:

This Court is not asked to decide to what extent compulsory education ought to be introduced for the "Native" children of the Territory, nor to what extent such a system ought to have been introduced in the past. Applicants submit, however, that the failure by Respondent to introduce any compulsory education, on any level, for any population other than the "European" is a manifest failure to promote the well-being or social progress of the inhabitants.

The main point was that "the policy and practice of apartheid is, *ipso facto,* a violation of international law." The core of the case, Gross insisted, was "the character and consequences of the policy of apartheid," under which, the Reply stated, "the accident of birth imposes a mandatory life sentence to discrimination, repression, and humiliation." There was no indication whether that use of "mandatory" was a conscious play on words.

In preparing the Reply, which the counsel for the Applicants regarded as their main accusatory document, Gross and his colleagues were especially mindful of the 1962 Spender-Fitzmaurice dissent. *Were* there objective criteria against which the conduct of the mandatory could be legally measured? Gross thought there certainly were, and on page 274 of the Reply, and for thirty succeeding pages, he zeroed in on them. His argument was that there existed an overwhelming corpus of universally accepted standards that pertained to the proper treatment by states of individuals— such as the 1920 League of Nations treaties concerning the rights of minority groups, the constitution of the International Labor Organization, the U.N. Charter, many General Assembly declarations on human rights, and further resolutions passed by such worldwide groups as the International Law Commission.

Furthermore, the Applicants went on, these standards had been so widely acknowledged that they had come to acquire the status of international law and had become what Gross called norms. Measured against these standards and norms, the Applicants concluded, apartheid could be said to belong to that outlaw category of human behavior that had theretofore sheltered three of civilization's most notorious villainies—piracy, slavery, and genocide. Later, during the oral proceedings, Gross was to put his line of thinking about standards into compact syllogistic form:

1. The major premise: International standards are accepted according to which racial discrimination is inherently and always incompatible with moral well-being and social progress.
2. As a minor premise: Apartheid is an extreme form of racial discrimination.
3. The conclusion: Apartheid is inherently and per se incompatible with the Mandate obligation to promote moral well-being and social progress, interpreted, as the obligation is to be interpreted, in the light of the applicable international standards, which is set out in the major premise.

207

The Respondent's lawyers, and the judges as well, seemed to share Gross's view that the arguments that began on page 274 of the Applicants' Reply were of particular significance, for from that moment on there were to be countless allusions to that page number, and to norms and standards, or "norms and/or standards," in the course of the proceedings. Sir Percy Spender, for instance, would observe from the bench that the Applicants had "anchored themselves" to page 274 of their Reply. Whether he meant that in his judgment they were stuck to it or stuck with it was—and in view of the Court's evasive action must presumably remain—anybody's guess.

South Africa's riposte to the Reply was a Rejoinder of one thousand eighty-two more pages that, *inter alia,* touched on some of the interracial aspects of contemporary life in the United States. The Respondent observed, with uncharacteristic understatement, "The [American] federal government's policy of nondiscrimination does not appear to have stimulated social integration between Negroes and Whites to any marked degree." And for the umpteenth time the Respondent favored the Court with its own analysis of apartheid:

In short, separate development is intended and calculated, negatively, to avoid the human tragedies which have occurred, and are occurring, in African territories such as the Congo, the Sudan, Rwanda, and others, as well as in the systems of ruthless dictatorship found necessary in so many other territories with a view to maintaining even a semblance of order. Positively, separate development envisages the establishment of a system of peaceful and friendly coexistence, based on mutual respect for one another's identity, culture, right to existence and human dignity, coupled with fruitful co-operation in matters of common concern. Attempted integration, on the other hand, involved inevitable injustice to minority groups—the highest and the least developed ones—inevitable retrogression in standards of economy and administration, and a very high degree of probability of a repetition of the human tragedies of other territories, or ruthless dictatorial rule, or both.

The usual mass of accompanying literature was filed with the Rejoinder. One item was the *Concise Oxford Dictionary of Current English*. It was just about the only time that conciseness figured in the South West Africa Cases.

On March 15, 1965, four years and four months after the proceedings began, the oral portion of them finally got under way. Many precedents in World Court history were established in this case. There was one that mid-March day when South Africa, *in camera,* raised a question "relating to the composition of the Court." It challenged the right to sit of Judge Padilla Nervo, of Mexico, who had been elected the year before. The apparent grounds for the Respondent's complaint were that while he had been his country's chief representative to the United Nations, Mexico had either sponsored or voted for several anti-South Africa resolutions in the General Assembly. Padilla Nervo was therefore conceivably biased. But of the twelve permanent judges then hearing evidence, seven had earlier participated in U.N. affairs in one capacity or another, Sir Percy of course among them. It would have been hard for the Court to consider prior U.N. service a cause for disqualification. Even so, the vote on that issue turned out to be another squeaker: eight to six (the two ad hoc judges rounding out the total) against South Africa.

The oral proceedings had hardly begun, *ex camera,* when South Africa tried to set another precedent. Only once before had the Court left its bench to make an *in loco* inspection, and then, in a dispute between Belgium and the Netherlands, it had got no farther from The Hague than the Belgian border. Now, the Respondent proposed that the judges, or any number of them they deemed sufficient, take a trip to South Africa and to South West to see for themselves what was going on there (the Respondent thought seeing would be enough—there was no reason for the judges to trouble themselves by asking anybody any questions); and, while they were at it, to visit Ethiopia, Liberia, and one or two other African states so they could compare well-being and progress in the one part of the continent with well-being and progress in the others. African reality, de Villiers argued, had to be seen to be appreciated.

In a sense, South Africa was reversing its position; it had said at the United Nations, more than once, that there was no need for outsiders to inspect its sovereign soil. Ernest Gross, for his part, had thought at the time he prepared his 1960 memorandum of law for Liberia that if the Court could get pertinent facts about South West Africa in no other way, maybe it ought to appoint a board of inquiry to go there. Now, in 1965, he too switched; the Court, he said, had all the facts that were necessary, and to take time off for a firsthand investigation would be fruitless and dilatory. There was still another factor, to which Gross tactfully did not allude: the average age of the twelve permanent judges was sixty-eight, and it seemed likely to some of the spectators at the Peace Palace that a few of the members of the Court not only couldn't stand a long journey but might not even stand up under antecedent inoculative shots.

Not until toward the end of the oral proceedings would the Court reply to South Africa's invitation; then the answer was negative. Back in Cape Town, *Die Burger* commented editorially that South Africa had

> wanted to open doors and let the light shine through into all corners. The fact that South Africa was willing to lay bare everything in South West Africa to a personal investigation by the World Court will in future remain a weapon in her hand when she is again accused of perpetrating underhanded dealings there which cannot stand the light of day. And when the World Court gives its final judgment next year, its responsibility will be all the greater because the proposed investigation did not take place.

Die Burger had evidently figured its country didn't have a chance in Court.

A few weeks after de Villiers had startled all concerned with his proposal of a novel kind of African safari, the South Africans professed to be equally startled by what they came to insist was a major change in the charges against them. This occurred when Gross declared that averments of fact submitted to the Court by the Respondent "may be treated as if incorporated by reference into the Applicants' pleadings." He qualified this statement, to be sure, by saying that the facts he was talking about—he had in

210

mind the texts of pass laws, job-registration laws, antiunion ordinances, and other official guidelines of apartheid—had to be "relevant to its [the Applicants'] contentions of law," but his caveat was brushed aside by his opponents, who began and continued to announce trumpetingly, both in and out of the courtroom, that Ethiopia and Liberia had acknowledged as fact all of South Africa's voluminous written submissions. Not only had *that* changed the case, said the Respondent, but so had the Applicants' disinclination to press charges of bad faith. Time and again, de Villiers played resounding variations on the changed-case theme, as when he told the Court:

> The abandonment of that charge of oppression, and the admission of the true facts which so abundantly refute that charge, had a very important practical effect on the Respondent's position, Mr. President, because that had the effect of clearing the Respondent's name of these charges, at least before this Court, and to a large extent before the whole world, if only the world will get to know about it, because, if I may say by way of parenthesis, that, with commendable exceptions, it does not seem as if the press of the world is, in general, keen to inform the world of these extremely important developments in this case . . .

After four more months of harangues, exhortations, orations, and perorations by the opposing advocates, still another World Court innovation got under way: the presentation of witnesses. In the past the Court had on rare occasions heard live testimony, as when in 1962 a geomorphologist gave oral evidence on terrain features while the Court was weighing the rival claims of Thailand and Cambodia to the Temple of Preah Vihear, which lay on their joint border. (Cambodia got the judicial nod.) In the South West Africa Cases the Applicants had resolved from the start not to produce witnesses. There were plenty of South West African exiles available who would have been glad to speak up against apartheid and its applicability to well-being and progress, but Gross and his associates felt that to put them on the stand—and thus, of course, to expose them to cross-examination—might have had little legal effect and might have led to a supercharged emo-

211

tional atmosphere in the courtroom. South Africa, however, had every intention of bringing in witnesses. It wanted to let the judges see for themselves that, in addition to their ad hoc colleague Mr. van Wyk and the de Villiers contingent, there were other men who believed in and practiced apartheid who did not look like ogres but like decent, rational, clean-cut human beings.

At first Gross tried informally to dissuade his opponents from carrying out this plan. He considered witnesses of any guise unnecessary; the international norms and standards in which he had embedded the anchor of his argument seemed to him impervious to what anyone might say. Later, as the parade of South African witnesses materialized and he began to cross-examine them, he changed his thinking. He concluded that the Respondent's witnesses were helping *him*. As he told the Court, "The witnesses brought to life in the courtroom the impact upon individual human beings of an official policy of racial discrimination in which, and according to which, inhabitants are classified by inexorable fiat as either non-European or European, as either White, or Native, or Colored, or Asiatic."

It might be worth noting that at no time in the proceedings, despite hours of rhetoric addressed to the specific point, were the two sides able to agree on a definition of "discrimination." But then they scarcely ever agreed on anything, a state of affairs that was exemplified by one remark of Gross's through which the judges had to pick their way:

As has been said, and must be assumed as an axiomatic premise, the Parties to the present proceedings share in common a desire to assist the Court in respect of any measures or procedures the Court may conclude to be helpful to such an adjudication. It is on the basis of such an assumption that the Applicants have confessed difficulty in understanding Respondent's earlier reference to the difficulty alleged to be perceived by Respondent with respect to our position on the matter.

The American member of the Court, Judge Phillip K. Jessup, may have been harking back to that sort of thing when in his dissent he referred to "a semantic swamp in which the argument frequently bogged down."

There were forty witnesses in South Africa's original roster. The list was eventually pared down to fourteen; the Respondent's given reason was that inasmuch as the Applicants had changed their case and conceded all its facts, so large a number would be supererogatory. Of the fourteen, only one was a resident of South West Africa. He was Kurt Dahlmann, the German-born editor of Windhoek's *Allgemeine Zeitung.* During cross-examination, over loud South African objections, Gross extracted from him the admission that in his youth he had belonged to the Hitler Youth. Eight witnesses were South Africans, and their testimony dealt more with their own country than with its mandated territory. Gross was delighted at this geographical turn of events. "This was putting apartheid on the line," he said afterward.

There was a second journalist among the witnesses. He was the editor of *Die Burger,* Piet C. Cillié. South Africa wanted to put on one witness who could talk knowledgeably about the nation's politics. Dr. Verwoerd would, of course, have been the one with the most formidable credentials. But to the men who were mapping the Respondent's strategy it seemed unwise to expose a prime minister to the barbs and thrusts of cross-examination. And any lesser government official might have seemed a mere mouthpiece. So Cillié was chosen. He is one of his country's most urbane and articulate Afrikaners, although, being a Capetonian, he is sometimes thought by the Nationalists of the Transvaal province to harbor excessively liberal leanings. (He once said to me, in Cape Town, "I sometimes think that the reason the rest of the world attacks us is that it can't bear looking at itself.") On the stand at The Hague, Cillié described his paper's relationship to the government as

a sort of marriage in which the partners never really think in terms of divorce but do think sometimes in terms of murder. . . . I don't think we have ever differed to an extent that would have given our persecutors any sort of comfort because the differences were always directed to better implementation, better and wiser implementation of the basic policy, to which we are utterly committed.

213

To a question about apartheid from Sir Percy, the editor responded:

You see, if you could strip the policy of all its side issues, I do think that you would find that it is the vast majority of the South African Whites who would support the basic principles of the policy, but there are arguments about implementation and there are different nuances. There are, in fact, also white people who do believe in a policy of integration. It is very difficult in politics to get an exact division; the issues are not always posed very clearly, they get muddled up.

"I am aware of that," the President of the Court replied.

Among the other South Africans who put in an appearance were a vice-chairman of the synod of the Dutch Reformed Church; a number of economists and educators, one of them the author of a book on games Northern Sotho people play; and one of five members of the Odendaal Commission. He was Johannes Petrus van Schalkwyk Bruwer, a minister and social anthropologist, whose basic language was Afrikaans but who acknowledged from the stand also a proficiency in Zulu, Nyanja, Nsenga, Kunda, Kuanyama, Ndonga, and Kuangari. To help the Court, he testified in English.

Dr. Bruwer, who probably knew as much about South West as any white man anywhere, was killed in a plane crash in March, 1967. He had first gone to the territory in 1954, and had served as Commissioner-General for Bantu Affairs. But he had quit that post because of a growing feeling that his government was less concerned about Africans' welfare there than in its own strategic interests. In 1966, a few months before his death, he brought out a book about South West Africa in which he said that the problem of South West Africa was twofold: the outside world was too far away to understand it, and the South African authorities on the scene were too close—not to mention being in some cases ignorant and incompetent.

On the witness stand he made no such concessions. In justification of apartheid and the proposed reshuffling of the population of South West, he explained that it would be just as intolerable for

214

Whites to encroach on lands reserved for non-Whites as it would be for natives to encroach on lands reserved for Whites. He himself had fleetingly entertained the notion, he said, of living in Ovamboland when he retired, but he wouldn't and couldn't do that because he'd have to get a house and that would require land and that would be encroaching.

Of the five non-South African witnesses, one was a British professor of international law, C. A. W. Manning, whom Gross had known slightly since 1931, when they met at the International School of Studies at Geneva. As young students they were trying to find a common approach to international law. In thirty-three years they had conspicuously failed: while Gross was preparing his aggressively antiapartheid Reply, Manning was writing "In Defense of Apartheid" for *Foreign Affairs*.

The other four men who testified in defense of apartheid were Americans. One was S. L. A. Marshall, the military historian, who confined himself pretty much to a refutation of a charge that South Africa, in violation of the League mandate, had fortified South West. The other three were professors. One of them, Ernest van den Haag, a Dutch-born naturalized American now teaching social philosophy at New York University, got into a jam when he testified that some of the anti-Jim Crow documentation accepted by the United States Supreme Court during the Brown v. Board of Education case had, in his blunt word, been faked; under pressure from Sir Percy, he retracted the allegation and ate crow.

Perhaps the most interesting of all the Americans was Richard F. Logan, a professor of geography at the University of California and an internationally recognized authority on arid zones. Professor Logan likes to testify for South Africa. When a U.S. House subcommittee began a series of hearings on that country in the spring of 1966 he went out of his way to get an invitation to appear. He told the congressmen that by his lights the bulk of South Africans enjoyed liberty. "The locking up of people has been—as far as I am aware—primarily because these people were Communists or were considered to be Communists," he said. Professor Logan had been to South West Africa three times before the World Court case began. He was there when the oral proceedings got under way at The Hague, and in describing his departure from the territory for the *Windhoek Advertiser,* he said, "I went off to protect world peace."

On his return to Windhoek he addressed the local Rotary Club about the court case. The *Advertiser* headlined its account of the occasion with "IF S.A. WINS WORLD CASE, 'ALL HELL' WILL BREAK LOOSE." Professor Logan told the Rotarians that Ernest Gross was "an impractical idealist" who "was not adept at cross-examination." South Africa's lawyers at the Court were far abler, he said; he would not have liked to have been cross-examined by one of *them.* These and other remarks he made about the litigation, which was then still *sub judice,* prompted Windhoek's leading attorney, Israel Goldblatt, to write to the *Advertiser.* A gentle, learned, man, born in London in 1897, Goldblatt has been a permanent resident of South West since 1920, the same year the controversial mandate began. He has in recent years given some legal advice to the territory's Africans. He never charges them fees, but some of his German neighbors, possibly because his name is Goldblatt, have accused him of getting rich at the expense of his black clients. In his letter to the paper Goldblatt said that Logan, not being a lawyer, couldn't possibly know what he was talking about and that, being a foreigner, he shouldn't have talked where he did in the first place, because he "should appreciate that propriety dictates that he should not interfere in the domestic affairs of this territory whether as a protagonist of the South African Government or otherwise."

Gross, for his part, was quite satisfied with his cross-examination of Logan. It was the Applicants' lawyer's contention throughout that South Africa's mandatory practices were inadmissible if under them a single individual could be shown to have been deprived, because of his racial categorization, of the rights, duties, and privileges that any other individual enjoyed. And had not Logan said under questioning that "in some cases it is necessary to jeopardize the absolute happiness of a certain very small proportion . . . in order that the set of circumstances, the set of conditions, and the set of plans be allowed to operate"? Had he not said, too, with respect to the Western-world concept of governmental concern for the dignity of the individual, "I am not thoroughly convinced that our Western way of life is absolutely

216

ideal"?

For twenty-eight days in all, Gross pounded away at South Africa's witnesses. He elicited from the vice-chancelor of the University of Pretoria the statement that an African family that had lived nowhere else but in white man's land for three or four unbroken generations could nonetheless be said to be entitled to no residential rights there but was, instead, "sojourning." From Dr. Bruwer, the social anthropologist who'd served on the Odendaal Commission, Gross drew the admission that a black South West African who had been born and raised in white man's land had no recourse against the restrictions imposed on him there, because of his color, other than to "escape."

Concentrating on the rights, or nonrights, of individual Africans, Gross asked witness after witness what each thought about the plight of a hypothetical African he concocted. This was a man who had somehow managed to become trained as an engineer. He couldn't work in the white zone of South West because of the apartheid laws, and in the native reserves, where he could work, there were no openings for engineers. What was he to do? Were his well-being and progress being promoted—at all, let alone to the utmost? Or was he doomed to suffer forever under what Gross called the "doctrine of inevitable frustration"?

The first witnesses seemed to Gross to be so flustered by the dilemma of his engineer that all the Applicants' lawyers became very fond of him. He figured more and more importantly in their private discussions. They even gave him a name—Tom. While mapping their strategy prior to cross-examination of a new witness, they would say to one another, "Let's take Tom off the bench today and throw him into action." *In* court one morning, Gross got so carried away with his imaginary frustrated engineer that while cross-examining one witness about this character the lawyer interposed, "Let's say his name is Thomas." One of the American's associates had to repress a snort.

Tom appeared to be so effective to his progenitors that they thereupon invented a sister character—an African nurse named Sister Teresa who was similarly frustrated because, by decree of apartheid, she was not allowed, no matter how skilled she might be professionally, to give orders to white nurses, except in dire

217

emergencies. How could a situation like *that*, Gross demanded of the witnesses, promote to the utmost the moral and material well-being and the social progress of any human individual? By the time Gross had finished with all the witnesses, he was elated. "We've extracted the anatomy of apartheid out of the mouths of its own witnesses!" he told a friend.

Gross's exultation was dampened, if not drenched, on July 18, 1966, when the World Court announced its verdict. Practically everybody, in and out of South Africa, had expected the Applicants to win some kind of decision. When they didn't, the bars in Windhoek stayed open all night. The U. S. State Department had no immediate reaction. It couldn't; all the statements it had prepared in advance had been predicated on the Court's ruling, in one fashion or another, against South Africa. (Our Ambassador to South Africa had publicly declared there, shortly before the announcement by the Court, that he hoped all parties would be bound by its decision, no matter what happened; South Africans are still reminding him of that.) The majority of the Court—two Sir Percy Spenders, that was, and six of his thirteen confrères—ruled that Ethiopia and Liberia had no standing to have their charges against South Africa adjudicated. In his closing arguments for the Respondent, Advocate de Villiers had dwelt at length on every conceivable point he could dredge up to bolster his country's case, but he never even mentioned the Applicants' right to have their case considered on its merits. Everybody thought *that* had been settled back in 1962.

But now the Court had reversed itself. It wasn't that any judge had changed his mind. It was just that illness and nonparticipation and the replacement of a judge from Egypt by one from France had combined to change a 1962 minority into (counting Sir Percy twice) a 1966 majority. The majority's line of thinking was summarized in a brief excerpt from its opinion: "Throughout this case it has been suggested, directly or indirectly, that humanitarian considerations are sufficient in themselves to generate legal rights and obligations, and that the Court can and should proceed accordingly. The Court does not think so." Individual states like the Applicants, Sir Percy added, had never—not even back in the

218

League days—had the right, as he put it, "to invigilate the sacred trust"; as far as he was concerned, *actio popularis,* however high a repute it might enjoy in this or that country's domestic legal system, had no place in international law.

There were seven negative votes and seven dissenting opinions. The Soviet Judge Koretsky observed that "the 'door' to the Court which was opened in 1962 to decide the dispute . . . was locked by the Court with the same key which had opened it." (Judge Koretsky became the Court's Vice-President in 1967; Sir Percy's successor as President was Judge J. L. Bustamante y Rivero, of Peru, the judge who had been ill. Since he'd been unable to vote, he ended up in nobody's bad graces.) The American Judge Jessup said that the verdict was "completely unfounded in law." He castigated the majority for "stopping at the threshold of the case" and said that its judgment that while Ethiopia and Liberia had the right to institute proceedings they weren't entitled to a decision on them "suggests a procedure of utter futility." In what he pointedly stated was his first dissent from the majority in five years on the Court, Judge Jessup continued, rhetorically, "Why should any State institute any proceeding if it lacked standing to have judgment rendered in its favor if it succeeded in establishing its legal and factual contentions on the merits? Why would the Court tolerate a situation in which the parties would be put to great trouble and expense to explore all the details of the merits, and only thereafter to be told that the Court would pay no heed to all their arguments and evidence because the case was dismissed on a preliminary ground which precluded any investigation of the merits?"

When Mr. de Villiers and the other lawyers who represented South Africa at The Hague returned home, they were welcomed at the Johannesburg airport as few attorneys can have been before anywhere. A flag-waving crowd of several hundred assembled and greeted them with cheers, prayers, and hymns. De Villiers, who had been a respected but not nationally celebrated judge before the litagation, became a chief spokesman for his country at the next session of the U.N. General Assembly. The University of South Africa announced it would set up an international-law center and name it after another South African advocate, who died while arguing for

219

his country at The Hague. Prospective contributors in South West were told of "the opportunity to pay grateful tribute to the work done for us . . . and to help safeguard our future. . . ." Citizens of Windhoek swiftly came through with a kick-off gift of forty-five thousand dollars. The vice-chairman of the Dutch Reformed synod was promoted to moderator. Professor Bruwer was installed as vice-chancelor of a new university at Port Elizabeth. The ad hoc justice, Judge van Wyk, returned home by ship. Prime Minister Vorster, then still Minister of Justice, went out on a cutter to welcome him. When the ship docked an Immigration man tried to detain Mr. Vorster because he hadn't taken along the right identification papers. "Is this a police state?" Mr. Vorster asked, in a variation on his favorite much-used quip.

Ernest Gross, once he could speak again, said to a friend, "Well, I think we've all helped the World Court grow. It will never be the same again." It probably won't. For some years to come, certainly, it will be hard for the Court to command much respect or attain much effectiveness. The venerable institution at The Hague may prove useful, in its way, for resolving small disagreements between nations, like the Minquiers and Ecrehos Case it handled with dispatch a few years back. That was a dispute between England and France about sovereignty over two tiny Channel islands with toothsome oyster beds, and the Court boldly declared for Britain. There were no repercussions. The repercussions from its failure to declare much of anything about South Africa will, like the English Channel's waves, long be rippling.

The jubilation in South Africa was not, however, untempered. An editorial in the *Johannesburg Star,* for instance, observed:

South West Africa as a stalking-horse for the opponents of apartheid and white rule has probably lost its value for ever. These great issues are firmly back where they belong in their broad South African context. Their focal point is Pretoria, not Windhoek. The onslaught will continue; the flank attack has failed.

The consequences will be far-reaching. The strategy of the campaign has shifted to ground which South Africa, due to its great economic strength, has found favourable. It has won time, time to wrestle with its great problems and its own conscience. South West Africa, the least suitable territory in Africa to be cast into the uncertain seas of international politics, was always a phoney issue, a marginal note in the documentation of African affairs.

The Court has erased it and sent its petitioners back to their studies of the real problems that confront them—and us.

Had the World Court decided against South Africa and ordered that country to do something, and had South Africa refused, or dilly-dallied, the Security Council might or might not have tried to enforce the order. As it was, of course, the South West Africa question was thrown right back into the lap of the General Assembly, where it had so often squirmed before. This gave a number of Afro-Asian nations, at the Assembly session that began in September 1966, a chance to take their own action. (While they were at it, they hit back at the Court, declining to augment its budget by $72,500—a sum it had already spent to defray the unusually heavy costs of the South West litigation.) On October 27 the Assembly overwhelmingly adopted Resolution 2145 (XXI)— South Africa and Portugal voting against it, the United Kingdom abstaining along with one of South Africa's small neighbors, Malawi. Two even closer and smaller neighbors, Botswana and Lesotho, were discreetly absent.

The resolution terminated the mandate and also set up a fourteen-member Ad Hoc Committee for South West Africa, which was instructed to "recommend practical means by which South West Africa should be administered, so as to enable the people of the Territory to exercise the right of self-determination and to achieve independence, and to report to the General Assembly at a special session as soon as possible and in any event not later than April, 1967."

The General Assembly had given the committee only a little over five months to report; it took nearly half that time just to form the group, which finally met on January 17. There were four African members—Ethiopia, Nigeria, Senegal, and the United Arab Republic. Once under way, these nations wanted to move fast. On January 24 they proposed that there be no further debate after January 27. Eventually, after prolonged debate well beyond that date, the African quartet recommended that the U.N. move right into South West, backed by an international police force, and that South West be granted independence not later than June 1968.

There were two other proposals. The United States was for deferring everything at least until the following fall and for holding consultations with the "existing governmental structure"—i.e., the incumbent government of South Africa, whose mandate America had already declared nonexistent. When the committee's report was finally published, on April 7, it was an astonishing document. It had no majority recommendation at all; it merely listed the proposals its factions had put forth.

Throughout the Ad Hoc Committee's inconclusive cerebrations, the government of South Africa seemed fairly unperturbed. Prime Minister Verwoerd had long before put it on record that his country was prepared to fight to the death against any international invasion. As for another possibility that had aroused speculation—an assault from the north of the continent by some combination of African nations—Prime Minister Vorster declared brusquely, "We can deal with them before breakfast." Mr. Vorster had also hinted from time to time that rather than put up with the U.N. any longer ("a so-called peace organization," *he* called it), South Africa might just pull out of it. (One Supreme Court judge in South Africa added his pinch of flavoring to the simmering pot by asserting that South Africa had never belonged to the U.N. in the first place, because of a technicality involving the manner in which Jan Smuts ratified the organization's charter at San Francisco in 1945.) Notwithstanding, the government in Pretoria—for the first time since 1947—submitted a report to the U.N. on its stewardship in the territory. It emphasized that this was a voluntary submission. The document ran to one hundred and ninety tightly packed pages, and there was hardly anything in it that, in one form or another, South Africa had not made public before.

Meanwhile, in South West itself, there had been considerable evidence of South Africa's determination not to leave the place.

222

In the spring of 1964, while the wrangling at The Hague was in full swing, the government had unveiled a new administration building at Windhoek, containing a handsome chamber for the territory's all-white Legislative Assembly. An opening-day brochure quoted the South West's Administrator as saying that the building was constructed with an eye to the future. Concurrently, South West officially adopted a new coat of arms, sporting a Welwitschia plant, a German eagle, various local animals, and the motto "Viribus Unitis."

Following the World Court's decision, in fact, South Africa tightened its grip on the territory. Until the summer of 1966, non-white political parties, which no longer exist in the Republic, had been tolerated in the territory. Clemens Kapuuo is the head of one, called the National Unity Democratic Organization, for which he claims twenty thousand members. True, many of the African leaders were in exile, but their groups continued to function after a fashion. (There were no elections for them to participate in.) And before the Court decision, the Republic's detention laws had not been applied to the territory. In the fall of 1966 they were, and among the first to be imprisoned, under the catchall Suppression-of-Communism Act, were three leaders of the South West African Peoples Organization, or SWAPO, and one of the South West African National Union, or SWANU.

The South African government has related these arrests to a fairly recent flurry of restlessness in Ovamboland, which has a common border with both Angola and Botswana, and into which outsiders can readily infiltrate. More than fifty of *them* have been arrested in the last couple of years. The government calls them "terrorists," and says that some it has captured or killed have been armed with Soviet-made weapons. That is quite likely; there is no doubt that many Africans in exile from South West, like their counterparts from the Republic, are hoping to have a chance some day to invade their one-time homeland and are in training for that specific purpose. In December 1966, an émigré SWAPO leader, Sam Nojuma, wrote to the *Windhoek Advertiser* from Lusaka, in Zambia; he said that SWAPO was in the forefront of the infiltrators' skirmishes with the South African police in Ovamboland. His boast from that sanctuary may not have been of much help to

223

any SWAPO men the police may have had suspicions about within the territory.

There are probably training camps for revolutionaries in Ovamboland itself. Nojuma, a burly, black-bearded firebrand who, like most SWAPO members, is an Ovambo, has said that he commands an army of four thousand who are ready to fight at his word. A liberated and independent South West Africa would, if his views prevail, be known as Namibia, and the broadsides that SWAPO periodically issues from his base at Dar es Salaam, in Tanzania, refer pointedly to the proceedings at The Hague as the Namibia Case. (SWAPO, however, has not changed its name to NAPO.) Until recently few outsiders had much of an idea what was actually going on within Ovamboland. The South African government, as part of its implementation of the Odendaal plan, has built a five-hundred-bed hospital in Ovamboland and has embarked on an airstrip- and road-building program (Sam Cohen has six subcontractors in the area), but aside from the hospital no one can figure out what all the construction has been for. The Ovambos do not much use cars or airplanes, and the new transportation facilities are widely thought to be strategically motivated. In any event, Ovamboland has long been a closed community. The late Dr. Bruwer invited me to go there with him in December 1966, and I accepted. But no White can visit Ovamboland without a permit, and when I applied for one the government told me that Dr. Bruwer had changed his plans. I never heard from him again before he was killed in the plane crash.

In the winter of 1967, with the Ad Hoc Committee in session, the South African government made two unusual moves. It invited diplomats from U.N. countries accredited to it to visit Ovamboland (only those from Portugal, The Netherlands, and Rhodesia were quick to accept), and it offered Ovamboland a chance to determine its own political future. The Ovambos—numbering nearly half of all the non-Whites in South West—were told, through a gathering of their chiefs and headmen, that they could have complete independence, if they wanted it, or "some other relationship with other nations." To what degree, if any, South Africa had in mind the Ovambos' maintaining a relationship with itself or with the rest of South West Africa was not made clear. South Africa prob-

224

ably visualized a Bantustan like the Transkei. This might not sit too well with the Portuguese, who control the Ovambos in Angola, for Portugal has never practiced apartheid. The proposal did at least give the Ad Hoc Committee its one opportunity to achieve unanimity; all its members said that the Ovamboland scheme was a violation of another provision of the General Assembly's Resolution 2145 (XXI), which had enjoined South Africa "forthwith to refrain and desist from any action, constitutional, administrative, political, or otherwise, which will in any manner whatsoever alter or tend to alter the present international status of South West Africa."

In Windhoek the Burgomeister, with the cooperation of the Territorial Administration, has been proceeding briskly with plans to construct a handsome new permanent municipal building. At the United Nations the special session of the General Assembly to hear the report of the Ad Hoc Committee met in the spring of 1967 and voted, eighty-five to two, to establish an eleven-nation council to take over South West on its behalf. The method of doing this was conspicuously omitted. South Africa and Portugal predictably voted against the resolution; this time thirty nations abstained, including Russia, Great Britain, and the United States.

It wasn't until June 13, 1967, a month after the resolution passed, that enough countries could be rounded up to serve on the council, and three of those that were—Indonesia, Nigeria, and the United Arab Republic—hardly seemed promising as progenitors of stability. (The council proceeded to do absolutely nothing, which didn't much bother South Africa; it had no intention of giving the new group the time of day.) By June 13, in any event, the Middle East crisis had begun, and nobody was paying much attention to South West Africa. After all, the United Nations is supposed to be principally a peace-keeping organization, and it is hard to demonstrate, in or out of a courtroom, that South Africa's administration of its mandate has constituted a serious threat to the peace of the world. The impact, if any, of South West Africa on the world's conscience is, of course, another matter. And who knows what might happen by the year 2000?

XI

Shortly before I set forth to South Africa, I met a businessman from there who was living in the United States. He asked me how long I expected to stay in his country. About three months, I said. "You'll have a good time if you forget about politics," he said. It was as if he had told Commander Peary to forget about snow and ice.

As a rule, the best way for most visitors to South Africa to escape its politics is to stop talking and listening to its people and to commune instead with its magnificent scenery or, even more distractingly, its magnificent animals. South Africans do that, too. Thousands upon thousands of them annually beat a path to their Kruger National Park, of which they are understandably proud. By and large, they are not a complaining sort, as their leaders are happily aware, but many of them protested loudly when, a couple of years ago, the government started to pave the Park's main roads. The citizenry thought this might inhibit the animals' freedom of movement.

Wild-animal watching, though, does not always guarantee immunity from political discussion. I was up a tree on night in a game reserve just outside Kruger, watching two lionesses sup on a haunch of zebra, when a man alongside me got to meditating aloud about the dilemma of contemporary white South Africans. He and I had spent a long day together, gazing respectfully at, among other species, giraffe, zebra, warthog, waterbuck, kudu, duiker, baboon, klipspringer, Bartlow eagle, mongoose, bush pheasant, ostrich, guinea fowl, hornbill, impala, vulture, hippopotamus, and squirrel. As a starter, we had arisen at daybreak to board a stripped Land Rover and head out cross country in search of white rhinoceros. In view of the importance attached in South Africa to the precise usage of words relating to color, one feels obliged to explain that a white rhinoceros is called that not because of the color of its skin, which is dark gray, but because of confusion resulting from the Afrikaans word for "wide," *wyd;* the beast has big, square lips.

Our driver, who was both white and square-lipped, was a textbook white hunter—born in India, where his grandfather had commanded a celebrated British regiment; professional tiger hunter there when the maharajahs still swayed regally in their howdahs; gentleman farmer in Kenya, later, through all that Mau Mau bother; rejected, on grounds of age, as a member of Colonel Mike Hoare's South African volunteers in the Congo; now ferrying chaps like me around, and turning up at dinner, in our rustic lodge, impeccable in jacket and tie. When he heard I was from America, he was quick to express his regrets that Barry Goldwater hadn't made it.

With the help of a sharp-eyed and keen-eared African who clung to the rear of our vehicle, our spruce guide steered us straight to—almost on a collision course with—a couple of satisfying white rhinos. One that must have weighed three tons seemed to be contemplating a closer inspection of us when he was only fifty feet away. Our hunter stopped him by coughing. (I had spent the previous five minutes suppressing a cigarette cough, never dreaming it might be a deterrent.) Then we bumped across a stretch of scrubby veldt and halted near some eland. The white hunter asked me if I had any sweets. We'd started out at five-fifteen, and it was now nearly seven, and we'd had no breakfast. I thought he was hungry, and offered him one of two oranges I'd brought along. "No, not for me, for the eland," he said.

Somewhat hesitantly, I extended an orange-bearing hand toward the big animal, which came loping up, its foot-and-a-half-long pointed horns looming larger with each stride. The eland gobbled the orange and then tried to climb into my lap. I wouldn't have minded too much except that he was sprinkled with ticks. I began to count them while he nuzzled my shirt, presumably seeking more sweets. "He looks as though he's learning to butt," said the white hunter, and started up his engine. The eland backed off, reproachfully. I coughed.

That was as close to a supposedly wild South African animal as I got, and it was close enough. On the tree platform, later, peering down while the lionesses tore at the zebra, I was glad to be out of nuzzling range. We had hoped for a male lion, too, but there seemed to be a shortage. A fierce and richly maned old paterfamilias, whose picture adorned the cover of a brochure put out by the place at which I was staying, had wandered off into a neighboring estate not long before, where shooting was permitted, and had been gunned down. The proprietors of my establishment were quite miffed.

It takes a long time to watch lions eat. While we were staring at them and munching cold impala-venison sandwiches ourselves, the man next to me, who was in mining, got to talking about race relations. He was concerned that I should understand the peculiar situation of South Africa's three million Whites, who I had already agreed with him are probably the most powerful, most prosperous, and most picked-on minority group on earth. "I guess the best way to describe us," my companion said, "is as survivalists. People will do almost anything to survive, even if it means submitting to a touch of totalitarianism."

Dr. Verwoerd used to talk along much the same lines. "The issue at stake is the self-preservation of a nation—nothing more,

228

nothing less," he said in 1963. "It is also the self-preservation of each individual member of this white nation. . . . The Whites in South Africa can see clearly what is expected of them. Whatever the cost, they must continue to survive." There was no doubt that the sharer of my platform, like his former prime minister, thought that the white inhabitants of the Republic were the fittest to survive, and of course—considering that they control the country's resources and weapons and have been the brains if not the brawn behind its vaulting economic growth—they may well be.

He went on for a while about the difficulty of being a white African on a nonwhite continent (when white South Africans describe themselves as a part of Africa they often take pains to say "inseparable part"), and then he stopped. The lionesses, sated, had drifted away in the dark, and after an interval of reconnaissance a hyena had slunk into the clearing beneath us and was having at the zebra. The way that poor zebra carcass was being savaged by all sorts of nonzebras drove my man into brooding silence.

The white South Africans have good reason to be perturbed. Not only are they outnumbered by five to one in their own country, but the rest of their continent has begun to march, and they often seem dismally out of step. In the spring of 1967 Mrs. Helen Suzman said, in Parliament, "We seem to work in a closed circuit, forgetting about the big world outside . . . while we live in a world two-thirds of which is colored, in a country in which we are a small minority and at the foot of a continent on which there are two hundred million nonwhite people."

My white friend up in the tree had told me that he took his citizenship very seriously, reminding himself each time he cast a ballot that he was in effect also voting for five of his unenfranchised countrymen. Mrs. Suzman's responsibility is more real and more burdensome. Her votes don't count for much in Parliament. She is the only M.P. from the Progressive Party, and she is never on the winning side of any issue. All the same, hers is usually the sole voice that is persistently raised in Parliament on behalf of the country's twelve and a half million nonwhite majority. When she visits an African township, Blacks cluster around her to shake her

229

hand; they know how ineffectual she is as a lawmaker, or law re-
pealer, but their admiration for her as a person is much like that
of American Negroes, in another era, for Eleanor Roosevelt.
Some months ago the *Rand Daily Mail,* whose political views
generally parallel Mrs. Suzman's, ran a poetic tribute to her, entitled "The Pluck to Stand Alone," that ended,

> Give thanks for her. She raised the cry:
> This thing is evil; let it die.

Mrs. Suzman was born just outside Johannesburg. Her father
was a Jewish merchant from Lithuania who dealt in animal
products—hides, tallow, and soap—and who ultimately became
wealthy by investing his proceeds in real estate. Helen studied
economics at the University of Witwatersrand, in Johannesburg,
and later taught economic history there. She married Dr. Moses
Suzman, who is now one of South Africa's pre-eminent physicians. After the National Party took control of South Africa in
1948, she became a political activist, and organized a branch of its
rival, the United Party, among her academic colleagues. In 1952
the U.P. needed a candidate to stand for Parliament from Hough-
ton, a northern suburb of Johannesburg where many wealthy Jews
reside. Mrs. Suzman undertook to recruit somebody, but got
turned down by everyone she approached. So, although she had
two young daughters to take care of, she ran herself, and she
won.

The United Party split in 1959, its more liberal members forming the Progressive Party, which espouses the abolishment of
segregation, though in a quiet, nonrevolutionary, gradualistic way.
Mrs. Suzman told her fellow M.P.s in Parliament during its 1967
session that she found it amusing that "here I am considered what
the honorable members call a sickly liberalist, a sickly humanist,
and I find that in the outside world I am considered to be a very
moderate, a very conservative person." She knows the outside
world better than do most South African M.P.s. On a recent visit
to the United States she was invited to go on *Meet the Press,* but
she finally decided against it on the ground that whatever she
might say about her country would offend many South Africans
and at the same time disappoint many Americans who wouldn't

think she had been offensive enough.

It is not easy or rewarding to be a Progressive in South Africa today. The party has only three elected spokesmen—Mrs. Suzman and two members of the Provincial Council of the Cape of Good Hope, who are white men representing colored constituents. The last general election was in the spring of 1966. To keep frivolous candidates from running, South African law requires every Parliamentary aspirant to put up a hundred and forty dollars. If he fails to receive one-fifth as many votes as the winner of the seat he's contesting, he loses his deposit. In 1966 twelve out of twenty-six Progressives had to forfeit. Money is not their chief concern; Harry Oppenheimer, their principal angel, is a golden-winged one. But Progs, as they are called, have to take a good deal of bedeviling from their fellow countrymen. "To stick at being a Prog here, you've got to have hair on your teeth," one of them told me.

Mrs. Suzman, who is physically quite normal, is the most successful Prog, and she comes in for the most abuse. The progovernment newspapers periodically run ugly caricatures of her in which she is depicted with a huge nose and thick lips, like something out of *Der Stürmer*. When she gives a party the Secret Police are apt to call a neighbor at six the next morning to ask about her guest list. There used to be two "Mrs. H. Suzman"s listed in the Johannesburg phone book. The other one, a nonpolitical housewife, got so many uncomplimentary calls in the middle of the night that to relieve her Helen Suzman had her own listing changed to include her first name.

Some South Africans think Helen Suzman is very brave. She says she is merely trying to enunciate a civilized viewpoint. "The most soul-destroying thing one can do in South Africa today is to live here and do nothing about the situation," she says, "to enjoy the fleshpots that are here for all of us, and do absolutely nothing about the basic injustice around us." In a curious way, her determination to do something has probably proved useful to the National Party. It is difficult for critics to say unqualifiedly that South Africa is a police state when it boasts two assets that vitiate the charge—a comparatively free press and the irrepressible Mrs. Suzman. The attention she gets as an antigovernment gadfly sometimes irritates the United Party, which is supposed to be the

231

major opposition group and holds thirty-nine of the hundred and fifty seats in the principal Parliamentary body, the House of Assembly. U.P. leaders grumble that while their M.P.s vastly outnumber Mrs. Suzman, she frequently seems to attract almost as much attention as all of them put together.

Parliament's home in Cape Town is a complex of Victorian buildings, with a statue of Queen Victoria out front. The National Party M.P.s, who have the strength to pass any law they fancy, once contemplated enacting one that would have removed from the scene this solid reminder of their onetime subservience to the British, but they forbore. After all, history is history. Parliament customarily meets each January, for six months, and while it is in session Cape Town is the nation's capital. The rest of the time that distinction is held by Pretoria, a stodgy city whose central square is appropriately dominated by a large statue of Oom Paul Kruger, that squat, strong, stubborn squire of the Afrikaner pantheon. Since 1906 Pretoria's streets have been lined with jacaranda trees—more than seventeen thousand of them at last count —and during the South African spring the sultry scent of their purple blossoms permeates the Calvinistic capital.

When the government moves to Cape Town the diplomatic corps and a good many political journalists tag along. The Prime Minister has an official home in each capital. (The one in Cape Town used to be Cecil Rhodes's place, and the one in Pretoria is called Libertas.) Inasmuch as the British and American ambassadors are just about the only other regular migrants who have permanent lodgings in both cities, there is a semiannual scramble for rented premises in Cape Town. Toward the end of December, in Pretoria, one is less likely to hear people discussing what they hope to give for Christmas than where they hope to live after New Year's. Some owners of desirable Cape Town quarters travel comfortably for half of every year on the harvest they reap from their Pretoria tenants.

There are two branches of Parliament: the House of Assembly, where most debates occur, and the Senate, which is primarily a rubber-stamp repository for elder statesmen, or at any rate for elder politicians. Compared to the legislators of some nations, the South African M.P.s toil under Spartan conditions. Many of them

232

answer their own phones, having no office staffs to shield them from doting admirers or dotty cranks. The thirty-nine-man U.P. delegation makes do with a pool of six typists. (One happy result of this clerical austerity is that the M.P.s cannot readily issue mimeographed statements or copies of their speeches.) South African M.P.s, however, don't need especially large staffs because, by and large, they follow the British parliamentary system. They don't initiate legislation; that is all done by government ministries. (The ministers can be powerful men; once the laws they've framed get passed, they have a good deal of latitude in interpreting them administratively.) There is little fraternization between rival party factions. In the Parliamentary restaurant, it would be most uncommon to find a Nat and a U.P. man lunching together.

One bar is reserved exclusively for members; Helen Suzman never goes in there because she hates to drink alone. She takes her isolation in stride, professing to be unflustered by the imprecations that are often tossed her way. "The minute I leave Parliament, I forget that it exists," she told an acquaintance after one particularly harrowing session had concluded. "I meet these characters on the street somewhere and I recognize them as M.P.s, but I can't remember their names." The characters who taunt her are Nationalists, and gallantry is not the forte of all of them. In the first few hectic seconds after Dr. Verwoerd was assassinated, a spectator in the visitors' gallery saw one hysterical Nat M.P. turn on Mrs. Suzman, who was sitting across the floor from the stabbing, and all but accuse her of having committed the deed.

During ordinary, nonviolent sessions, M.P.s are supposed to pause as they enter or leave the chamber and bow to the Speaker, a wispy man with a wispy white goatee peeking out from his black robe. As Mrs. Suzman was going through this ritual recently, she stopped beside two craggy-faced Nationalist frontbenchers. They looked at her, turned away, nudged each other, exchanged a few words, and burst into uproarious laughter. They both resembled tillers of the soil—until recently, many Nationalist M.P.s were farmers—and one could sense that whatever it was they said about the honorable lady was fairly earthy. The Nats sometimes get even madder at a man among them, a U.P. M.P. named Japie Basson. He used to be a Nat himself, but was

233

drummed out of the party for taking a moderate stand on racism. "I'm a Nationalist in everything *but* race," he has subsequently said. That single wayward lapse from Nationalist grace made him so unloved by his former brethren that Prime Minister Vorster once called him a traitor on the floor of the House, and the two men haven't spoken since.

Mrs. Suzman gives as much as she takes. She has a sharp, unflagging tongue, and many a session has been enlivened by some acerb comment of hers about a prime minister or one of his stalwart henchmen. Once, when Dr. Verwoerd ran the government, she accompanied some other M.P.s on a visit to a mining town. Their attention was directed to a massive slab of granite. "Ah," the lady murmured sweetly, "the Prime Minister!" She has had many a public verbal duel with Mr. Vorster, but they get along reasonably well *in camera*. They meet now and then for coffee, and have found they have at least one thing in common: they are both fond of the same sugarless sweetener.

Mr. Vorster, since he became Prime Minister, has been likened by latter-day emulators of Mrs. Suzman to flexible granite. It is one of the seeming contradictions in terms to which South Africans are addicted. In the flesh, actually, he more nearly resembles hard sponge. A red-faced, pudgy, indifferently dressed man of fifty-two, he could pass anywhere for a third-echelon midwestern American businessman. He is casual and informal. At National Party gatherings he is apt to stick his hands in his pockets during the hymn singing. (The Nats like to blend hymns and homilies.) He is a heavy smoker, even while on public platforms; a golfer, too, he holds his cigarettes with a cupped grip. There can be few other chiefs of government who, like him, appear on rostrums with smoke curling from their nostrils.

In Vorster's case, the rest of the world would probably not be surprised if he emitted flames, for he has a dragonlike image. He earned it himself; as Minister of Justice he was probably more responsible than any other South African for implementing his country's detention laws and overseeing its ubiquitous Secret Police. (South African politicians' wives are not noted for modishness. After Mrs. Vorster turned up at one function wearing the kind of lumpy headgear that her set finds fashionable, much of

234

which, even when new, looks as though it had come from a thrift shop, an onlooker said, "I really don't see why the P.M.'s wife has to have her hats designed by the Special Branch.") He has had a hand in so many arrests and imprisonments that, after he became Prime Minister, one South African not especially fond of him waggishly replied, when asked what sort of person he was, "The Prime Minister speaks with a deep sense of conviction."

Since Mr. Vorster assumed his present high office some of his admirers have suggested that he was not really as wicked a man as he was portrayed while he administered Justice; that, in fact, Dr. Verwoerd had deliberately made Vorster look bad so that he himself would look less bad. (If that was Verwoerd's intention, there is little evidence that his scheme worked.) Prime Minister Vorster was born in the Cape of Good Hope, South Africa's most tolerant province, but in a part of the Cape near the border of the Orange Free State, the most intolerant. That gives him a nice geographical balance for Afrikaner politics. Like all the other prime ministers, he attended the University of Stellenbosch. In the Second World War he was interned. Along with many other chauvinistic young Afrikaners, he had joined the National Party. There may be some doubt as to whether the group wanted the Nazis to win the war, but it certainly didn't want them to lose. Many Nats belonged to an ostensibly cultural organization, the Ossewa Brandwag, which was founded in 1938. Its name means "Sentinels of the Ox-wagons." It was dedicated to "the perpetuation of the spirit of the ox-wagon in South Africa; maintaining, amplifying, and giving expression to the tradition and principles of the Dutch-Afrikaner; protecting and promoting the religion, cultural and material interests of the Afrikaner; fostering patriotism and national pride, and harnessing and uniting all Afrikaners, men as well as women, who endorse these principles and are prepared to make energetic endeavors to protect them."

The Ossewa Brandwag—which was ecumenical to a degree, its members employing in their rituals variations of both the Nazi and fascist salutes—devoted some of its energies to blowing up Allied troop trains and committing other acts of sabotage. Vorster was its second in command. For carrying on like that while his

235

country was at war, he was probably lucky not to have been hanged. As it was, he spent several months in prison. He now maintains that he was in solitary confinement, but the assertion is hard to prove or disprove; after the Nats took over the government in 1948 they spirited off and tucked away a good many archives of the war period, and South Africa is not the sort of country where anyone is likely to step forward and give oral testimony to dispute the Prime Minister's word. In any case, after 1948 the wartime saboteurs and traitors were acclaimed as national heroes and sold their reminiscences to South African magazines. When Vorster became Prime Minister one South African war veteran exclaimed, "My God, it's as if the British had given their best job to Lord Haw Haw!"

Since Vorster's ascent to power, his countrymen have found it a popular indoor sport to compare him with his predecessor. Verwoerd was not as well liked personally, it is generally agreed, but was held in much more awe, and the mere manner in which the two men are referred to is illustrative. "John's practice is to do what the *plattelanders* want him to," one South African told me. "The Doctor did what *he* wanted to." Vorster can and does delegate authority to his cabinet ministers; a meeting of Verwoerd's cabinet was compared to a shark swimming around in a tank full of minnows. Vorster has a propensity for changing his mind and often makes jokes at his own expense; in that respect, at least, he is similar to John F. Kennedy. When at a banquet the man introducing him somewhat stuffily told how he had traced the Prime Minister's ancestry back to an ancient Dutch household, Vorster roguishly urged him not to do any further research, lest he arouse the interest of the Minister of the Interior; the joke, as any South African knew, was that the Minister of Interior is the man with the ultimate authority to decree whether a South African is white or nonwhite.

It is hard to conceive of any circumstances in which, even in jest, Dr. Verwoerd would have alluded to the possibility of his being tarred with the stigmatic brush. Verwoerd was a humorless autocrat who thought he had a pipeline to God and was unswervingly persuaded of the righteousness of his peculiar apartheid philosophy. A record album put out in his memory by the South

236

African Broadcasting Corporation was called, simply, *He Was a Man*. After Verwoerd's death, Alan Paton credited him with having pulled off the tricky achievement of finding strong moral motives for actions that nearly the whole rest of the world thought decidedly immoral; another South African writer characterized him—though not, for obvious reasons, in print—as "the most magnificent creator of intellectual fiction ever known."

Verwoerd was apartheid's theoretician; Vorster is its practitioner. Since he took office there has been some relief expressed both in and out of South Africa that his behavior has been more moderate than his performance as Minister of Justice would have led anyone to believe. Notwithstanding, there has been little in his domestic programs to give much comfort to the non-Whites whom these principally affect and afflict. A progovernment Afrikaans-language newspaper editor said to me one day, "The one mistake we made in this country was to legislate too much about the non-White." But if Vorster shares that view, he has proposed nothing to undo any of his party's errors. Indeed, a number of pieces of legislation his government has offered to Parliament have been even more restrictive than past laws. The very definition of who is a white man and who isn't is being narrowed. It has been pretty much agreed on among South Africa solons, in the course of their Alice-in-Wonderland deliberations, that a nonwhite man is not a white man, but what is white? One would think they thought they knew by now.

Not at all; they devoted interminable hours in their 1967 session to debating the ticklish question, like a pack of theologians pecking away at a single pesky adjective in the Bible. In discussing an amendment to the nation's Immorality Act, they eventually reached concurrence on this definition of "white": "Any person who in appearance obviously is a white person and who is not generally accepted as a colored person, or who is generally accepted as a white person and is not in appearance obviously not a white person." But appearance is not all it appears to be. While amending the Population Registration Act, the legislators came up with, "In deciding whether any person is in appearance obviously a white person or not a white person, his habits, education, and speech and deportment and demeanor in general shall be taken into account." Woe betide the drunk or untidy or epileptic white man who comes up for a hearing on his color without supporting affidavits!

Mr. Vorster's comparative reasonableness—comparative, that is, to Dr. Verwoerd's intransigence—has been most evident in his foreign policy. South Africa's relations with the rest of its continent, for all its claims of inseparability, have for a generation been minimal. It is the *bête blanc* of the Organization of African Unity. Its airline, South African Airways, cannot fly over or land in most of the other African nations. S.A.A. flights between Europe and Johannesburg have to detour around the bulge of West Africa and to touch down en route at Las Palmas, in the Canary Islands, a Spanish possession; at Luanda, in Angola, which belongs to Portugal; and at Salisbury, Rhodesia.

It is a long trip. I've made it. By the time I reached the Jan Smuts Airport I was too weary to react in any startled way, as most new arrivals to South Africa supposedly do, to the country's Customs and Immigration forms, which require the traveler to state whether he is White, Asiatic, or Other. I was more taken aback by having to depose whether I was carrying any used beehive appliances. A South African visa stipulates, rather dismayingly, that "this visa does not guarantee admission into South Africa or South West Africa," but once I had mine, qualified though it sounded, I had no difficulty getting in or out of the country. Customs never even opened any of my luggage, though I was known to be a working foreign journalist. And at my final departure the final words addressed to me on South African soil by a South African came from a uniformed Afrikaner—Passport Control or some such, I guess he was—who said, "Thank you, Sir. Much obliged. 'Bye now."

Just a few days before Dr. Verwoerd's death he had had his picture taken shaking hands with Chief Leabua Jonathan, of the then British High Commission Territory of Basutoland. When that protectorate, which is entirely surrounded by South Africa, became independent as Lesotho, Chief Jonathan became its prime minister. A good deal was made in South Africa of that clasping of black and white hands—perhaps a bit too much, for up to 1961, when South Africa was still in the British Commonwealth,

238

its prime minister would routinely shake the hands of African chiefs of state at Commonwealth conferences; and, since then, South Africans posted to the United Nations have been seen in the Delegates' Lounge drinking—though not in the presence of photographers—with representatives of African nations that accuse Pretoria and all its emissaries of unmitigated villainy.

Even so, it was something for the granitic Verwoerd to make that manual gesture. Vorster has gone considerably further. He has seemed to sense that South Africa, already its continent's most vigorous and most industrialized nation, could lead all of Africa to incalculable glory if only it could somehow become acceptable—or at the least not hateful—in the rest of Africa's eyes. Vorster not only shook hands with Jonathan after he became Lesotho's Prime Minister, but had him to lunch at the Mount Nelson Hotel in Cape Town, where thitherto a non-White of any nationality had had about as much chance of eating a meal as swallowing a white rhinoceros. Mr. Vorster has said that he will get together with the head of any African state on an equal basis. He has welcomed a trade mission from nearby Malawi, and has waved a friendly palm toward neighboring Botswana. Then, the Malawi delegation, while visiting Johannesburg, stayed at the Langham Hotel, another normally all-white citadel. The English-language *Star* sent a nonwhite reporter around to try to get an interview with the transient Africans, but he was barred from the premises. "Mischievousness" and "trouble making," sputtered the Afrikaans-language *Dagbreek*.

Dr. Verwoerd once hoped that South Africa would ultimately take over both Botswana, which is larger than France and has five hundred and fifty thousand people, and Lesotho, which is about the size of Belgium and has a million. Both are now politically on their own, but economically they are dependent on South Africa. That makes it difficult for their black leaders to spurn a proffered white hand. The two fledgling nations belong to a South African customs union and they use South African currency. Most of their citizens' wages are earned in South Africa.

Lesotho is the worse off. Among the world's free nations it may well have the fewest resources, natural or man-made. (An exception is a 601¼-carat diamond that one of its indigenes stumbled

239

on not long ago and sold to a South African dealer for $302,904.) Much of its land is mountainous and arid. It has practically no electricity, railways, or paved roads. It has quite a few college graduates, but no jobs for them. Were it not that something like a hundred and fifty thousand of its people work, at any given time, outside its borders and within those of South Africa, it would be absolutely destitute. Botswana is in a little better shape, but not much, and it is so conscious of its proximity to the potent, rich Republic that it has lately been deporting South African political exiles who had earlier sought haven in it.

I didn't have a chance to visit Botswana or Lesotho, but I did get to Swaziland, the only one of the three former British protectorates in Southern Africa that is not yet fully free. It is well on its way. In April 1967 Swaziland, which is a bit smaller than New Jersey, has a population of nearly four hundred thousand, and is all but surrounded by South Africa, became a protected state. Britain, through a resident Queen's Commissioner, still handles its defense and security, and some of its finances. When, probably toward the end of 1968, Swaziland achieves independence—it may keep that name or, as a noncolonial gesture, call itself Ngwane, after one of its early rulers—its chances of being economically sturdy are infinitely better than those of Botswana or Lesotho.

Even today, Swaziland's exports exceed its imports in value. It has been one of the world's major producers of asbestos for almost thirty years, and three years ago it began exporting iron ore. It has a railroad, which was originally built, mostly with South African money, to transport the iron ore. (The asbestos is shipped to a South African rail terminal via alpine cable cars that traverse more than twelve crow-flying miles.) There are few Swazis, so far, who can handle managerial or administrative jobs; most of its businessmen, and indeed some of its clerks as well, are white South Africans or Englishmen.

Like Botswana and Lesotho, Swaziland is primarily an agricultural region. Unlike them, it has plenty of water, and fertile soil. In addition to growing its own maize, for home consumption, it exports substantial quantities of sugar, rice, and citrus fruits. Its two major cities are Manzini, its business capital, and Mbabane, its political capital, which is situated in a district with the arresting name—arresting to Westerners, anyway—of Hhohho. Between Manzini and Mbabane, which are twenty miles apart, shuttle a fleet of nondescript jitneys, one of which calls itself Sputnik Bus Service. The buses sometimes slow down as they pass a tilled area so the passengers can read the latest intelligence posted on a sign there in Swazi and English: something, as a rule, like "Maize harrowed, hoed, and cultivated—Cotton cultivated, hoed, and thinned—The next step: Side-dress Maize—Beware stalk-borers —DDT 5%—Side-dress cotton—Spray if necessary."

The acreage where this information and advice is furnished is called the King's Field because, like much of Swaziland, it belongs to Sobhusa II, the Ngwenyama—the Lion—of the Swazis, who was born at the turn of the century and has reigned since 1922. He controls a political party called the Imbokodvo (Grindstone) National Movement. When members of Swaziland's first legislative assembly were chosen in the spring of 1967, the Imbokodvo won every seat that was voted on. Sobhusa, in accordance with the newly adopted Swazi constitution, had the right to appoint six legislators. Interestingly, four of his selections were white men. As undisputed ruler, the King is above partisan politics; the Swazi with his nose closest to the grindstone is the Prime Minister of the new nation, Prince Makhosini Dlamini, a portly, courtly nephew of Sobhusa's who used to be a rural-development officer under the British. The Prince is quite urban and urbane, now; he has traveled around the world, and on being invited recently to a Manzini businessman's home to meet an American who was passing through, had his secretary call to inquire if he should wear a dinner jacket. A number of Swazi politicians have a better firsthand acquaintance with the outside world than do many South African leaders; another relative of the King's recently spent six months in a Swazi jail for assaulting three prostitutes, but before that misadventure he had seen a good deal of the globe himself, getting to, among other stimulating cosmopolitan centers, Moscow, Havana, and Peking.

Swaziland is a polygamous nation. Sobhusa has had four or five dozen wives, and a good many of his subjects are understandably his kin. Still another relative and political leader, a man named

241

Simon Nxumalo, has spent much of the last six years trying to cope with one of Swaziland's gravest problems: It has the world's highest illiteracy rate. Nxumalo's parents, like three-quarters of contemporary Swazis, could not read or write. He, as a partial consequence, doesn't know exactly when he was born. He is pretty sure it was a Thursday in July, and he suspects the year was not before 1936, because he knows a man younger than he who was ascertainably born in 1937. As for the day and the month, Nxumalo did some checking and learned that around the time of his birth cattle in his neighborhood went to the dipping tanks on Thursdays, and that on the day of his birth a cow couldn't be dipped because she was calving, and her calf was named "July" by a neighbor who knew a little English.

Polygamy gave Nxumalo his educational start. His father had thirty wives, all of them totally uneducated. The elder Nxumalo married two more women on condition that they start a school for the other thirty, and various of his children took advantage of the academic opportunity thus at hand. Simon went on to a number of other schools, including Syracuse University; he also put in a couple of years at a South African gold mine, where, while above-ground, he became proficient at tennis. Since 1961, when not in politics, he has been running the Swaziland Sebenta Society, which has brought a measure of literacy to a thousand persons a year.

The main difference between the protected state of Swaziland and the Republic of South Africa can be illustrated very briefly: Simon Nxumalo has a blond, white, English secretary. Racial discrimination is illegal in Swaziland, though some social organizations, like the Manzini Club, blackball nonwhite applicants. One white South African of my acquaintance spent a couple of weeks at Mbabane on business. The day after his arrival he had to mail a letter. He went to the post office and wasted nearly half an hour trying to find the entrance; there were a lot of black people using the only entrance he could see, and it never occurred to him that that was supposed to be his entrance, too. White South Africans are confounded also by other spectacles; in Swaziland one is apt to see a black man walking along a road carrying a rifle. It would be unheard of in the Republic. Some white South

Africans have difficulty adjusting to all these strange patterns of behavior. Other South African men, however, have adjusted so quickly that they regularly cross the border to carry on weekend dalliances with Swazi women, in defiance of the immorality laws they zealously uphold at home.

Another attraction that Swaziland offers to citizens of the neighboring Republic is legal gambling. Off the Mbabane–Manzini highway, in a glen known as the Valley of Heaven, is an improbable establishment called the Swaziland Spa, which looks like a package that had been ordered by Las Vegas or Grand Bahama and had been wildly misdelivered. The Spa is a luxurious gambling resort with sulphur baths, a golf course, and nightly floor shows. While I was there music was provided by a Portuguese combo with the odd, seemingly incomplete name of Los de Buenos Aires. The entertainment consisted of three tired-looking white girl dancers from Johannesburg. A few days later they flounced out of Swaziland in a huff, one of them complaining about wolf whistles on the streets of Mbabane, the second saying that she thought it was repugnant to see white men dating non-white women, and the third saying she objected to being called "baby" or "darling" by men to whom she had not been properly introduced, whatever their color.

The Spa's principal *raison d'être* is an all-night casino organized by a consortium of South African and Italian investors. Before they got an exclusive gambling concession in Swaziland, they had to stipulate that Swazis would be allowed to buy a 50 per cent interest in the venture. But of the nearly two million dollars needed to get the place going, in 1966, the natives came up with only about thirty thousand. The Swazi government gets 40 per cent of the take, which has not yet amounted to much. The prospects, though, are beguiling. South Africans are a sporting lot, and at home nearly all public night life, thanks to the dicta of the Dutch Reformed Church, has to shut down at midnight. A dusk-to-dawn casino only two hundred miles from Johannesburg, the proprietors of the Spa reasoned, was bound to be magnetic. So confident were they of its special appeal to night owls that when they designed the place, although they put in three big bars, they provided only sixty bedrooms.

243

Another singular institution in Swaziland, though its uniqueness is just about all it has in common with the casino, is the Waterford School, perched high on a hillside outside Mbabane. It is a nonracial private boarding school for boys, the only one of its kind in southern Africa. Waterford opened its doors in 1963. It was founded, and is run, by Michael Stern, a Cambridge graduate born in Egypt of English parents. He came to South Africa in 1955 as headmaster of a mission school in Johannesburg. Later he started an all-white boys' school there. Stern hoped it could eventually be integrated; like a number of other South Africans, a decade ago, he thought the country would become more liberal. "I guessed wrong, and realized I'd have to do what I wanted to do elsewhere," he says. He has already done a lot: Waterford has attracted international attention, and, on its own scene, one of its boys has broken the all-time Swaziland record for the hop-skip-and-jump.

Waterford's symbol is a phoenix, to memorialize the emergence of the Swaziland school from Stern's charred South African aspirations. He is not highly esteemed by the South African government, but some of its citizens—and other sympathizers in England and the United States—have contributed three quarters of a million dollars to Waterford. Stern's goal is an enrollment of around two hundred students. He now has enough buildings to accommodate just over one hundred. Half of them are white, and half are nonwhite—Indians, Chinese, and Africans from South Africa, Kenya, Mozambique, Botswana, Lesotho, and, of course, Swaziland itself. There are also a few boys whom he categorizes —though only for illustrative purposes—as Eur-Africans; among these is a son of the Prime Minister of Botswana, Sir Seretse Khama, whose wife is a white Englishwoman. It is indicative of the enormous gap Waterford has bridged that one of Sir Seretse's son's schoolmates is a descendant of Oom Paul Kruger, a patron saint of white supremacy. The faculty is nonracial, too; one of the instructors is the first and so far only South African of Cape Colored designation to have graduated from Harvard.

Stern is often asked by visitors or people he approaches while fund-raising how, so close to South Africa and so inevitably affected by that country's racial policies, his boys get along together. "Color is genuinely ignored because it is soon not noticed," he has replied. "To us it is not remarkable, because we expected nothing else, but even if we had, a week or two of lessons and games and swimming and eating would have finally removed our prejudices and preconceptions. It is just physically impossible to go on worrying about color when it is so patently irrelevant. Why can't people understand this?"

supremacy in an attempted process of integration, and which seeks to bring about free, self-governing communities which can co-operate with one another as the nations of the world do in matters of mutual economic and other interest.

The Republic of South Africa's relations with the rest of the world are far chillier than those it has been guardedly establishing with its immediate neighbors. Prince Makhosini of Swaziland told me one day that when his country became independent and joined the U.N. it would never vote for sanctions against South Africa. There is nothing that most other African nations would more enthusiastically endorse. The likelihood of any such punishment being effectively inflicted on South Africa, short of its invading one of its neighbors, is slight. As long ago as 1947, before the National Party was voted into power and when the country was far less sturdy than it is today, its Foreign Minister declared, "To remain master in our house and to maintain white civilization in this country is of greater importance than the maintenance of trade relations."

There has been no indication of a change in that basic posture. In any event, it would be all but impossible, as the world is constituted today, for South Africa to be made to change its ways by mere economic pressure. As for military pressure, South Africa would rather fight than switch. By global standards it is a small nation, and it wouldn't stand a prayer against an armed attack by a major power—not that any seems likely to mount one in the foreseeable future. But South Africa could probably turn aside any assault from its own continent. Most white South Africans can handle firearms, and twenty thousand of them get military training each year. The country is now spending about three hundred and fifty million dollars annually on its defense forces, and an additional eighty million on its police. It manufactures its own armored steel and automatic rifles, and it has a missile-development program under way.

When the United States, which for most noncommunist countries would be the logical source of heavy weapons, imposed an arms embargo against South Africa, the Republic simply looked elsewhere and quickly found France, which was glad to supply it with jet fighters and helicopters. In the spring of 1967 Paris and Pretoria agreed to a further transaction, involving three brand-new French submarines. South Africa boasts that it has a first-rate radar-warning net, and in December 1966 its Minister of Defense announced that a new secret weapon, made by and for his countrymen, was at hand. He did not amplify his statement, and there has been practically no speculation in South Africa, where even presumptive breaches of security are severely dealt with, as to just what he might have been talking about.

South Africans, even without knowing how formidable their arsenal may be, profess not to be afraid of anyone. They are worried and aggrieved, though, at their relations with America. They are so unable to comprehend how distasteful their apartheid laws are to outsiders that they cannot see why the United States should be censorious of them. Why should America pick on *them* for their own solution of their own native problem, South Africans persistently inquire, when America has so shabbily treated its own native Indians, not to mention its imported Negroes? Many South Africans spend far more time mulling over the plight—or their version of the plight—of American Indians than do non-Indian Americans. South African government officials visiting the States make special trips to Indian reservations, seeking firsthand confirmation of their widely expressed qualms about discrimination toward indigenes. (That Indians can vote and that men of admittedly Indian ancestry have served in Congress and have been in charge of the Bureau of Indian Affairs is less widely reported than are the poverty and listlessness and drunkenness that characterize many Indian communities.) On the other hand, the eminent South African historian, Leo Marquard, who is one of his country's staunchest liberals, once wrote that while it might be true that Americans tried to exterminate their Indians, and Australians in their turn their aborigines, white South Africans would probably long since have exterminated all their black compatriots had there not been so many of them that it would have been too expensive.

Many white South Africans, inevitably, feel a bond of sympathy with unreconstructed American southerners. The feeling is mutual. (Some American corporations send southerners to represent them in South Africa, on the theory that they will more

249

readily adjust to the environment.) Many Americans of the George Wallace persuasion have the impression that *all* white South Africans share their views.

Not long ago a decent, nonracist businessman from South Africa was visiting Alabama. He met a states-rights advocate who, on hearing where he was from, said that birds of a feather had to stick together and wondered if the visitor could tell him of some South Africans who might be solicited for funds to help bring about the downfall of interfering northern big-city radical anti-segregationists. The businessman, after a moment's meditation, straightfacedly named Alan Paton and a few other prominent integrationists. The Alabama man, who had never heard of any of them, was profuse in his thanks. Whether or not he ever acted on the prankish tip is uncertain. The American tendency to lump all white South Africans together is equally observable up North. The same South African was strolling along a Brooklyn street one night with a white friend when a Negro panhandler accosted them. The South African gave him a quarter. His companion couldn't resist saying to the beggar, "Do you know where your benefactor's from? He's from South Africa." The Negro threw the coin in the gutter and walked away.

South Africa's incumbent Minister of Foreign Affairs, Dr. Hilgard Muller, addressing Parliament in April 1967 on relations with the United States, reminded the assembled M.P.s of a statement he'd made the year before: "We try to avoid those points of friction and concentrate on the large number of points of common interest." Anticommunism, of course, is one. Science is another. America has missile-tracking stations in South Africa, and NASA allocates nearly four million dollars of its annual funds to Pretoria for assistance in its space program.

In February 1967, when the United States aircraft carrier *Franklin D. Roosevelt* was heading home from Vietnam, our Defense Department announced that it would put in at Cape Town for refueling. Two years earlier, when our navy had proposed it might be nice if some of the air crews on the carrier *Independence* could have brief shore leaves in South Africa, Dr. Verwoerd had raised a rumpus by gruffly saying that no planes could land at any of his airfields if they had Negroes aboard. What the

250

American Defense and State departments had in mind when they announced the *Roosevelt*'s itinerary is hard to fathom, but what Prime Minister Vorster had in mind was obvious. During his administration a half dozen small American naval vessels with multiracial crews had paid liberty calls at South African ports without any furor. Vorster planned to use the arrival of the *Franklin D. Roosevelt* as a demonstration of South African amicability toward the United States.

Elaborate plans were made—with American concurrence—to entertain the carrier's crew ashore at Cape Town. Hostesses were not discouraged from inviting American Whites and Negroes to their homes simultaneously, and the South African police were instructed to look the other way if Negro crewmen entered public bars normally off-limits to non-Whites. When at the last minute Washington, under pressure from civil-rights groups, changed its mind and backed off—as if it had just suddenly remembered about apartheid—and confined the crew to its ship while it was refueling, the South Africans were puzzled and hurt, but even then Mr. Vorster refrained from any angry outburst.

The upshot was that in South African eyes Mr. Vorster's government gained a victory over the United States in, of all unlikely areas of competition, that of tolerance. The crew of the carrier sent a letter of thanks to the President of South Africa for his country's intentions, and South African newspapers gleefully printed letters from individual American sailors expressing gratitude for the proffered hospitality and upbraiding their own country for not letting them take advantage of it. Subsequently, some Capetonians organized a Goodwill Fund Committee, the stated objective of which was to raise enough money to defray the transportation to South Africa of widows of men who had died in Vietnam while assigned to the embarrassed carrier. In many aspects of its conduct of foreign affairs, South Africa sometimes seems obtuse, but in this instance it demonstrated its awareness of one cardinal principle of public relations: during wartime, always stick up for the fighting man.

Both before and after the carrier incident, the Foreign Minister's views notwithstanding, there has been a good deal of anti-American feeling in South Africa. When the Minister of Defense proposed several months ago that all South African soldiers not only receive military training but be indoctrinated against the evils of communism, *Die Transvaler,* a newspaper that usually reflects government thinking, urged him to indoctrinate them also against American liberalism, which the paper regarded as no less pernicious. Many white South Africans blame what they take to be America's failings on our State Department, which they believe to be riddled with Communists, or what they take to be Communists. Senator Joe McCarthy could have convinced these South Africans of *anything,* and by them his presence on the American scene is sorely missed. Their American villains are his kind of villains.

White South Africans, for the most part, cannot find a good word for Judge Jessup, of the International Court of Justice, who voted against their country in the South West Africa case. They do not like Congressman Barratt O'Hara of Illinois, the chairman of the House subcommittee that has been holding hearings on South Africa, which, though scarcely mentioned in the American press, have been faithfully reported in South Africa. They can get splenetic thinking about Senator Robert F. Kennedy, who during his visit to South Africa in 1966 asked one group of Afrikaner editors if they thought God was black—a blasphemous question to some South African ears, though a stimulating one to some others; who stood on the top of a car in Durban and sang "We Shall Overcome," which had been banned by the S.A.B.C.; and who in Johannesburg gave the right-thumb-up salute of the African National Congress, which has been banned, too. When the editors presented the Senator with a book on apartheid, he countered by passing out copies of a statistical volume called the *American Negro Reference Book.* He also distributed some John F. Kennedy half dollars, as souvenirs. One woman who had seen an African delightedly accept one remarked that she thought Kennedy was trying to buy appreciation. The recipient, a professional man with two college degrees, retorted, "I don't really think the Senator figured that fifty cents would see me through the day."

President Johnson isn't a particularly heavy villain, because he hasn't said much about South Africa. The chief American blackguard, of late, has been Arthur Goldberg, who has said a lot. A

252

few days after he made one particularly strong antiapartheid speech at the United Nations, our ambassador in Pretoria, William Rountree, found himself suffering from a respiratory problem, and went around to see an Afrikaner nose doctor of firm National Party convictions. While jabbing a sharp instrument up his patient's nostrils, the doctor suddenly paused and asked, "Tell me, Mr. Ambassador, what do you *really* think of Arthur Goldberg?" There are times when a diplomat has to be heroically diplomatic.

Whatever the temperature of American-South African governmental relations, relations between the two countries' businessmen have remained fairly normal. At last count, two hundred and fifty American corporations were doing business in South Africa. Practically all the familiar names are there, including, of course, Coca-Cola, which in 1966, as a promotional scheme, introduced the yo-yo to South Africa. (There are many areas of difference between the English-speaking and Afrikaans-speaking white South Africans, but in one respect they have been found to be remarkably alike; a couple of years ago, Coca-Cola discovered from a market-research survey that 44 per cent of the English-speaking crowd, when asked what brand if any of soft drink they'd consumed the day before, replied "Coke," and that 40 per cent of the Afrikaners gave the same answer.) The total American investment in South Africa is not colossal; a billion dollars is the largest estimate anyone has yet made, and that may be a bit high. "We've been here since 1924 and I doubt whether our total investment adds up to more than fifty million dollars," a Ford man told me at Port Elizabeth. "That's peanuts by our standards."

Peanuts or watermelons, money is money, and most of the Americans in South Africa seem to have no concern other than to make sure that theirs brings a suitable return. (It almost always does—on the average, something over 20 per cent.) They resolutely shy away from provocative topics. One South African woman told me of being invited to a dinner party by a hostess who begged her not to bring up politics—which South Africans nearly *always* discuss at dinner—because some General Motors bigwigs from the States would be present. American businessmen in Port Elizabeth or Johannesburg or Cape Town are not, as a

253

rule, outspokenly pro-South African. They are practical men, and much as they want their products to appeal to South African customers, they don't want to do anything that would get them into unnecessary trouble with twenty-two million American Negroes who constitute a larger potential market than all South Africans put together. So, American businessmen in South Africa tend to be scrupulously noncommittal about internal South African affairs. When anything comes up that they might have to express an opinion on, they often take a tack that has been found useful over many years by English businessmen in that country: they go off and play golf.

The United States is most harshly criticized, not surprisingly, by South Africa's right-wingers. What may be surprising is that there are people in South Africa who are considered right-wingers by Nationalists, whose most sinistral members, by worldwide criteria, are rightists themselves. Some South African politicians are so far right that they have divorced themselves from the Nats, whom they regard as irredeemably leftist, and have formed two splinter parties, neither of which has made any headway. The story is told of a Natal man who, visiting the Transvaal, met an organizer of one of these minuscule groups, was impressed with his spiel, and said he'd like to join the branch in his home province. He subsequently got a membership card, with a number on it—"1."

Most of the rock-hard conservatives are Afrikaner Nationalists. A notable exception is an English-speaking South African in Pretoria named S. E. D. Brown, the editor of the monthly *South African Observer,* which he calls "a journal for realists." It is the kind of publication that is distributed at John Birch Society gatherings, and it usually contains reprints from two or three American journals that follow the Birch line, such as the *Daily Advance* of Lynchburg, Virginia, which many of Lynchburg's white citizens have deplored as excessively anti-Negro. Until 1962 Brown served the government as an official censor, and his journal used to receive a small subsidy from the National Party, but that was stopped; he was getting to be an embarrassment to the South African establishment. Not only does he attack Arthur Goldberg and others considered fair game in South Africa, but he has aspersed, among institutions that are close to the government, the respect-

254

able daily, *Die Burger.* Brown calls its conservative editor, Piet Cillié, "the intellectual of Afrikanerdom's new radical movement and spokesman-in-chief for the Afrikaner liberal establishment." That is about as mild a criticism as he makes of anyone.

Brown was very much in evidence, in the fall of 1966, at an international conference on communism held in Pretoria. There, intellectuals and radicals and anybody whom any speaker chose to call an intellectual or a radical were inundated under waves of calumny. The English-language newspapers sent reporters around to cover the gamy affair. Some of them were thrown out, with Afrikaners in the audience pleasantly suggesting, as they were being shoved toward the door, that their hair be set afire.

A participant who appealed hugely to that caliber of audience was an American named Edgar Bundy, a professional anticommunist who presides over something called the Church League of America. Bundy, who spent some time in the United States Army and clings to the title of major, is not very well known in the United States, except out on the far-right flank, but he has a considerable celebrity in South Africa, which cottons to a man who professes to know all about communism and its machinations. It is astonishing, in a way, that he hasn't accused South Africa of being a communist state. After all, Afrikaners smoke Havana cigars made under Castro; they are excessively fond of "hammer" as a verb; and, like Russians, they have their own odd pronunciations of the English letters "g" and "h"—the only difference being that Russians give our "h" a "g" sound, and that Afrikaners make our "g" come out very "h"-like.

Many South Africans are obsessed with superlatives. They are pleased that geologists have credited them with what may be the oldest part of the crust of the earth—some granitic rocks near Barberton, in the Transvaal province, that are supposed to be three billion three hundred million years old, or about half a billion years senior to any other country's rocks. (When it comes to that, one scientific theory has it that human life originated in the Transvaal.) Supremacy is a South African desideratum; farmers vie to grow the biggest cabbages or pumpkins, and municipalities compete for the distinction of having the tallest rugby uprights of any of the nation's playing fields. The South African writer Uys Krige has even commented on his fellow countrymen's pride in

255

being "the greatest brandy drinkers in all Christendom." (But, he went on rhetorically, "surely true greatness is more likely to be found where there is less self-consciousness about it?") It is thus perhaps to be expected that many South Africans regard themselves as the foremost anticommunists on earth.

In grappling with communism they are a bit behind the times —few of them yet seeming to have detected any cleavage between China and Russia—and they do not appear to be faced with any grave internal threat from that source: one of their rightest-wing publications asserted in 1966 that there were 48,502,900 Communists around the world, of whom 800 were thought to be in South Africa. The Communist Party itself has been outlawed there since 1950, and in a 1966 poll of white South Africans only 3 per cent of the sample thought communism was the country's greatest problem. Seventy-three per cent thought race relations was.

Over the years, of course, South Africa has had its share of Communists. Apartheid is the kind of dirt that is hospitable to its propagation. One South African Communist, the Afrikaner lawyer Abram Fischer, was awarded the Lenin Prize in 1967 by the Soviet Union, a twenty-five-thousand-dollar award that could do him little good, inasmuch as he was sixty and serving a life sentence in a Pretoria jail. When it suits their purposes, the Nationalists define communism fairly loosely. They tend to equate it not only with socialism but with liberalism and intellectualism and rationalism and secularism and humanism and something they call panhumanism. Liberalism is an especially aggravating bugaboo, as it keeps sprouting up all over the place and is hard to suppress, only rarely taking a form that can be called seditious. But it is kept under careful surveillance. Not long ago, for instance, an official of the South African Association for Technical and Vocational Education—which one might think would devote itself chiefly to practical matters and leave abstractions to others— declared that liberalism was anti-Christian and that schoolchildren—presumably even those being taught how to operate lathes and blowtorches—should receive instruction about its dangerousness.

As a political force, liberalism has got practically nowhere in

South Africa. Mrs. Suzman's Progressive Party, as she herself has said, would be quite middle-of-the-road anywhere else. South Africa does have a Liberal Party—which stands for immediate outright equality between races—but it is a shadow of a shell. A few years ago some of its members, persuaded that they could never change their country's unacceptable ways by nonviolent means, engaged—rather clumsily—in sabotage or attempted sabotage, and when the government caught them it had all the excuse it thought it needed to crack down on their political associates. The Liberal Party itself was not outlawed. It was effectively hamstrung, though; nearly every one of its African organizers was banned, and thus taken out of political circulation; so were five editors in a row of a publication the party tried to keep going.

In Cape Town, the country's most liberal city, the Liberal Party had at last reports fewer than four dozen members. And not even all of them were active. When a meeting was called to discuss the possible dissolution of that feeble contingent, one Capetonian who'd been a nominal member for years, but had never participated in any of its affairs, wondered if he should attend. Should he turn up at this conceivably terminal meeting, he kept asking his friends, even though the Security Police would doubtless be taking down names? Would that be fair to his family? Did he have more of a responsibility to attend this crucial session, because of his past remissness, or less? He argued with himself for several days until one of his children got sick, which gave him a legitimate excuse for staying away, but his conscience has been bothering him ever since.

One adamantine member of the Liberal Party who knows his mind, and often speaks it, is Alan Paton. Now sixty-five, with thin white hair and a wizened, saddened face, ruddy from gardening, he lives fifteen miles outside of Durban, in a comfortable suburban home with a detached *rondavel*—the circular, thatch-roofed hut in which millions of Africans reside—as a study. Paton has not been banned, as many Westerners seem to think (indeed, *Cry, the Beloved Country* is prescribed reading in some of the correspondence courses of the University of South Africa), and has been free to travel around his country, although sometimes when he does his windshield gets mysteriously shattered or his tires are unaccountably deflated. He might even be free to travel abroad. He wouldn't know for sure unless he applied for a passport, which he hasn't done for several years. If he were to, he might be issued one on condition that he refrain from speaking publicly about South African politics while overseas, and he couldn't agree to that. "I think it's better to be silenced than to keep silent," he says. So, in a sense, he is a voluntary prisoner in his own beloved country.

Much of the time he sits in his snug *rondavel*—one of the few objects hung on its walls is an incongruous sight in South Africa: a framed certificate attesting to his life membership in the National Association for the Advancement of Colored People— attending to correspondence, receiving visitors, and writing articles and speeches for home consumption. His last book, a biography of the Afrikaner statesman Jan Hofmeyr, was published in South Africa without interference, and it sold fairly well, but the episode was another reminder to the author of his peculiar status in his homeland: not a single one of the progovernment, Afrikaans-language newspapers in the country carried a review of it. "Some of my friends reckoned this was a compliment," Paton says.

South Africa's extreme right-wingers might be passed off as a disagreeable joke were it not that one of their elder statesmen— among other things, he presided at Major Bundy's symposium on communism at Pretoria—happens also to be an elder of the Dutch Reformed Church and an elder brother of the Prime Minister. He is Dr. Jacobus D. Vorster, whose nickname is "Koot." That is about the only informal touch to him. He invariably wears the stiff white collar and white necktie affected by Dutch Reformed *predikants*. These ministers are not, by and large, a fun-loving group, though an extraordinary number of them do seem to get caught, despite the Immorality Act they esteem, embracing young African girls. (One twenty-eight-year-old Dutch Reformed minister, a family man, went on trial not long ago for enticing a sixteen-year-old African girl into the yard of his home. He was not accused of immorality, only of conspiracy, because before he could do whatever it was he'd had in mind a detective spying on him from behind a bush had clumsily toppled out of his cover.

The minister's lawyer vainly argued for his acquittal on the ground that "the worst did not happen.") One *predikant,* occupying a lofty position in the Dutch Reformed hierarchy, told me that some of its other ministers believe that Dr. Vorster, who gets his kicks making unannounced inspections of what he considers juvenile vice dens, sleeps in black pajamas.

Dr. Vorster, who is the chairman of the National Council Against Communism (its emblem is a red star with a dagger thrust through it), is an actuary of the church. The title goes back to the middle of the nineteenth century. There was a shortage of Dutch ministers in the Cape Colony, and the British, who were in charge, wouldn't let any more be recruited from Holland. However, the British said, there weren't any basic inconsistencies between that church and the Presbyterian Church of Scotland, so they taught some Scottish Presbyterians Dutch and shipped them to Africa. The Scots being Scots, each church had an actuary to scrutinize its finances, and that custom was shipped south, too.

Actuary Vorster is a very public figure in South Africa. He told a high school graduating class in Port Elizabeth that their country was the only one on earth where white people could properly live. He was accused of blasphemy by the United Party for saying on another occasion that every leader of the country except Jan Smuts—the one leader the U.P. most cherishes—had been handpicked by God for his high post. One of South Africa's principal political journalists was permanently barred from the press gallery of Parliament for, among other lese majesties, irreverently reporting, after noticing that Jacobus Vorster was sitting up in the visitors' gallery one day while Balthazar John Vorster was speaking on the floor, that Big Brother was watching. The Reverend Martin Luther King can't get a visa to South Africa, but this past winter the Reverend Jacobus Vorster got one to the United States. He was escorted around the right-wing lecture circuit by, inevitably, Major Edgar Bundy, and the Prime Minister's brother told one Chicago audience, without disclosing his sources of information, "Your President Kennedy and our Dr. Verwoerd were both killed by Communists." He also suggested that there might be something sinister in the coincidence that the chief United States delegate to the U.N. and a notorious South African saboteur both

259

had the surname Goldberg.

The Dutch Reformed Church is not a state church, but it is close enough so that the government now and then feels impelled to deny that it is one. As one associates windmills with Holland or temples with Thailand, so does one come to think of South Africa as a land whose nearly every inhabited community of any size is dominated by a Dutch Reformed church with a characteristically steep roof and high bell tower. (Pretoria's central downtown plaza is called Church Square.) The Afrikaner, especially the rural Afrikaner, would not dream of skipping church on Sunday, though from his expression as, scrubbed and suited, he goes to worship, one might wonder how much the experience exalts him. Watching one group of countryfolk respond to the call of their bells, a nonchurchgoing South African friend of mine remarked, "Gee, you'd never know love entered their religion."

There are limited alternatives to churchgoing on South African Sundays. In most of the country, sports events for which admission is charged are taboo. In Natal, where the Dutch Reformed influence is weakest, this rule is not always observed, but the Monday-morning radio reports of Sunday results are discreetly worded and merely say that this rugby game or that cricket match was played "over the weekend." In the Orange Free State, where the church's influence is strongest, Sunday fishing is prohibited. A few years back the church nearly succeeded in getting public swimming pools shut down on the Sabbath, and it did push through in that compliant province an ordinance requiring people who go to public pools on any day of the week to sit with their bodies at least twelve inches apart. Hand-holding is out, even from a distance, and there may be no mutual application of suntan lotion by persons of opposite sexes. In the Free State a ten-year-old girl was not long ago ejected from a public bath for wearing a bikini.

There are actually three Dutch Reformed churches, though their differences are slight and they are often considered a single institution. The oldest and much the largest of the trinity is the Nederduitse Gereformeerde Kerk, which originated in the Cape of Good Hope. Then there is the Nederduitsch Hervormde Kerk, which began in the Transvaal, where it *was* for a while a state

260

church. The remaining branch, the smallest and most Calvinistic of the three, is the Gereformeerde Kerk. All together, they have nearly three million adherents, two-thirds of whom are white. The non-Whites have their own ministers and worship separately. One of South Africa's staple antiapartheid stories has to do with a black man who was found down on his knees in a white Dutch Reformed church, and was asked what he was doing there. "Praying," he said. He was thrown out. An hour or so later he was back at the same spot, down on his knees again, scrubbing the floor, undisturbed. Some of the nonwhite officials of the Dutch Reformed Church are themselves conspicuously narrow-minded. One of the body's colored elders objected recently to his six children being taught in school that the earth was round. He knew it was flat, he said, though he conceded that the only book he had ever read in his entire life was the Bible.

South Africa naturally has other denominations, too. The British had no hesitation, during their heyday, about sending down Anglican ministers. Some of the latter-day advocates of that faith have, by South African standards, been markedly liberal—that is, they have opposed apartheid—and foreign Anglicans are periodically declared persona non grata and have to leave. The present head of the Anglican diocese of Zululand and Swaziland is an African, Bishop Alpheus Zulu. Several clergymen of other faiths attended his installation in August 1966, but not a single Dutch Reformed minister turned up. Subsequently, the government refused Bishop Zulu permission to occupy the residence that goes with his office, since it happens to be in an area that has been proclaimed habitable only by Whites. He did not have the bargaining power of a group of fellow clerics from the Anglican, Methodist, Congregationalist, and Presbyterian churches, who a few years ago established the Federal Theological Seminary, for nonwhite students, in a white area. They were able to do that because they made a real estate deal with the government, getting the site they wanted in exchange for some land that the government very much wanted and that happened to belong to the Church of Scotland.

There is even a Unitarian church in South Africa—a small one in Cape Town with an American minister and a congregation of a

261

hundred and fifty families, of which five are colored. It is so feeble an institution that nobody bothers about it; the Dutch Reformed Church doesn't even acknowledge its existence. Actually, a number of other South African churches conduct integrated services. In principle, the Roman Catholics do not condone segregated worship; in practice, their masses are mostly segregated. More than eight hundred thousand of South Africa's one million Catholics are nonwhite, but even so the white-area Catholic churches do not attract many nonwhite communicants. One reason is that the nonwhite residential areas are usually a long way from the churches most Whites attend. Another is that many Africans don't especially like white services. They tend to be too brief. Africans generally favor protracted worship, with a great deal of singing; at white services, in Catholic churches and others, they feel short-changed. They want their religion to be fun, and in some of their own independent sects they concentrate on enjoyment almost to the exclusion of spiritual matters. One small separatist African church has a peculiar open-air ritual that begins with a lively tug-o'-war, proceeds from there to a picnic, and concludes with another tug-o'-war.

There are almost three thousand independent African churches in South Africa, with more than two million adherents. Some have unusual names, like the Castor Oil Death Church and the FM Radio Church. The rites of a number of them consist principally of dancing. I asked a communicant of one of these churches if it wouldn't make sense for some of the tinier ones to merge, instead of going their own fragmented ways. "If you had two million of us dancing together," he replied, "half of us would get crushed to death." The creeds of these sects, by and large, are an amalgam of Christianity and witchcraft, which still plays an important part in African life, whether rural or urban. At Christmas time, in the big-city townships, sheep and goats are sacrificed, in ancestors' memory, and after they're eaten their bones are buried in trash-littered back yards to placate tribal gods. Few Africans are prosperous; few African witch doctors are not. Their services are regularly besought by, among others, workers in sophisticated industries, who buy potions to slip into their supervisors' tea so that the bosses will be nice to them.

262

One independent South African sect that is very decidedly not nonwhite and that isn't a religion, either, though to many of its members it is the holiest of holies, is the Broederbond, a secret society of some eight thousand Afrikaners that was founded in 1918, ostensibly to create "healthy and progressive unanimity among all Afrikaners" and the "awakening of national self-assurance among Afrikaners." Secret societies are supposed to be illegal in South Africa, but the Broederbond's right to exist has not been challenged, largely because it runs the country. Its carefully screened and selected members are thought to include the Prime Minister, his actuary brother, and almost every other Afrikaner who is prominent in government, education, business, and the armed forces. The man widely believed to be its chairman is also the chairman of the South African Broadcasting Corporation.

Probably five hundred of the country's sixteen hundred Dutch Reformed ministers are Broederbonders. Some years back the arcane fraternity assigned a few of them to pore over the Bible and cull examples of scriptural sanction for apartheid. One of the men assigned to the task was the Reverend C. F. Beyers Naudé, a member of a distinguished Afrikaner family. He couldn't come up with any citations that convinced him, and he was glad; he hadn't liked apartheid to begin with. Soon after that he quit the Broederbond, and subsequently divulged some of its mysteries. That would have been enough to make him suspect in Afrikanerdom. But he did something even more unbrotherly. In 1963 he was one of the organizers, and has since served as full-time director, of a multiracial ecumenical group called the Christian Institute of South Africa, in whose ranks *predikants* have rubbed shoulders with Anglican ministers and Catholic priests—though not, since the Institute requires of its members an allegiance to trinitarianism, with any Unitarians.

The Institute's stated goals seem harmless enough. Its avowed ambition is to teach people, through Bible-study groups and pamphlets, that the principles of Christianity have a place in everyday life as well as in church affairs. "We stand in no other service, nor do we wish to stand or have ever stood in any other service," the Reverend Naudé has declared, "than that of the Word of God." The Institute hadn't been in existence for forty-eight hours, nonetheless, when Dr. Verwoerd, presumably because it was nonsegregated, alluded to it as a danger to the nation. At the start, two hundred and fifty Dutch Reformed ministers joined up, but they have been drifting away. The Reverend Naudé himself was given the option by his church of giving up his ministry or giving up the Institute; he chose the Institute. He was subsequently branded a liberalist heretic and a traitor by other men of God, and the Security Police, for their part, have several times raided his home and his office, looking for subversive literature or anything else they might find that could incriminate him.

In November 1966, after the Reverend Dr. Vorster had denounced Naudé and the Institute at a synod of the main branch of the Dutch Reformed Church, the assembled clergymen voted to forbid all members of their church to belong to the Institute. Those who didn't quit it would be liable to excommunication. "We can only pray that God through His Spirit will bring about a change of heart among the leaders as well as the members of this church," was Naudé's reaction, "so that they may take grateful note before God of the blessed activity of the Institute."

Meanwhile, Naudé and another liberal Dutch Reformed theologian, Professor Albert S. Geyser, became involved in South Africa's most consequential libel suit. A fundamentalist professor of theology wrote three articles for a Dutch Reformed Church journal in 1965 in which, without mentioning any names, he accused two fellow theologians of all sorts of wicked behavior, ranging from encouraging a multiracial international society to showing sympathy for African barbarians to selling their souls to the devil by hobnobbing with the World Council of Churches—from which last, in 1961, the South African Dutch Reformed churches, led by the busy Dr. Vorster, had formally withdrawn. (The author of the articles also called the Christian Institute a communist front.) Naudé and Geyser concluded that he had them in mind, and took him to court. The World Council of Churches raised money to defray their expenses. Dr. Vorster helped raise money for their antagonist; several Nationalist M.P.s generously contributed to his cause. The trial began in February 1967, and in June the Supreme Court justice presiding over the case handed down his decision. He ruled that the two clergymen *had* been libeled, and awarded them each fourteen thousand dollars in damages, along with costs. The Dutch Reformed Church was severely shaken.

It somehow seems characteristic of South Africa that while its three million Whites fight for survival in a three-billion-person world, one faction of one church of one minority color group of that whole thousandth of humanity should be in litigious battle with another. There will soon be more South Africans to rail at one another. (There will, of course, also be more of the rest of humanity to decry South Africans' heterodoxy.) By the year 2000, according to present projections, South Africa's population will have increased by over 100 per cent. The country will then have six to seven million Whites, and around thirty-five million non-Whites. The turn of the century is supposed to be a critical time for South Africa; it is then that they expect their dreams of fully self-governing Bantustans to come true. But the lands that the Whites have allocated to the non-Whites simply can't accommodate anything like that large a crowd. Many, if not most, of the additional non-Whites would have to do what today's non-Whites are doing—hang around, rejected, on the edges of the white urban communities that demand their labor and demean their pride. The South African plan of separate development may be doomed, if by nothing else, by the weight of statistics.

South Africans are forever talking about their problems. Perhaps their principal one is not that there are too many Blacks in their country but too many Whites. In an editorial headed "Pity We Are White," the *Johannesburg Star* not long ago said, "The South African problem would be viewed more objectively by the world at large if it was recognized for what it is: an African problem concerned with contending national groups within an African country." Some thoughtful South Africans believe that outright partition of their nation among the contending groups is its only hope for a stable future, but there is no meeting of minds as to how the country should or could be carved. "I can understand why white people here reject the idea of race integration," says Laurence Gandar, the editor-in-chief of the *Rand Daily Mail*. "It is a desperately difficult problem. It isn't just a gap of color; it's

265

culture and economics and education, too. For us to integrate would be superhuman. I'm not sure we could pull it off. But if people here spurn that solution, they must accept the implications—that is, they must adopt a meaningful separation policy. The separation policy we have, such as it is, doesn't stand up to ten minutes' serious investigation. Our solution either has to be integration or genuine partition, like that of India and Pakistan, and South Africa isn't moving seriously in either direction. It's a tragedy that our leadership isn't giving us proper guidance. Why don't the Nats say, 'Let's separate the races in a meaningful fashion'? A prerequisite of genuine partition would be a manifestly fair division of land, natural riches, and developed resources. Then, moreover, whatever settlement there might be would have to be a negotiated one, and not one decided unilaterally by the Whites. And after that there'd have to be genuine autonomy for non-Whites. And after *that*, once the country was divided, there'd have to be an end to race discrimination against the non-Whites remaining in the white area, and vice versa. Otherwise, the thing doesn't make any sense. But considerations of this sort are never really discussed, and as a result, because of the dilemma of unacceptable alternatives, the country is immobilized."

Of course, there would be no problem if the Whites would just pack up and leave. They won't. "The white man of South Africa is not expendable," Prime Minister Vorster has said, and there is no doubt that his white compatriots resoundingly agree with him, as most of them also do when he says, as he often does, "We will solve our problems in our own way, without the help of anybody from outside." (Now and then, in an especially confident mood, he will say that South Africa already *has* solved its problems.) But if the solution requires some major change in South Africa's posture, it is hard to see that coming from inside. It is not often that haves voluntarily yield up their rights, privileges, advantages, and comforts to have-nots. The English educator Robert Birley said, after three years in South Africa, "The world doesn't realize that in demanding that South Africa do something, it's demanding an extraordinarily creative act of statesmanship."

In any event, there is little hard evidence that the white power structure *wants* to change. The Nationalists could have a long time ago if they'd had any such bent. They have so much authority they could change anything they wanted to practically overnight. What they have seemed to fail to realize, among other things, is how useful it might be for them, without their having to sacrifice any real perquisites or power, if they would merely make some token little gesture—like, say, repealing a few of their most pernicious laws—that would give the rest of the world an opportunity to reassess them, and maybe stop hectoring them. Such a gesture would surely help at home, too. If the non-Whites in South Africa thought the pressures on them were being relaxed, they'd be less likely to explode—and it is hard to visualize them going on too long as second-class citizens without erupting. "You can't slap people in the face forever without having them revolt," one African told me. "We only have to have a call from somebody, and everybody will be ready."

Revolution is probably far from all that imminent. There is no organized African opposition in South Africa today. Some former leaders of the African National Congress, looking for any kind of group to belong to that won't be pounced on by the government, have turned for want of any better alternative to Moral Rearmament. South Africa is not seething and bubbling. As one African who used to be militantly active against the government put it to me resignedly, "There's no question but that we have peace here today—the peace of the grave." It seems unlikely that that mock peace will be shattered for quite some time to come.

Still, there is little permanence in politics. The Nats firmly believe that they are on the right and proper course (a belief enhanced by the conviction of many of them that they are innately superior to non-Whites), but they can readily shift if it seems to their advantage to do so. Their party is solid, but it is not monolithic. If Prime Minister Vorster continues to seek warmer relations with the rest of the world, he is bound to further irritate the already aroused members of his own party who want to be as detached as possible from that extraneous part of the globe and don't give a hoot for its opinions. But there are other Nats who are more and more arguing within their own ranks as to whether some of their old-fashioned notions may not need reappraising, and

267

may even be outmoded; and who are wondering what new notions, if any, they could safely embrace without having the reins of power slacken in their tight-clenched hands. One hears conservative white South Africans saying these days that while of course a multiracial state would be unthinkable in their lifetime, it might work out all right for their children and grandchildren.

One thing seems sure. Sooner or later, something will have to give. The authors of a contemporary book on South African attitudes say, "The present policy holds for white South Africans little glory—only certain disaster." Just how much longer these poor rich Whites can continue to survive is impossible to predict. They won't go away, and there is probably very little they can do as long as they cling to the system of apartheid that, ironically, has in the end made them themselves the one group on earth so sadly set apart from the remainder of mankind. One searches for glimmers of hope. Maybe I espied one as I was leaving the country. As I was driving to the Johannesburg airport my taxi came up on two men on horseback who were cantering spiritedly along a shoulder of the highway. I noticed them first because they were matching stride for stride, so perfectly synchronized that it was as if they'd rehearsed. Then I noticed the color of the horses. One was gray and one was brown. Then, as we drew abreast and overtook the well-coordinated pair, I noticed the color of the men. One was white and one was black.

Index

Abraham, J. H., 108
Ad Hoc Committee for South West Africa, 221–22, 224–25
African Field Reports, 197
African National Congress, 13, 49–50, 252, 267
African Self Help Association, 87, 117
Afrikaans, language, 13, 15; press, 62–65, 69; history of, 70; literature in, 71–73; in politics, 76, 78; Society for the Maintenance of Afrikaans, 81; terms in: *laager*, 13, 36; *hou links*, 15; *sjamboks*, 17; *swart gevaar*, 24; *kragdadigheid*, 126. *See also* apartheid
Afrikaanse Woordeboek, Die (dictionary), 71
Afrikaners: characteristics of, 13–14; ancestors of, 14–15; fear of Blacks, 22–23; and term "apartheid," 23; birthrate of, 79; involvement in economy, 125; toughness (*kragdadigheid*) of, 126–29; as businessmen, 129–31
Afrikanse Studente Bond, 140
alcoholism, rate of, among Coloreds, 53–54
Allgemeine Zeitung (newspaper), 173, 213
American investment in S.A., 253–54
American Negro Reference Book, 252
Anatomy of South Africa (Hudson, Jacobs, and Biesheuvel), 20
Anglican Church, 261, 263

Anglo-American Corporation, 116
Angola, 113, 223
anti-American sentiment in S.A., 251–52
anti-Communist sentiment in S.A., 255–56
apartheid: Verwoerd on, 16; origins of, 25–26; areas of life effected by, 26–35; and curfew, 39; and sports, 43–46; and the Indian population, 47–51; and reclassification of color, 51–52; cultural, 56–61; reactions to by the press, 62–69; passbook regulations and, 90–94; detention laws and, 97–99; banning and, 99–100; in prison, 100; in courts, 100–02; and the Bantustan concept, 103–04; in the mines, 112–19; and job-reservation policy, 123–24; and education, 132–41; and housing, 141–47; as issue in South West Africa Cases, 181–225 *passim;* definitions of, 246–48; as breeding ground for communism, 256; in African churches, 260–65
Associated Press, 67
Athlone Advice Office, 93

banning, as security measure, 99–100
Bantu, 12–13, 27, 42
Bantu Administration and Development, Department of, 91
Bantu Affairs and Development, Department of, 27, 39, 86, 91, 109, 172

currency, rand, basic unit of, 16
Curtis, Mallet-Provost, Colt & Mesle, 192

Himba, 205
Hoare, Colonel Mike, 227
Hoffenberg, Dr. Raymond, 100
Hofmeyr, Jan, 258
Hottentot, 25
housing, 141–44
Huddleston, Father Trevor, 143
Hudson, Dr. William, 20
Human Resources Laboratory of the Chamber of Mines, 118

"I.D.B." (illegal diamond buying), 117
Ilanga Lase Natal (newspaper), 68–69
illiteracy rate, among mineworkers, 114–15
Imbokodvo (Grindstone) National Movement, 241
immigration, encouraged by government, 80–81
Immorality Act, 74, 237, 258
Independence (U.S. aircraft carrier), 250
Indian National Council, 50
Indians (American), 249
Indians and policy of apartheid, 47–51
Information Service of South Africa, 107–08
International Court of Justice. *See* World Court
International School of Studies (Geneva), 215
interracial gatherings, 34–35

Jacobs, Gideon Francois, 20
Jan Smuts Airport, 238
Jessup, Philip K., 212–13, 219, 252
Jews, as subgroup in South African population, 14–15
job reservation, policy of, 123–24
Johannesburg: population of, 12; apartheid conditions in, 28, 30, 39; droughts in, 37; burglar-alarm systems in, 37–38; gold mining in, 39; Gary Player Health Center, 45; mining industry, 113; Sophiatown, 142
Johannesburg Star, 46, 78, 121, 220, 239, 265

John Birch Society, 66, 254
Johnson, Lyndon, 252
Jonathan, Chief Leabua, 238–39
Jongilizwe College, 106
jury system, in S.A., 100

kaffir, 12, 32
Kapuuo, Clemens, 169, 171, 202, 223
Katatura, 171–72
Kennedy, Ethel, 96
Kennedy, John F., 148, 162, 252, 259
Kennedy, Robert F., 58, 96, 140, 252
Kerouac, Jack, 60
Khama, Sir Seretse, 244
Khan, Sir Muhammed Zafrulla, 188
King, Martin Luther, 259
Koo, V. R. Wellington, 188–89
Koretsky, Vladimir, 198, 219
Krige, Uys, 73, 256
Kruger National Park, 226–27
Kruger, Oom Paul, 232, 244
Kupugani, 89
Kutato, Hosea, 169
kwashiorkor, 88

laager philosophy, 13, 36
League of Nations, and the South West African Mandate, 165–66, 181–225 *passim*
Lenin Prize (1967), 256
Leroux, Etienne, 72
Lesotho, 33, 238–40
Leutwein, Theodor, 165
liberalism, 256–57
Liberal Party, 21, 257
Liberia, as plaintiff in the South West Africa Cases, 181–225 *passim*
Lippmann, Walter, 188
literacy program, for mineworkers, 114–15
literature, in S.A., 71–75
Logan, Richard F., 215–17
London Daily Mail, 67
Lourens, Oom Schalk, 75
Louw, Eric, 191
Luthuli, Chief Albert, 35, 60, 99

272

274

South African Colored National Convention, 52–53
South African Institute of Chartered Secretaries, 131
South African Institute of Race Relations, 79, 114
South African Observer, 254
South African Security Police, 94–97
South African Table Tennis Board, 44
South West Africa: Theodor Leutwein as colonial governor, 165; League of Nations mandate for, 166; compared with micronesia, 166–67; topography of, 168; population of, 168–70; climate of, 170–71; housing in, 171–72; trilinguality in, 172–73; German influence in, 173–76; fishing fleets of, 176–77; resources, 178–79; Sam Cohen's influence on, 179–80; ownership case before World Court, 181–225 *passim*
South West African National Union (SWANU), 223
South West African Peoples Organization (SWAPO), 223–24
Soviet Union, fishing fleets in Walvis Bay, 177
Soweto (South West Townships), 141–44
Spender, Percy C., 183, 188–89, 199–200, 207–09, 214–15, 218–19
sports, apartheid conditions in, 43–46
Stern, Michael, 244–45
Suidwes-Afrikaner, Die (newspaper), 173
Sunday Times, 64
Suppression-of-Communism Act, 61, 74, 223
Suzman, Helen, 22, 229–34, 257
Suzman, Moses, 230
Swakopmund, 175–76
swart gevaar ("black danger"), 24
Swaziland, 33, 240–44
Swaziland Sebenta Society, 242
Swaziland Spa, 243
Swazi tribe, 85
Syracuse University, 242

Tanaka, Kotaro, 195
theater, in S.A., 56–57
Tjimba, 205
trade unions, 116, 124
Transkei, 65, 225; foundation of, 104; legislature, 105–06; education in, 107; Commissioner-General of, 108; medical conditions in, 109–10; agriculture in, 111; recruiting of mineworkers in, 112
Transkeian Legislative Assembly, 105
Transvaler, Die (newspaper), 62, 70, 73, 252
Tsafendas, Demitrio (Verwoerd's assassin), 147–164 *passim*
tsotsis, 143
Tubman, William V. S., 192, 197

U Thant, 190
Unitarian Church, 261–63
"Unitas," motto of S.A., 33
United Nations, and the problem of South West Africa, 167–68, 172, 176–77, 181–225 *passim*
United Party, 58, 230–33, 259
universities, structure of, 74
University of Cape Town, 73, 138
University of Fort Hare, 136–37
University of Natal, 75
University of Potchefstroom, 59, 139–40
University of Pretoria, 76, 129, 139
University of South Africa, 137–38, 219, 257
University of Stellenbosch, 73, 138–41, 235
University of Witwatersrand, 135, 140
Uys, Stanley, 20

Vaderland, Die (newspaper), 80
van den Berg, Willem Martin, 152
van den Haag, Ernest, 215
Van der Merwe (fictional character), 75–76
van Riebeeck, Jan, 51
van Wyk Commission, 162–63
van Wyk, Judge, 189, 212, 220
Versailles Conference of 1919, 183–84

Verwoerd, Hendrik F., 13, 16, 44–45, 62–63, 73, 75, 77–78, 103–05, 116, 119, 147–64 *passim*, 177, 203, 213, 222, 228–29, 233–39, 250, 259, 264
Voortrekkers, 13
Vorster, Balthazar John, 12, 16–18, 37, 44–45, 58–59, 62–63, 78, 90, 98, 119, 135–36, 140–41, 220, 222, 234–39, 251, 264, 266–67
Vorster, Jacobus D., 258–59

Wallace, George, 250
Walvis Bay, 175–78
Warren Commission, 162
Waterford School, Swaziland, 244
Watts, California, riots in, 25
Welwitschia mirabilis, 168, 170
Wessels, Albert Jan Jurie, 130–32
Western Cape College, 73–74
whipping, as punishment, 95
"white," definition of, 237–38
Whyte, Quintin, 114–15
Williams, Mennen G., 23

Wilson, Woodrow, 184
Windhoek, South West Africa, 169–75
Windhoek Advertiser, 216, 223
Winela. *See* Witwatersland Native Labor Association
Winiarski, Bohdan, 189–90
wiretapping, 97
Witwatersland Native Labor Association, 113–14
Women's Defense of the Constitution League, 92
Woods, Donald, 65–66
World (newspaper), 68–69, 96
World Council of Churches, 264
World Court, and the South West Africa Cases, 181–225 *passim*

Xhosa tribe, 13, 85, 104, 106
Xhosa National Unit, 108

Zulu, Bishop Alpheus, 261
Zulu tribe, 13, 85

276